CALL ME J

CALL ME
Jimmy
The life and death of Jockey Smith

CALL ME JIMMY

Published in Australia by
Floradale Productions Pty Ltd and Sly Ink Pty Ltd
March 2003

Distributed wholesale by
Gary Allen Pty Ltd,
9 Cooper Street,
Smithfield, NSW
Telephone 02-9725 2933

Copyright Damian Boyle, 2003

All rights reserved.
No part of this publication may be
reproduced or transmitted in any form
or by any means without the
publishers' permission

CALL ME JIMMY
The life and death of Jockey Smith
Damian Boyle

ISBN – 0-9579121-1-0

Cover design, typesetting and layout
by Write Impression Publishing

CALL ME JIMMY

> 'Only a jockey boy,
> foul-mouthed and bad you see,
> Ignorant, heathenish,
> gone to his rest …
> What did you do for him?
> – bad was the best.'

– Banjo Paterson, *Only a Jockey*

CALL ME JIMMY

The author

DAMIAN Boyle is a freelance journalist and teaches Media Studies at Belmont High School in Geelong. He was founding editor of *Gathering Force*, a literary magazine for fledgling writers, and completed the first take of *Call Me Jimmy* as a master's research thesis at the University of Queensland. He has lived and worked in various states of Australia, including 20 years running a beef property in the Otway Ranges where he first began the research for this book.

The author wishes to acknowledge that two chapters of *Call Me Jimmy* were originally published as short stories in *Kalimat,* a Sydney-based literary magazine.

CALL ME JIMMY

Index

Prologue		1
1	Bad news	3
2	Jockey turns apprentice crim	21
3	Ronald Ryan's little mate	45
4	An early Christmas present	69
5	The conspiracy	81
6	Taking a hike	101
7	Captured	127
8	The jury	149
9	Out for the count	185
10	The bookie murder	209
11	Doing time	231
12	Free as a jailbird can be	243

CALL ME JIMMY

Prologue

WHEN the phone rings an hour before midnight, Jean Smith is lying in bed. The radio is on, but she hears the insistent bell through the soft music and news bulletins that are the background noise of many a widow's lonely nights.

She sits up, swivelling herself around awkwardly until she can touch the floor with her foot.

A wooden crutch is standing in its place beside the bed. She grasps it and, with a practised heave, hauls herself up and stands erect.

The living-room is dimly lit by the weak light filtering from the bedroom door but, after 20 years of practice, it doesn't matter to Jean. She negotiates the sofa and a small occasional table as she makes her way to her armchair and lowers herself, groaning softly with effort, before collapsing into its depths.

She snatches up the receiver with a trembling hand.

If the caller gives his name, she doesn't take it in. The anxieties and fears of half a lifetime have narrowed to this instant and the urgent, eager voice in her appalled ear.

CHAPTER 1

Bad news

IT'S the house she and Daniel rented at first, then bought. It's hers alone now, with Daniel dead. A cheap little box of a house with concrete walls bolted together, in a modest housing estate at Corio on the outskirts of Geelong, a provincial city that has changed a lot since its origins as the exit port for wool, meat and grain from Victoria's wealthy Western District.

It isn't much but it is hers, with its flourishing garden of gladdies, phlox, geraniums and ornamentals, which she has tended lovingly on one knee all those years. There's a vegie patch and fruit trees out the back. The garden redeems the house. Now she maintains it alone: this ageing, one-legged, spirited woman of nearly 70. Her face is lined with worry and a lifetime struggle to make ends meet.

There's no sign of luxury here, though it is cosy, with touching signs of the respectability she has strived for most of her life. On the little occasional table beside the sofa is a little of her set of best china. The chair in which she now sits, nearly

CALL ME JIMMY

as old as she is and just as strong, is where she sits to receive visitors, and to view the framed photographs, trophies and childhood bits and pieces lining the walls. And from which she makes and takes telephone calls ...

The handpiece is in her hand, the voice on the line talking fast, too fast, with the speed that comes from nerves. His name doesn't register with Jean. Why should it? She can think only about the question he asks ... 'Mrs Smith, do you know your son's been shot at Creswick?'

It is the question she's feared for years, but she half expects it. There had been a warning half an hour earlier on the 3AW radio news bulletin. Then, she had willed herself to ignore it, to dismiss it as just another hoax, like the time her son's obituary appeared in the Melbourne *Sun* newspaper, years before.

As far as she knows, her son is somewhere on the central coast of New South Wales, safe with friends. But there is something in the reporter's voice, an urgency, an excitement, which she knows confirms the worst. This time her son, James Edward Smith, known to police and the underworld as 'Jockey', really is dead.

Jean Smith slumps in her chair, grief-stricken and oblivious to the reporter's pressure to respond. She doesn't want to believe. She has to find out for sure. She telephones Ballarat police and waits as the switchboard operator puts her call through to a senior officer. Gently, he tells her it's true.

BY midnight, at the Creswick police station, Senior Constable Ian Harris had handed a tape recording and a written statement to Senior Sergeant John Morrish of the homicide squad. The two were an odd couple. Harris was taller, with the beginnings of a middle-age spread; Morrish short and stocky, with the air of a street fighter. Harris's eyes glazed with shock; Morrish's blue ones hooded and watchful, like a hawk's.

BAD NEWS

That night was hell for Jean. For her, it was the culmination of years of worrying that one day her son would be taken from her. 'I don't remember much about that night. Oh, the telephone rang constantly with friends and well-wishers wanting to offer their sympathies. People were wonderful, but it just didn't register at the time. For a long time I just sat there asking myself, "Is it him, is it him?" .'

Early next morning Jean called her son Ron and asked him to identify his brother's body.

For Harris, it was a long night of questions, statements, telephone calls from superiors and avoiding the media. Until that night, there had been nothing remarkable in his record of service. He'd worked in a few stations, a uniformed policeman who spent most of his time on routine patrols or doing office work. He was married and, until now, had enjoyed a relatively quiet life, turning up to work each day and turning off at the end of a shift. Now, he had been blasted into the spotlight as suddenly as the bullets had blasted from his service revolver hours earlier. The boundaries of his world had blurred and there was an odd sense of guilt to deal with, even though what had happened wasn't his fault. He'd just been doing his job. But that wouldn't stop him being thrust in to the unforgiving glare of the media spotlight.

Smith's death was a big story. Not only was he a criminal celebrity whose life had drawn persistent media coverage but his death was yet another police shooting in Victoria – where there had been so many shootings it was becoming notorious. In New South Wales, went the black joke, when the cops caught crooks, they just robbed them or copped a bribe; in Victoria, they shot them.

The number of people shot by Victorian police in controversial circumstances had reached double figures in a few years. Loose allegations of police 'executions' had made headlines.

CALL ME JIMMY

All in all, it was no wonder the media now converged on the place of Smith's last stand.

AT Creswick, the harsh lights set up by television crews played against the brick Victorian-era buildings as the cameras panned the street either side of the crime scene and lingered on Smith's body where he had fallen, sprawled on his side facing the driver's door of a police car. Images of the scene were splashed on television screens across Australia.

Police crowded the area – some from the homicide squad, others from forensic and more from Ballarat, there to control the crowd. Witnesses gave impromptu interviews and became momentary celebrities in the biggest story of the day. Reporters chased comment from any police officer who would talk to them.

At least one television station aired a glimpse of the bloodied, stiffened corpse. Next morning, the *Sunday Herald Sun's* headline was **Top Crim Dies in Shootout.**

The newspapers had hit the streets before Ron Smith was able to formally identify his brother. The body had been taken to the State Coroner's centre in South Melbourne.

One side of his face was smeared with congealed blood, coughed up as he died. A gold watch was still strapped to his wrist and a money pouch holding more than $1000 was still around his waist, a giveaway that the shooting hadn't happened in Sydney, where it would be odds-on that the first detectives on the scene would ensure the money belt was 'found empty'.

One bullet had lodged just below his neck, another below his rib cage.

Ron was taken to the St Kilda Road police complex in Melbourne and questioned about his brother's most recent movements. Not that it really mattered any more.

BAD NEWS

IN the weeks before his death, Smith had stayed at a house in Kingcumber Avenue, Davistown, a secluded settlement near Gosford on the New South Wales central coast, about an hour north of Sydney.

Steep bush led down to the hidden coves of Brisbane Water, a tidal inlet joining the ocean through a narrow opening not far from Ku-Ring-Gai Chase National Park on one side and the competition surf of Copacabana Beach on the other.

The network of waterways, which offered many avenues of escape, had suited 'Jockey' perfectly. The rented house backed down onto Empire Bay, where he had a boat waiting. With only one land approach, strangers could easily be seen when a lookout was in place, though neither Smith nor those with whom he was associating were fully alert.

Instead, he spent much of his time at nearby stables, or the racetrack. Even when at home, he was less than vigilant. Jimmy Smith was getting sloppy; years behind bars had not dulled his instinct for self-preservation, exactly, but it had turned him into more of a creature of habit, like one of the stabled racehorses he was so fond of: flighty and potentially dangerous, but used to being looked after.

Keeping a lookout around the clock would have been tedious, time-consuming and would have demanded sustained self-discipline of a sort rarely found outside elite armed services. Smith was armed, but he was no commando. He was a crook who hated coppers and loved easy money and had a weakness for racehorses and various games of chance.

In January 1992, Smith had been released from Silverwater Jail after serving more than 14 years of a life sentence. He had satisfied the judicial arm of the law, but not his enemies, it seems. Just two days after he arrived at his wife Valerie's flat in Bondi, an unknown gunman had shot and almost killed him, pumping five shots into him in the stairwell of the flats late one night. It was rumoured that the would-be assassin was on the payroll of police who hated Smith and who, some said then and still do, feared he would or could expose police corruption.

It was as good a theory as any, given that bent police are probably the most dangerous denizens of the dark side of life. They have more to lose than most criminals, like a career, respect and reputation, and are well-versed in the best ways to get away with murder.

After recovering at St Vincent's Hospital, Smith moved to Davistown. Valerie was settled in Bondi and stayed there, but visited him on weekends. It was easier that way.

In November 1992, the drug unit of the New South Wales major crime squad moved into Smith's neighbourhood. They believed that a resident of the house in Davistown, Garrick Norman Joseph, was supplying large quantities of amphetamines and cannabis to users on the central coast.

A 'bug' was surreptitiously installed and monitoring started on November 19. Tape recordings of conversations revealed that, apart from Joseph, two others were thought to be involved in a conspiracy to supply prohibited drugs – Julie Anne Cashman and Smith, who was using the name 'Tom Price'. All three were identified when the surveillance team photographed them.

While Garrick Joseph was known to police only for juvenile offences, Julie Cashman had worked hard at establishing a criminal profile that included convictions for importing marijuana, breaking and entering, armed robbery, forgery and escape from lawful custody. She had been dubbed 'The Angel of Death' by the press because two men in her life died as a result of their association with her.

In 1979 Bruce Kennedy, the father of her daughter, had helped her escape from Mulawa Training Prison in New South

BAD NEWS

Wales and the pair headed for Brisbane with a plan to go straight in Western Australia. While they were visiting a fortune teller in Brisbane, police were tipped off and, in trying to escape, Kennedy was run down by a police vehicle. He died six months later of spinal injuries.

Ray Wright, like many prisoners who'd known Kennedy, contributed to the funeral fund and met Cashman a couple of years later. The attraction was mutual and strong. The pair set up a marijuana farm, which was raided. Wright escaped, Cashman was caught, but skipped bail.

The pair were on the run for two years, but in 1983 Cashman was caught again following a car accident at The Rocks in Sydney. She returned to prison but cut her hand with a broken bottle and was taken to Westmead Hospital for stitches. Wright was waiting to help her escape and, together, they were on the run again.

On 29 September, 1984, Wright, Cashman and another man held up the pay office at the Wolston Park Psychiatric Hospital in Wacol, an industrial suburb west of Brisbane city. The hospital was set on lawned acreage with its own network of roads next to the Wacol Golf Course.

The armed grab netted $230,000 and cost Wright his life. The hold-up was planned weeks in advance and dummy runs took into account all eventualities – times of the armoured van's arrival and departure noted, disguises in place including Cashman dressed and padded out to look like a man, and a seemingly foolproof getaway planned. But the robbers hadn't calculated on two undercover Armaguard officers being present in the office after the van left and, having battered down the pay office door and filled their bags with cash, Ray Wright was shot through the base of the skull while fleeing to the getaway car.

Cashman came back for her man, saw he was dead and fled

CALL ME JIMMY

with the driver across the adjoining golf course and to one of the two stolen cars waiting at the nearby Wacol railway station.

Cashman stopped in Sydney on her way to a safe house in Melbourne but police were closing in. As one half of a Bonnie and Clyde style partnership, she was listed as one of Australia's most wanted criminals. A prize scalp for police.

About six weeks after the robbery, and following a two-day chase through the rugged terrain of the Dandenong Ranges east of Melbourne, Cashman walked out and gave herself up to uniformed police officers. She was extradited to Brisbane and sentenced to 11 years, spending 3½ years at the infamous Boggo Road Jail before being transferred to New South Wales to face escape charges there.

Cashman was a model prisoner. She studied by correspondence at Deakin University in Geelong and later at the University of Technology in Sydney whilst inside. And she became a voice decrying the allegedly glamourous life of crime. Prison officers, social workers, solicitors, psychologists and religious folk praised her efforts at self-rehabilitation. She was released late in 1990 and, within two years, was actively involved in the drug scene again, this time with Joseph and Jockey Smith.

All three had been at Davistown planning a 'job' and Smith had been recorded offering to supply Joseph and Cashman with ten pounds of cannabis leaf – about ten mature marijuana plants with a street value of between $30,000 and $40,000. If caught, he was risking three to six years jail.

It was almost inevitable that Smith would turn his hand to drugs. He had already spent most of his adult life in jail, mounting endless defences against charges of murder, armed robbery, escape and conspiracy. Outside prison he had no other skills to rely on except those of the felon – except, perhaps, working for a few dollars an hour as a stablehand, strapping

BAD NEWS

racehorses, which was about the most humble form of hard labour around. Anyway, since the shooting, he was in fear of his life and wanted to stay well out of sight.

Smith had a pot of cash, collected by friends when he was in hospital, but that wouldn't last. He needed fast money. But his days as a stick-up man were behind him. The man who once headed Australia's Most Wanted list was 50 now, overweight and suffering the pain of arthritis. After 14 years behind bars, the underworld he re-entered had a new focus. The easy money was in drugs.

Ten days after police monitoring began, Smith set off alone on the journey that would eventually end with his death at faraway Creswick. That afternoon, in Grace Brothers' store at Erina Fair shopping complex, security staff spotted him shoplifting. They followed him out of the store. He made a run for it but, after a short chase, they caught him.

Desperate to escape, he threatened his pursuers with a revolver. Even worse, he commandeered a car, thereby technically abducting its two elderly occupants, albeit for only a few seconds.

It was a crazy move, and one that ensured he would get a long stretch for kidnapping on top of any other charges if he were caught. It was a decision made in a split-second and, when it came to rash behaviour, Jockey had plenty of form, all of it bad. But there might have been some method in his madness. At the time, any suggestion of being back in custody might have been enough to tip him over the edge because he had reason to think that a return to courts and jail would make him an easy target for those who wanted him dead. On the loose, at least he could try to dodge.

Monitoring of the group continued and, although Joseph, Cashman and Valerie June Smith were overheard talking about disguises and leaving the area by train, police did not pounce, perhaps because the conversation was muffled and no specific details were recorded.

In his statement to the coronial inquest following Smith's death, NSW Detective Sergeant Stephen McClelland, a senior investigator with the Central Coast Drug Unit, would reveal that Joseph, Cashman and Hill did not stay at the monitored premises that night but booked into a motel room, possibly with Smith.

The following day Joseph and Cashman returned to the house, discovered the listening device and were arrested. They were charged with conspiring to supply cannabis leaf and amphetamines. Valerie Smith was not charged, with the implication she was either not involved in the conspiracy or was not recorded by monitoring equipment during the surveillance operation.

Radio reports warned Smith he was, once again, a wanted man and, until he turned up at Creswick a few days later, police had no idea of his whereabouts.

Afraid of the police and their underworld connections, he moved in secret. He caught a train from Gosford to Sydney, where he was met by friends. From there he was driven to Victoria in a panel van belonging to a mate. Just outside Werribee, on the Geelong side of Melbourne, he was greeted by the familiar smell of the sewerage farm and another 'friendly' panel van, which took him to a safe house somewhere around Ballarat in the old goldfields district of central Victoria. Friends monitored the entire journey by mobile telephone.

WHEN 5 December, 1992, dawned, Smith had hours to live. He entered a farm on the Daylesford-Malmsbury Road at Glenlyon, a pretty district popular with hobby farmers and weekend getaway fanciers less than two hours drive from Melbourne.

BAD NEWS

Without knowing it, he had walked into a trap. The farmhouse, known by its address as RMB3697, was under surveillance by police attached to the Victorian Special Operations Group. Their job, codenamed Operation Farnsie, was to recapture an armed robber and jail escapee, Christopher Dean Binse. A surveillance team had been in place since five o'clock that morning. They had a clear view of the main gate and the driveway into the property, but a restricted view of the house because of the geography and vegetation.

Officers watched from the tops of hills either side of the property. But the area was rough and heavily timbered and the mists that settled morning and night blurred movements. It was hard to tell, sometimes, what was human activity and what were goats grazing in nearby paddocks.

The farm entrance was at a bend in the Daylesford-Malmsbury Road, itself a narrow, winding ribbon of bitumen carved along the contour of the hills. The track in to the house, short by farm standards, was studded either side by regularly spaced poles protruding about three metres from the ground – perhaps the beginnings of some ornamental structure to give the entrance an avenue affect.

As the track wound closer to the house, the place looked more and more like a secondhand market, with fridges, washers, bathroom pedestals, crates of bits and pieces scattered about. Sheds were overflowing with farm machinery and a tractor or two stood idle nearby. Chooks roamed freely and bushy native trees and conifers added to the seclusion of the house, a low-roofed pine bungalow with ceiling to floor windows. Despite surveillance difficulties the police, keen to get Binse, were able to get closer to the house at times without being seen.

Why police had failed to apprehend Binse at least twice when he was spotted at the farm at first appears puzzling to an

CALL ME JIMMY

outsider. If the purpose of the surveillance, as outlined in police statements, was to arrest Binse then why wasn't he taken at the earliest opportunity?

There were four police officers in two strategically located cars observing the farm. They were in constant contact with a command centre at nearby Daylesford, a small town famous, along with nearby Hepburn Springs, for its natural mineral waters. Had police converged on the farm at 6.20pm they would have captured not only Binse and his girlfriend, Lorna Skellington, but Smith who, according to police statements, was there from as early as 8.50am – although he hadn't been identified then.

However, others in the know, including Binse, claimed Smith arrived at the house after 6pm. Binse should have known, because it was he who had collected Smith in Ballarat. Had police taken the initiative earlier there was a very real possibility that Jimmy Smith would have been taken alive and that Senior Constable Ian Harris would not have been put in the position where he had to shoot to survive. On the other hand, storming the farmhouse might have resulted in even more deaths, as it may have resulted in a shootout between armed men with a taste for violence – Smith and Binse in the house and the Special Operations Group outside it.

The farmhouse was rented by Binse, who had used the name Bob, and Skellington, calling herself Candy. It appeared they persuaded the caretaker, Giuseppe Corso, that they were from Tasmania and looking for a holiday farm on which to relax for a couple of weeks. It didn't look like a conventional tourist getaway, but that didn't appear to worry the 'Tasmanians'. They paid $400 for the privilege of having the farm to themselves.

On the day Smith arrived at the farm there was some coming and going of vehicles. In fact, the property was being used as a

BAD NEWS

safe-house in preparation for a big bank robbery in Melbourne and an arsenal of weapons had been put together for the job. According to their subsequent statements, the police did not realise Smith was at the farm and when, around 8.20pm, a white Ford panel van left and headed west towards Daylesford, they didn't know who was driving it.

At that time a police telephone intercept recorded a call from the farm, which indicated a man named 'Tony' would be leaving the property soon, going to Daylesford and returning. 'Tony' was James Edward Smith, driver of the panel van. He pulled out from the farm track onto the bitumen and turned left, towards Daylesford. Surveillance did not follow because their target was Binse. They could not know they had let one of Australia's most wanted men slip through their fingers.

It was raining and he was concentrating on the road, travelling well within the speed limit. He reached the Midland Highway and turned left again, still heading towards Daylesford. Several hundred metres away a police car was rapidly making ground on him.

Senior Constable Harris was on routine patrol in a marked police car. Stationed at Ballarat, Harris had been the relief officer at Creswick for the previous week and was returning to base after a routine sweep of the area. That day he'd started his shift at 2pm and, as usual, was equipped with a .38 calibre Smith & Wesson police revolver.

Around 8.25pm he was travelling west along the Midland Highway towards Daylesford. In the distance he noticed the tail-lights of a vehicle, caught up with it and clocked it travelling at 80kph in a 100kph zone. Suspicious of the slow-moving vehicle, he was to explain later, he drew close enough to note the particulars of the panel van, including the registration number. He radioed Ballarat D24, the police communications

CALL ME JIMMY

network operating throughout Victoria, and asked for a vehicle check. It turned out the panel van had been stolen from Northcote the previous day. Harris followed it.

At Daylesford, Smith's panel van was spotted at 8.31pm driving past the Special Operations Group command post where officers were still in contact with surveillance teams at RMB3697 – the farmhouse Smith had just left at Glenlyon. They made no attempt to intercept the van. Officers at the command post were not aware Harris had already contacted D24 and was following a stolen vehicle.

Ballarat D24 maintained contact with Senior Constable Harris while he tagged Smith to Creswick, about fifteen minutes from Daylesford.

Sensing it was time for action, D24 arranged for back-up. But events moved too quickly. Moments after Harris radioed his mobile position, he called in again. 'Creswick 202,' he gave his call sign, 'the vehicle has just pulled up outside the Farmers Arms Hotel. I'm going to have to intercept.' Harris spoke normally; this was routine, but D24 was cautious, acknowledged his position and passed it on to a support vehicle in the area with the added request for urgency, 'It's not known how many heads on board ... 650, if you can, head in that direction at light speed'.

A police divisional van was also backing up when D24 sought confirmation from Harris that all was well. 'Affirmative, mate,' he replied, 'the keys are in the ignition so it may not be a stolen vehicle as yet'. It was the last radio link for some time.

FOR the last five minutes of Jockey Smith's life, Harris followed him into Creswick. Smith pulled up out the front of the Farmers Arms Hotel; Harris pulled off the road a short distance away. Maybe Smith had arranged to meet someone at

BAD NEWS

the hotel or maybe he was there simply to buy alcohol. Knowing he was being tailed by police, he might have chosen to stop there with the intention of making a run for it, if need be, by creating some confusion amongst those at the bar and slipping out the back door.

He'd been told the van wasn't 'hot' – a mistaken belief on his part, which might have caused the sequence of events that killed him. In Smith's mind, if the police weren't pulling him up over the van, then they knew who he was and wanted him for the offences at Erina Fair.

He never made it to the bar of the hotel. Senior Constable Harris was out of his police vehicle too quickly. To run now would obviously draw more attention, so Smith decided to bluff it out. Harris asked who owned the car; Smith said it belonged to a mate. The two were standing face-to-face, midway between the two vehicles – the policeman towering over the short suspect.

Harris asked for some identification. Smith said he'd left his licence in the panel van and returned, ostensibly to get it. He backed out of the van, carrying a small folder, and turned towards Harris. There were just a few steps between them. Smith walked over to Harris, the folder still covering his hand. When he got close to Harris, Smith flipped the folder away and revealed a small revolver in his right hand.

Instinctively, Harris went for his gun. He was scared; this was his first experience at the other end of the barrel. But he was trapped out in the open, a few metres from the protection of a vehicle and a long way from the safety inside the Farmers Arms. Both vehicles had pulled off the road onto a wide expanse of bitumen outside the hotel. There was nowhere to run, nowhere to hide. It was like a scene from an old cowboy flick where the sheriff and the bad guy face each other in the main street of town while the gals from the saloon run upstairs

CALL ME JIMMY

and the drinkers inside take to the protection of upturned tables. Only, in this case, it looked like a rigged game; the bad guy had produced an ace from up his sleeve … the revolver.

'Don't touch the gun,' ordered Smith.

Harris replied, 'No, don't, don't'. Harris moved his right hand towards his gun.

Smith brought the pistol to Harris' chest and repeated, 'Don't touch the gun'.

'I'm not,' Harris said, raising both hands in the air. He edged along the side of the police car, away from Smith. There was a chance he could put some space between himself and Smith, enough distance to allow him to take cover and draw his weapon. Smith was having none of it. He moved forward and leaned towards Harris with his left hand outstretched to take the policeman's gun, but Harris turned side on, making access difficult.

Harris kept edging towards the rear of the police car and yelled, 'Help, help, someone help me'.

They were both distracted when a brown Holden station wagon pulled off the road and stopped behind Harris. A Creswick local, Darren Neil, had been driving by when he noticed the policeman in trouble and decided to lend a hand. In an act of spontaneous and reckless bravery, he got out of the station wagon, leaving his two small sons in it, walked across to the gunman and pushed him in the chest.

Smith fired a shot into the ground. Neil's boys screamed. Neil backed off to his station wagon, drove the children to the entrance of the hotel and left them with patrons inside. He returned to the station wagon, ready to go on with it.

Moments later, a second shot was fired into the ground. 'Don't touch your gun!' Smith ordered. Harris still had his hands raised. A handful of patrons outside the hotel watched

BAD NEWS

helplessly. Others had taken cover, peeping through the windows of the hotel.

'Ring for back-up, ring for back-up,' Harris yelled at them.

Two more shots were fired – one into the air and one into the ground. Smith could have shot Harris at any time – or Neil, for that matter.

The bottle shop attendant, Craig Clark, dialled 000 and was connected to Ballarat D24. The message was passed on to the radio operator, who was still calling car 202 while directing all available resources to the area. Harris appeared shaky on his feet, which was natural enough. Neil was getting into his station wagon and Smith screamed at Harris: 'Lay on the bonnet!' Using his left hand, Smith grabbed Harris by the shirtfront, ripping off the two top buttons. 'Don't touch your gun,' he ordered.

'No, no, I won't.'

Smith pointed the gun at Harris's head and said: 'I'm going to kill you.'

'Run over him!' screamed Harris. 'Run over him!'

A lot of people might not have done it. Others might have been too slow to react. But Darren Neil wasn't one of them. He drove straight at the gunman, but stopped short of Smith, who turned and pointed the revolver in his direction.

There was time to fire but Smith hesitated. Harris seized the opportunity, dropped his right hand, drew his service revolver and fired three rounds at Smith. Two bullets hit home. Smith lurched back two or three steps. Patrons went to ground. Harris and Neil ran to the rear of Neil's station wagon.

It was 8.55pm and almost dark. Jockey Smith had seen his last sunset.

HARRIS was stunned and distraught. He radioed for help: '202 urgent.' The message was garbled. 'Three shots have been fired

CALL ME JIMMY

... and I shot him. Can you get an ambulance please?' Meanwhile, Darren Neil took Smith's gun and placed it on the boot of the police car.

Harris, leaving the radio, picked up the gun by the trigger guard and placed it inside the car's boot. It was eventually returned to its approximate position next to Smith's body in an attempt to keep the crime scene intact, in line with police training procedures. Harris and Neil marked off the area with police crime scene tape.

Drinkers came out of the hotel. A couple of them attempted to resuscitate Smith. Others stood by, numbed by what they'd witnessed. In the sleepy township of Creswick, with its wide streets and rambling buildings, Jimmy Smith had made his last stand. And no-one even knew who he was. Yet, anyway.

WITHIN an hour of Smith's death, news bulletins alerted Binse and Skellington. Police moved quickly to arrest them. They were taken to Melbourne where Binse was later to claim he was beaten savagely enough to warrant hospitalisation. He was eventually convicted on a number of charges and sent to Barwon Prison – not far from Jean Smith's home – where he was leg shackled 23 hours a day because prison authorities considered him an intractable prisoner.

The coronial inquest into Smith's death found no culpability on the part of the policeman Harris. Darren Neil was awarded the Star of Courage.

CHAPTER 2

Jockey turns apprentice crim

JAMES Edward Smith's arrival in this world was far less noteworthy than his departure.

His parents, Daniel and Jean Smith, had survived the Great Depression of the 1930s as children, to be confronted by World War Two as young adults. They married on 19 October, 1940, and settled in Colac on the edge of the Otway Ranges, where dwindling rainforest overlooks the wild waters of Bass Strait to the south and the plains of the Western District to the north. It is beef and sheep country, prime grazing land prone to fires in summer and floods in winter. Colac, with a population of around 8000, serves the local farming and timber industries, and has changed little since the time the Smiths lived there, although Daniel, if he were still alive, would note immediately the disappearance of the saleyards from the centre of town to the shores of Lake Colac a few kilometres away.

On 29 July, 1941, nine months after the Smiths settled into their home in Pound Road, across from the Colac Cemetery,

CALL ME JIMMY

Jean gave birth to their first son, Ronald William. On 3 October, 1942, James Edward arrived. It was a time of large families and, in all, Jean delivered eight children in 11 years. Her fifth child, Elaine, died soon after birth. It was a strong, united family held together by the indomitable spirits of both parents.

Daniel worked hard all his life to provide for his family. Like his second son, he was a small man, with brown hair and eyes. He was quiet and gentle with no time for anything but the care of his family. Written references from G.J. Johnstone and Co., an old Colac stock and station agency, and from the Fyansford Quarries in Geelong, testify to his willingness to work and his ability to get a job done unsupervised.

Daniel was respected by employers. When he worked at the saleyards as a general hand he often brought home day-old calves for the family to rear to supplement their income. And, like others who had battled to survive through the Depression, he went rabbiting, using ferrets to flush his quarry out of their burrows. Jean would skin the catch and, next day, push the pram full of rabbits around town, selling to whoever would buy her 'underground mutton'.

Jean loved her children, but Jimmy was special to her. All the family liked him. The only times she can remember him crying was once when she hurt herself and again when he saw a dog run over.

As a youngster, he was full of life. He delivered papers every day and, at 13, spent his weekends picking peas for pocket money. The Colac police ran a boxing club and Jimmy and some of his friends went along. An old school friend remembers their early days together at the police boxing club. It was a place to go, a place to hang out. He wasn't a villain then and certainly showed no violent tendencies.

People had some respect for young Smith. Like most of the other kids, he could hold his own in the ring and later tried his

JOCKEY TURNS APPRENTICE CRIM

luck in the boxing tents of travelling shows. He did the circuit of towns in the Western District, but gave it away when he started working.

Jimmy Smith's passion was horses. Agile and confident, he thought nothing of riding the horse in the paddock opposite his home without a bridle or saddle. He had energy to burn.

Each day would start with a country breakfast of eggs and toast or spaghetti on toast – or, if there was a lot of work to be done, a portion of the lot. It was important to Jean the children started the day with a good meal in their bellies, energy for the hike up the hill to Elliminyt, a little settlement on the outskirts of Colac, and school.

The children went to Sunday school and on special days Jean attended all the services – if there were three church services that day, she went to the lot. And, on school or church picnics, she was the first there, cutting sandwiches and making raspberry vinegar. The Smith family was part of the community and helped where it could.

They established a reputation as excellent tenants. One Colac landlord reduced the rent from 12/6 a week to 10 shillings and, in the 14 years the Smiths lived there, never raised it. He was happy to have a family prepared to maintain the garden and house.

JEAN'S story begins early last century. She was born into a family of battlers while the Great War was reaching its highest pitch of slaughter. A world away from the European battle-fields, near a quiet country town in the far west of Victoria, Jean began a country childhood where life was governed by seed-time and harvest and the leisurely swing of the seasons.

Teams of massive draught-horses, whose muscle built Australia, were familiar to her. And the distinctive double 'ting – clang' from the blacksmith's shop as he forged the horseshoes to fit each giant hoof was a sound so constant that it could be

CALL ME JIMMY

ignored. After autumn rain, she saw the horses pulling ploughs through the damp earth, leaning into their collars while behind them the plough-shares, polished to bright silver, sliced the rich soil, curving it over in neat, straight lines that stood out, dark across the pale pasture.

She saw the first hint of green intensify to transform her visible world into a temporary version of a gentler climate. Then summer once again scorched the grain into ripeness and galvanised men and horses to the concentrated effort of the harvest. Paddocks gradually filled with wigwam-shaped stooks of hay. Wagons loaded high rumbled slowly to the railhead, iron wheel-rims crunching the gravel. Vast rectangular stacks of bags packed tight as drums rose in the railway yards, built by sweating, straining men carrying four bushels of grain on their shoulders up ladders.

It was then that the train lines were busy. The family led a life so frugal that for Jean even 'tuppence worth of broken biscuits' was a rare treat, but there was plenty of fresh air and plenty of exercise, for Jean walked to school. She had grown into a healthy, hardy child used to the two-and-a-half mile hike twice each day.

Sometimes, in winter mornings, she stamped crackling ice on frozen puddles in the pot-holed road, along fences where every wire was sheathed in ice. Sometimes, on summer afternoons, when the children had been released from the purgatory of a school-room roofed with galvanised iron hot enough to fry eggs, Jean made her way home again through heat that hurt. And nearly always there was the wind. Sweeping in from the west it snatched hats and flung grit and grain-dust into screwed-up eyes. Horses turned their tails to it. Even the trees were shaped by its constant pressure as they grew.

One blustery February morning, when harvesting was in full

JOCKEY TURNS APPRENTICE CRIM

swing, Jean, now just nine years old, was on her way to school, buffeted by turbulent squalls that filled ears and snatched sounds away. At the railway crossing, she saw her friend on the other side, waiting for her. And that's when it happened …

IT is February 3, 1927. Jean's mother is heavily pregnant with her last child. That morning, like any other, Jean starts her long walk to school. It is summer but the weather doesn't know it. A cold wind blasts the small settlement of Salisbury, near Nhill, not far south of the Big Desert, in the north-west pocket of Victoria where grizzled men hack at the scrub, clearing for crops. Sweat-stained shirts washed once a week.

Heaps of mallee roots dot the landscape, waiting a turn to burn in the fire of someone's hearth. Nhill, home to the mallee fowl, a no-man's land where the rainfall barely wets the soil – soil prone to take flight in raging dust storms that blanket the city hundreds of kilometres away. Intense summer heat, 'bugger all' shade. Winters cold enough that the children suck ice from frozen puddles at the edge of the dirt road on their way to school.

The Nhill of Jean's childhood isn't much more than a railway station and a few wheat silos. Next stop, Bordertown in South Australia …

Jean fought her way against the freezing squalls. She battled forward, her eyes cast down against the dust, except the once, when she looked up to take her bearings and sees her friend on the other side of the tracks, waving. They always met at the crossing.

Further along the track, near the silos, a railway worker was struggling against the wind to uncouple a pair of empty grain carriages. Finally, the pin gave and the cars rolled free, a few feet from the rest of the train. The man went about his business thinking the cars would lose momentum and stop. Which they did – but only when they hit another car, fully loaded with wheat, further down the track. The impact was enough to stop the first cars, but the laws of physics ensured the collision caused the loaded car to roll away.

All the while, Jean was nearing the tracks and still waving to her friend.

She didn't see the loaded wheat carriage making its way silently towards her along the tracks. She stepped onto the cold steel at precisely the wrong moment.

It happened so quickly. One second Jean had two legs, the next only one. When the railway truck hit her, her leg was completely severed. The rapid loss of blood and the onset of shock should have killed her, but she cheated death.

Jean's friend watched helplessly from the other side of the tracks as eight wheels carrying 25 tons of wheat and steel rolled over her friend. The girl sprinted home and screamed for the wheat agent, a man who had no family and was fond of Jean. He rushed to the scene with Jean's mother, who removed the boot and sock from the severed leg and wrapped it in white baby towels. The next hours were crucial and, despite the shock of the moment, Jean's memories of that time are vivid.

A LIFETIME later, she relates the story sparingly and without drama. 'They took me six miles to Nhill. I wanted to go to sleep; my mother wouldn't let me. I would have died. A young doctor, he was only 26, gave me an injection and advised us to go to another hospital a mile away because I had no pulse through loss of blood. They took the rest of my leg off above the knee on February 11.'

Hospital staff had to stabilise her condition before they could make a clean amputation and tie off the veins. After six anxious

JOCKEY TURNS APPRENTICE CRIM

weeks she went home on crutches. Jean was always a fighter. Not long after leaving hospital, determined not to be beaten, she made another attempt to cross the railway line. Thinking herself more nimble on crutches than she really was, she tripped on the line, fell and broke the knee of her good leg.

But, after this injury healed, she joined in the games her friends were playing, including cricket and branders in the ring. She'd hop around on one leg or scuttle about on her crutch and the peg leg she'd been given at the hospital.

By the time she left school at 15 she was riding a pushbike and going to dances.

On the day she turned 16 Jean went to work and was to spend the rest of her life working at one thing or another. When she was 18 she moved to Dimboola, midway between Nhill and Horsham, and within sight of the rocky outcrops of the Grampians, to take up general work on a dairy farm.

The farmer and his wife had 14 children and one of Jean's tasks was to look after them. She milked the cows and washed the clothes in 'one of those machines you had to thump up and down'. Although it was a demanding life, Jean enjoyed it. She loved children and when she went home for a weekend to see her own family she often took the farmer's two-year-old daughter with her.

JEAN alternated between working at the farm and looking after the house of two elderly ladies in Horsham. She pleased them so well they offered to pay for an artificial leg to be made for her. But she already had money for this; the local farmers so admired her tenacity that they had organised a collection and she had put the money aside until she turned 21. An artificial leg was out of the question until she was fully grown.

Saturday was dance night in Horsham. At the first dance she

went to Jean was a wall-flower. Perhaps the young men thought she might not be able to dance because of her peg leg. The master of ceremonies walked up to her and said, 'I don't know who you are, girlie, but you're welcome to come to these dances every Saturday night and I'll have a dance with you'.

Jean made friends easily. She had an invincible spirit and a wonderful sense of daring that others found attractive. She was not deterred by her missing limb and enjoyed the pursuits that others her age did.

Eventually, Jean had an artificial leg fitted. Her sister-in-law had a brother called Daniel. Jean had to go to Melbourne for treatment to her leg and Daniel offered to drive her in his truck. It was a whirlwind romance. Within a few months they planned to make a home together ready to rear their brood. Ironically, after Jean's artificial leg was fitted she discarded it for many years, preferring the peg leg because it allowed her to be more active, especially when her children were young and she had to chase them around the house.

When it came to chasing, Jimmy was the one who was hard to keep up with. He was a tenacious child with an insatiable curiosity. Jean remembers warning him, 'You do that again and I'll kick your bum'. He turned around with a grin on his face and replied, 'You try it, Mum'. Ten people living in two rooms created problems, and although Jean talks about disciplining her children, there is a gentleness behind the gruff voice.

She never saw them wanting and made sure they ate well. As the years passed and the number and size of the children grew, some of the little treats dwindled, but the solid basis was always there.

Jean was involved in an astonishing number of organisations – Brownies, Sunday School, Glastonbury Mothers Club, Geelong Youth Club and, later, Corio Youth Club, the scouting

JOCKEY TURNS APPRENTICE CRIM

movement, kindergarten committees, Norlane Fire Brigade, Red Cross, community friendship groups and more. She is and has been a member of the Colac radio station's Sunshiners' Club since 1942. She cooked for an invalid man in Colac for some time. She took in boys from youth clubs for the weekend. And when she cooked, whoever was in the house never left without eating first.

In 1956, after the family had moved to Geelong, Daniel cut firewood at Modewarre, about 20 kilometres from where they were living. It was hard, backbreaking work, but he did it because there was nothing else available at the time. There was no chainsaw to make light work; Daniel slogged away with axe and crosscut saw. He quickly established a reputation for the quality of his workmanship.

One government timber inspector commented to a group of woodcutters about a heap of firewood: 'I can tell you who cut that wood. There's only one man stacks wood like that and cleans up the branches – Danny Smith of Colac.'

Jean was proud of her husband and proud of her children. She was fiercely loyal and deeply enmeshed in the daily toil of a family that had to pull together to overcome the odds. It was a close family in the way of large families of that time. In many ways Jean was the mainstay, the backbone of the family, a courageous woman in the mould of many other women of her time and station in life.

THE Smiths moved to the Geelong area in 1956, the year of the Melbourne Olympics. They moved into a house about 30 minutes' walk from the city centre, near the imposing towers of a building that was, then, the Glastonbury orphanage. A state school attached to the orphanage was a bonus because the younger children could go there. They cleaned up their new home so well that the delighted owner gave them three months' rent and, when they left in 1961, forgave them another 20 pounds.

Geelong, with its deep berth for ships on the edge of Corio Bay at Moolap, was expanding to cater for new industries such as the Alcoa aluminium smelter. The phosphate industry was doing regular shipping business to keep farmers supplied with fertiliser. Taxis supplied the merchant seamen, many of whom had been at sea for months at a time, with quick but costly rides. They would go to regular haunts such as the Ocean Child Hotel in North Geelong, which was close to Corio Quay where the ships were berthed.

If sailors went into central Geelong, many would end up at the Golden Age, where they could get legless and keep an eye on the sea. Then it was another quick ride to one of the brothels for an even quicker ride in time to get back on board ship in time for muster.

The move to Geelong let Jimmy Smith pursue his love of horses. It had started with the horse in a paddock across the road from his childhood home. Lacking a saddle and bridle, he had learned to ride without benefit of either, starting a lifelong fascination with horses.

For all that, his first real job wasn't in a stable. After he left school he found a job at the Godfrey Hirst woollen mill on the banks of the Barwon River in South Geelong. It was hard, manual work. Going to the mill and back each day made him feel independent and he saved every penny he earned.

One day, he caused a sensation by arriving home with a horse. It was 21 May, 1957, and he produced the receipt signed by one J. Day. The horse had cost him 20 pounds, with threepence in stamp duty. He fussed over his purchase as if it were a favourite child, feeding and grooming it. He even taught it tricks –

JOCKEY TURNS APPRENTICE CRIM

kneeling and crawling under various barriers in the paddock. He had learned from his father to care for animals, that they reciprocated in kind and wanted more than anything to please. His skill and patience were noticed. When he was 16 he was approached by Murray Hoysted, a local trainer, who asked if he would like to work with horses. Jimmy jumped at the opportunity and quickly won a reputation as an apprentice jockey who knew how to handle a horse.

Jimmy was smaller than average and lean, even for a jockey. But he was strong, well able to manage any horse wanting its head. His natural ability was noticed by others and, before long, he moved to Williamson's stable in Caulfield, where he lodged with other jockeys in a loft. Jean recalls being there for breakfast one morning and being surprised by the meal of 'two little rissoles'.

From Caulfield, he was lent to Vic Moloney, who was training in Geelong at the time. Vic was later to train at Terang, a dairying district in Western Victoria, but in the late 1950s he operated from his home near the Geelong cement works, a 20-minute drive from the local racecourse at Breakwater on the city's western edge.

Here, for a while, the young Smith was probably as happy as he was ever going to be. Every day at dawn he rode work, crouched on the back of horse after horse, knees jammed tight into the pads of the exercise saddle, feet thrust forward in the stirrups to act as a lever against the hard-pulling thoroughbred, arms pumping in time to the ancient rhythm of galloping hooves.

Racing was a tough game for tough people, not for the faint-hearted nor for those who would grow too heavy too fast, but for a lad of Smith's humble origins, it might have been a way out of poverty and a lifetime of manual labour. Smith was good

CALL ME JIMMY

enough at it to have a chance, but it wasn't to be.

Years later, Vic Moloney remembered his former apprentice clearly and with some affection. The boy might have turned out better 'if everyone had paid their way', he was to say.

At the time, Moloney had about ten horses in training and plenty of work for a young, game rider. Jimmy lived with the family. Moloney was to say later the boy had every opportunity to steal but there was never an occasion to doubt him and nothing ever went missing. There was often loose cash lying around the house and plenty of equipment at the stables – temptation enough for light-fingered lads.

They were happy days and Jimmy learned his trade to the level where he was riding in races regularly. He won several races, more than one on a horse called Arbilot. He rode on the circuit of country tracks – Bendigo, Burrumbeet, Camperdown, Cranbourne, Cobden, Colac, Geelong, Mornington, Pakenham and Terang. His future looked bright and as secure as anything can be in an industry that is in essence a four-legged lottery, with danger thrown in.

In racing the one sure bet is that nothing is a sure bet. Moloney ran into bad luck and reduced the number of horses in work and this made life tough for his riders.

The time came when there wasn't enough track work for Jimmy, so Moloney arranged for him to ride work for a couple of other trainers after he'd finished with his own stable's horses each morning. A deal was done to everybody's satisfaction. Jimmy was guaranteed rides in races if he rode three or four horses in work for the other trainers each morning. He was to receive ten shillings for each track gallop, which should have earned him a couple of pounds on top of what Moloney was paying him each day.

Jimmy learned the hard way that the one thing more common

JOCKEY TURNS APPRENTICE CRIM

in racing than slow horses are empty pockets and emptier promises. Not only did the trainers not pay him for riding track work, the promised race rides didn't eventuate, either.

The trainers offered the excuse that the owners wouldn't put him on. Moloney believed that the trainers misled Smith and exploited him. If Jimmy was soured by the experience he hid it well from his master.

Eventually, Moloney's stable of horses dwindled to the point where Jimmy had to be put off. By then, he had a proven record and was immediately snapped up by an owner-breeder who needed someone to work his horses.

It sounded like a sweet deal – a 1948 DeLuxe Ford sedan with petrol supplied and five pounds a week. Jimmy was keen, but not for long. The owner paid up the first week, but then reneged on the deal. By the second week he had reduced payment to two pounds and, after that, he didn't pay at all. In fact, he declared that Smith would have to work for nothing if he wanted petrol for his car. Jimmy was young and naive; as he was to tell it later, he accepted the situation for several months before becoming thoroughly disenchanted. He believed the owner was cheating him. In retaliation, he was to say, he stole some goods from the shed believing it was owed to him.

It was a turning point. The owner set the police onto Jimmy and his life of crime had begun.

Meanwhile, he used to contact Moloney at Christmas and occasionally at other times. It was through this contact and newspaper reports that the trainer followed Jimmy's progress into crime.

Years later, he ran into his former apprentice in the streets of Geelong and the latter related a tale about the automatic, self-serve petrol pumps that existed for a time in that city. A motorist would pull up to a pump, insert two shillings and a pre-set

CALL ME JIMMY

amount of fuel would flow into the tank. The more 'two bob' coins, the more fuel.

Apparently, Jimmy had pulled into the Winter & Taylor service station in Mercer Street, Geelong, to refuel. The garage was closed for the evening, but the automatic pumps were working. While feeding the meter with coins Jimmy had time to ponder the situation. Later that night, he came back, broke into the pump and helped himself to the store of coins, then bolted and hid his loot behind the door trim of his car.

Moloney wanted to know why he did it and Jimmy replied, 'Well, I wondered where all the two-bob pieces went and just followed them up.'

Eventually, Smith was nabbed for this crime when police questioned him about a series of other robberies, but his progression into harder crime wasn't inevitable.

Vic Moloney has always seen Smith as a victim, especially at first, and believes he might have turned out differently if everyone had been honest in their dealings with him. His last memory of Jimmy Smith is of a telephone conversation with him shortly before Smith was killed. Jimmy had phoned out of the blue and wanted to see Moloney, almost as if he knew his time was nearly up and he wanted to say goodbye to an old friend. Smith had a lot of friends, even though many saw him as a loner.

None of those he worked for in the racing game doubted his tenacity and determination to best any situation. Ray Nellis, another Geelong trainer of that era, tells the story of the seven-gallon cow. It seems the ranger at the racetrack was given a cow that allegedly milked seven gallons a day.

'But she was the wildest cow you'd ever seen and, as the ranger had never milked a cow before, he was advised to get rid of it,' Nellis recalls. 'The next thing we know, Jimmy is racing

JOCKEY TURNS APPRENTICE CRIM

out with a pail. He propped the pail under her udder and went to work. She kicked and bucked and gave Jimmy hell. He had cuts all over him, but he never hit her, just continued trying to milk her. That's the kind of kid he was; he would never be beaten.' According to Ray, it didn't matter what it was, Jimmy always tried.

Ray lost contact when Jimmy went to prison for the first time in 1961. Even so, Jimmy sent him a Christmas card every year. Nellis had time for Smith who, he said, would never 'split' on his mates.

'You get that from the racing game; the old fellows were tough on talking about upcoming races and the horses they were racing.' Like Vic Moloney, Nellis used to leave money lying around, and Smith would never touch it, he says.

He remembers the first time Smith was arrested. 'He was lost. He didn't know what to do. But, once he got into prison, he lost his fear. He was a kind lad, one of the best. I remember an old bloke we had living at the stables. We were going to take him to the races but his trousers were putrid. Jimmy was with us but disappeared for half an hour. When he came back he had a brand new pair of trousers, paid for with his own money and still with the receipt in his hand. He didn't have a lot of money in those hard times but he'd raced into town and bought the trousers for the bloke. He didn't like to see anybody go without.'

SIMILAR stories are told by many people in the racing industry. In his own small circle, Smith was respected, even admired, by some. He was in the process of establishing a promising racing career, but doing time in jail didn't do a lot for his prospects. Apart from the racing authorities taking a dim view of 'licensed persons' being convicted of crimes, Smith hit

CALL ME JIMMY

the one obstacle few jockeys can beat: during his stint in prison he put on weight. It meant any chance of a comeback to racing at the top level was gone. He would be just another could-have-been, one of the hundreds of promising kids who got too heavy and dropped out of sight.

Maybe he would have gone straight if, as Vic Moloney suggests, those he dealt with had honoured their promises. But perhaps Ray Nellis's theory is a little closer to the unvarnished truth. Nellis said if Smith hadn't started running around 'with a few bad lads stealing things' he might have ignored temptation.

Interestingly, neither of these views tallies with Jean Smith's.

His mother loved Jimmy as much as any mother could love her son. But she came from stern stock and had weathered the harshness of life, through injury, depression and war and the poverty inflicted by too many mouths to feed. She had seen and overcome difficulty, had never taken anything she was not entitled to, and had instilled this into her children.

So, why did her Jimmy choose a life of crime?

Jean describes him as 'a Jekyll and Hyde'. She believes he was a kleptomaniac who couldn't help himself. He might have a pocketful of money and still walk into a shop and steal something, anything; often things he didn't need.

Oddly enough, some criminals who knew Smith said the same thing. One who served many years in Pentridge Prison was to recall prison lore about Smith ... that he was 'so mean he'd bite the head off a shilling'.

And that even if he had robbed a bank and had thousands of dollars he would steal something worth almost nothing, regardless of the risk. On one occasion, it was said, he had the proceeds of a huge robbery, but went down the street and stole a new rubbish tin.

Jean Smith always maintained that she had taught him right

JOCKEY TURNS APPRENTICE CRIM

from wrong and that the road he took was one of his own choosing. She never made excuses for him.

It was cold comfort on those nights, later, when she lay awake wondering where he was and if he was all right. She feared every knock at the door in case it was the police or, worse, Jimmy himself. She was torn by her desire to see and touch her son and yet was afraid that she might be drawn into his shadowy and increasingly dangerous world by implication.

In his way, Jimmy was a good son. During all his years outside the law, he never gave his mother any proceeds of crime. He was careful never to involve her and told her nothing of his activities, merely saying, when asked why he did what he did, 'It's my life, my burden. You don't have to worry about me'.

But Jean did worry. She had made it clear she didn't approve of his wild and increasingly wicked ways and, even if it had been offered, would never have taken money from him.

But Christmas and Mother's Day cards were another matter. He sent them every year and Jean treasured them. He would often sign them under assumed names; sometimes they weren't signed at all, but she always knew they were from Jimmy.

Jean Smith harbours a bitter resentment towards some officers in the police force, not particularly because of Jimmy's experiences, but more as a result of the way the police treated the rest of her family.

She talks about raids and harassment she says she and her family suffered, and says some police made false accusations and threatened violence and trumped-up charges against other members of the family as a way to 'get at' Jimmy.

It's not surprising that someone in Jean Smith's position would resent police, and that such feelings might be embellished, but there is a ring of truth in her criticisms of the way she

CALL ME JIMMY

says her family was treated. The findings of various inquiries into police corruption in Queensland, New South Wales and Victoria bear out her contention that some police made up their own rules. Certainly, the criminal world agrees with her. So, too, do many lawyers … and even a few police officers who have spoken to the author off the record.

Smith's sister, Norma, believes he ran foul of the law some time before his first conviction in 1961.

He was living at Williamson's stables at Caulfield at the time and came home to Belmont in Geelong every second weekend. Once, he was making his way home and was within sight of the house next to Glastonbury orphanage when two Colac detectives in plain clothes stopped him. When asked his name he replied, 'Smith'.

Perhaps it was the way he replied or the use of the cliché false name, butt of a million jokes about discreet hotel bookings, which made the detectives suspicious. They didn't believe Smith was his name and wanted to know where he lived. He replied that he lived across the paddock and pointed in the direction of home. 'That house over there with the light on.' The detectives didn't believe him. They wanted to know what was in his bag. When he opened it, they could see there was nothing but his racing silks.

None of which would matter much, except for one thing. According to Norma, after each question the detectives punched him. He was beaten badly and finally arrived home a bruised and bloodied mess. It was one of the few times Norma saw him cry.

She believes this episode caused his contempt for police and his decision to embark on a life of crime. It was, she thinks, a twisted form of 'revenge' formed in the impressionable mind of a powerless and inarticulate adolescent. Providing they picked

CALL ME JIMMY

contents of many more.

It was this first job that led, in part, to his first conviction. Police, aware that an organised gang was responsible for a series of crimes in the area, were closing in.

Herb Jeffery was the first policeman to arrest Jimmy Smith. Jeffery joined the police force in 1957 before retiring in 1963 and establishing a reputation as an Olympic swimming coach. Stationed at East Geelong, he had been gathering information on robberies in the area.

Reports had filtered through that a particular vehicle, with five occupants, had been seen around the town a lot, often in the early hours of the morning. Five 'heads' in a car after midnight wasn't a good way to go unnoticed and, sure enough, they were noticed.

A favourite haunt was the infamous McCann Street, a short, narrow street lined with cafes and pinball parlours in the centre of the city – part of the block around which carloads of young men would burn rubber into the night. It was a wild, lively scene where youths set out to impress each other while girls, grouped together on corners, watched the testosterone-fuelled display.

Jimmy Smith was there from time to time in his recently acquired 1958 Customline, a mean-looking sedan he'd picked up in exchange for a debt. For most of these 'blockies', the night dragged aimlessly on into early morning with the only trophy a set of bald tyres, a hangover and a mild dose of carbon monoxide poisoning. Divisional vans regularly toured McCann Street and police would make an occasional arrest, at which point the hoonish behaviour would cease – for a while.

Herb Jeffery, together with several other officers, had marked Smith's vehicle for attention – along with another car driven by some of his mates. The police had seen the other car at a house

JOCKEY TURNS APPRENTICE CRIM

their targets shrewdly, it was a time when police could hand out beatings with relative impunity. Who would challenge two policemen, swearing their version of affairs on oath, against some rough little stablehand?

The story of the beating might have been enhanced over time. However, it seems reasonable to deduce that something took place all those years ago and that it may have contributed to an 18-year-old's desire to 'get even' with authority.

But, even if it was his treatment by unscrupulous people in the racing industry that first soured Jimmy Smith, it was certainly his own choice to continue to commit crimes rather than turn his hand to honest work.

The reasons for his straying into petty criminality can be speculated about endlessly. But there is no doubt that, once started, he deliberately embarked on a life of crime that fitted a classic pattern of increasing seriousness. As 'Jockey' Smith got heavier, so did his crimes.

After petty thefts he took on safe-blowing. It was the next step up the criminal ladder in that pre-drug trafficking era. Time and re-telling distorts facts with fabrication and many versions have been given of Smith's prowess with explosives and the frequency of his attempts to crack what the underworld call 'tanks'.

But his first attempt at blowing a safe should have turned him off explosives for life. He used far too much and almost blew himself and his accomplice to an early retirement. As it was, the safe remained firmly locked so the pair made an embarrassed exit, safe in hand, to the nearby banks of the Barwon River.

After several more unsuccessful attempts to open it they gave up and tossed it into the river in an attempt to hide the evidence. The safe was later found, but not before Smith had improved his technique with explosives and had helped himself to the

JOCKEY TURNS APPRENTICE CRIM

in Isabella Street, in Geelong West, an older part of town where mostly small, semi-detached houses opened onto the streets.

Jeffery searched the house and found stolen goods in the garage. When the car returned, Jeffery arranged for police back-up. The three occupants were arrested and taken back to the station. Jimmy Smith was not one of them.

However, once the questioning began, Smith was implicated in the thefts. Later, Jeffery was tipped off by a neighbour who had seen Smith returning home at 4am and had then seen him washing mud off his clothes and boots.

While Smith refused to talk, one of his accomplices wasn't so staunch, and revealed the whereabouts of stolen property and the safe, which was retrieved from the river. Jeffery, in company with detectives, then headed for the Geelong racetrack.

A quantity of guns and equipment stolen from garages was found at the back of the grandstand. It was a clever hiding place because the cypress hedge had wedged itself against the grandstand to form an almost impenetrable barrier. The hiding place was Smith's idea and might have remained undetected had not one of the arrested youths given him up.

Smith and his three associates were charged with shop-breaking and stealing, garage-breaking with intent, and garage-breaking and stealing. On a bleak day in August, 1961, in the Geelong Court, Smith was sentenced to 18 months with a minimum of five months before being eligible for parole. He was 18 years old.

There was no appeal. Smith was taken to the Geelong Jail, a forbidding 19th Century bluestone and brick prison overlooking the city and the Geelong Hospital and not far from St Mary of the Angels, with its towering spire, a Gothic cathedral built nearly a century before Jimmy Smith was born. Like the sombre facade of St Mary's, the jail was a cold, bleak place

CALL ME JIMMY

with huge timber doors cut into the perimeter wall of bluestone and the sort of bricks known as Old Geelong Blues.

New prisoners were issued with uniforms and blankets and told how they were to behave. A series of narrow, steel stairways led to cramped, musty cells where there was nothing on the windows but iron bars. The bars stopped the prisoners getting out, but not the weather getting in.

Smith claimed later he was beaten severely by a particular warder just before his release. Those who came to collect him found him waiting outside the prison's gates, 'black and blue' with bruises. Smith's solicitor wanted to press charges, but he refused to co-operate and the incident was forgotten. Maybe he sensed he would be returning to prison and didn't want a hostile reception.

Smith was released three days before Christmas Day, 1961, but immediately started committing crimes and was arrested for the second time just five weeks later, on 29 January, 1962.

For all its harshness, prison had proved no lasting deterrent to the young Smith. A lifetime friend – and partner during his safe-cracking days – recalls Smith asking a couple of prisoners what they wanted for Christmas before leaving the jail. Everyone thought he was joking but, that night, he climbed the wall of the prison and left a bottle of wine for each in their lockers. It's a good story.

On 5 June, 1962, following his arrest in January, Smith was convicted in the Geelong Court of one count of garage-breaking and stealing and sentenced to six months. The magistrate also directed him to complete the unexpired portion of his parole from the previous offence.

He was released on 7 September 1963, aged 21. He had spent more than two of the past three years in jail. The die was cast. Many racing people, and certainly Smith's family and friends,

JOCKEY TURNS APPRENTICE CRIM

thought a jail term for a first conviction was tough. They argue it was unfair that Smith received the stiffest penalty when each of the other three in his gang had prior convictions. But Herb Jeffery felt the punishment was warranted because Smith had committed several crimes before being arrested.

Jeffery has a vivid memory of Smith as a young adult. He saw Jockey Smith as a tough lad 'who would never split on his mates'. Smith copped a charge if caught red-handed, but refused to talk about other offences police had linked with him. In fact, Smith was often to prove an irritant to police when he was subsequently arrested because he usually refused to make a written statement or sign any statement made on his behalf.

At this stage Smith was probably no more than nuisance value and considered little more than a petty crim.

While his thefts may have begun as a means of getting what he believed was owed him, there was obviously an element of adventure and risk associated with committing crime that appealed to him.

Some of his activities seemed almost more comical than sinister. Once he paid neighbourhood kids to let down the tyres of the Geelong Prison Governor's car. It seems the governor was fond of a woman who just happened to be a neighbour of Smith's family and he couldn't resist the prank. But he was involving himself deeper all the time and so became increasingly cautious.

When he needed a car for a 'job' he would take two and hide them in different places. He put pieces of string or brown paper in the doors of each car so he could tell if either had been found. He watched police movements and treated every situation as if it could be a trap.

Following his release in September 1963 from his second term in prison, Smith was soon active again. Lindsay's department store in Geelong, which sold clothing and a variety of

CALL ME JIMMY

homeware goods, seemed an easy target.

With his mates, Smith did his shopping out of hours. They entered through a skylight, leaving no trace to indicate unlawful entry. The group never took more than a few items of clothing and goods they could use day to day so that any missing stock would be attributed to shoplifters.

It worked several times without raising suspicion – until Smith raided the office and stole a quantity of cash.

Anticipating the police would be called in this time, Smith and his mates abandoned Lindsay's and looked elsewhere for excitement and easy money.

CHAPTER 3

Ronald Ryan's little mate

WHILE an apprentice jockey at Caulfield, Smith had met Ronald Ryan. They had friends in common, the Richards brothers. Ryan was a gambler; he loved the punt and couldn't leave it alone. He had a psychological addiction to winning and losing as a gambler – and crime was a way to feed that.

It was, perhaps, the ultimate gamble, one that eventually led him to stake his life against the odds. But that was later. Ryan wasn't long out of jail and, when Jimmy Smith was released a little later, Ryan offered him temporary digs at his home in Cotter Street, Richmond, then a cramped, working-class inner suburb just east of Melbourne's central business district.

Ronald Ryan had first gone to prison in August 1960, convicted of breaking and entering, and escaping. The latter charge resulted from an attempt to flee custody outside the courthouse moments before he was due to appear. He was 34, married and the father of three young daughters. It was not his first appearance before the bench – in 1956 he had been put on

CALL ME JIMMY

a good behaviour bond for receiving stolen goods and, just a few weeks later, he copped a five-year bond for passing bad cheques.

Ryan was an intelligent man and his first prison term affected him. He was separated from his children and it upset him. He was determined to change his attitude to life. He studied for his matriculation and worked so diligently at prison jobs that he was regarded as a model of successful rehabilitation by some of those in authority. Within three months he was earning four shillings a day, a princely sum for any convict at that time.

Ryan was transferred from Pentridge to Bendigo Prison in October, 1961. Here he met Governor Ian Grindlay, a man he admired and respected, a man who watched three little girls rush to their dad every month during visiting hours.

Grindlay had established a reputation as a humane jailer, one who believed in the possibility of rehabilitation and who encouraged prisoners to make use of their time by learning skills appropriate to re-entering society.

When Ryan was released after 3½ years Governor Grindlay might have expected him to settle down with his family and find honest work. But Ryan, 38, and Smith, not long 21, teamed up. They planned a job on Smith's home turf.

It was 15 December 1963. The target was Foy & Bilson's store in Murray Street, Colac. It was a midnight raid. Smith and Ryan broke in by jemmying free a section of the external cladding. They stole cigarettes and tobacco, tinned and raw hams, packaged groceries, suitcases and clothing, liquor, electrical appliances and footwear. The total value of their haul was more than £2000 – the price, in modern terms, of two new family sedans.

They made their way to a loading bay at the rear of the premises, opened the door and found a small truck with the key in the ignition. Smith drove it, laden with loot, down the Princes

RONALD RYAN'S LITTLE MATE

Highway towards Geelong, en route to Melbourne. Ryan kept pace in another car. His job was to look out for police. As one of the arresting officers put it, Ryan was 'jockeying' the truck driven by Smith.

Sometimes he would be half a mile in front and then drop back and travel half a mile behind the stolen truck. About 20 kilometres from Colac, the truck was spotted by an employee of Foy & Bilson's, who became suspicious and phoned police from the public phone box outside the general store at Birregurra, a little town off the main highway between Colac and Geelong.

He reported the stolen truck and noted that a Wolseley sedan appeared to be travelling as escort. D24 despatched a message for police in the vicinity to be on the look-out for a yellow Bedford tray truck. Near Moriac, about 50 kilometres from Colac and just 10 minutes from the city of Geelong, the truck was pulled over by a divisional van.

First Constable Clinton Harris got out of the divvy van and went to the driver's door of the truck, followed by Constable David Richmond. As Harris approached, Smith jumped down from the cabin, faced him and produced a gun. In Harris's statement he alleged Smith raised the pistol and aimed it at the policeman's chest. In response, Harris raised his service pistol and ordered Smith to 'drop that bloody thing'. Smith dropped his revolver to the ground and Constable Richmond retrieved it. Smith was arrested and taken to Geelong police station.

There, Smith was held in the muster room to await the arrival of a CIB detective. He was guarded by Harris and, according to Harris's statement, both men were seated. Without warning, the policeman later alleged, Smith lunged at the only window in the room in a vain attempt to escape. Harris said he managed to grab Smith by the right leg and, so constrained, Smith swung around and kicked him hard on the side of the head with his left foot. However, on his copy of the police statement, Smith drew a picture detailing the layout of the interview room that showed the only window was above the top of the door and to its immediate right.

He wrote, 'If I was sitting on the right and dive across the table wouldn't I dive into the brick wall not the window and if I was on the right and jump up on the table and you (referring to Harris) was on left wouldn't you have grabbed me by the left leg.'

It was a good question, but it didn't cut much ice with the authorities. Smith was subsequently cautioned and charged with four offences – theft of goods from Foy & Bilson's, illegal use of a motor vehicle, use of a firearm to prevent lawful apprehension and attempted escape from custody.

The police credited the quick thinking of Foy & Bilson employee, Keith Reginald Taylor, for Smith's arrest. Aware none of the company's trucks were scheduled for work at that time of night, Taylor had passed the truck and waited some distance ahead, having stopped his vehicle in a side road. The truck passed and it was then Mr Taylor noted the Wolseley following behind. He memorised the car's registration number – GCD 454.

Taylor's presence at that place at 3.10am on a Sunday was lucky for police, but left a few questions in the suspicious mind of Jimmy Smith. He claimed that Taylor's statement was fabricated, that he'd not been anywhere near the stolen truck on that early Sunday morning.

It's not hard to understand why Smith was sceptical. If, as Taylor's statement testified, he was parked in a side road when the truck passed, it must have been nearly impossible for him to see the registration plate of the Wolseley sedan.

It is assumed he was far enough off the road to avoid

RONALD RYAN'S LITTLE MATE

detection by the occupant of the truck. It was dark and number plates were more dimly lit then than today. Smith thought it unlikely that Taylor was able to identify all letters and numbers on the registration plate.

During the interview back at the Geelong police station, Constable Harris told Smith 'a man named Ryan' had often been seen driving the Wolseley and suggested that Ronald Ryan had been involved in the robbery as well. But Jimmy Smith gave up no names and, when the case came to court, no mention was made of the Wolseley registered GCD 454 and Ronald Ryan did not appear. Smith took the fall alone.

Of the four charges against Jimmy Smith he was found not guilty on one charge only, that of using a revolver to avoid lawful apprehension. He was convicted on the other charges and sentenced to two and half years in prison. His subsequent appeal was refused and he remained in jail until 6 May, 1966.

While Smith returned to Geelong Prison in February 1964 for his involvement in the Foy & Bilson's robbery, Ryan's near escape didn't stop the latter from chasing the 'quick quid' to fuel his gambling habit. A few months later Ryan was back in Pentridge, convicted for theft and possession of explosives and sentenced to 14 years.

It is now part of Australia's criminal history that Ryan, with a young prisoner called Peter Walker, planned an escape for 19 December, 1965, reasoning there would be fewer warders to contend with because that day was the warders' Christmas party.

Ryan and Walker were in the yards when Ryan gave the nod – the escape was on. They scaled the inner wall and made for the catwalk on the outer wall where a guard called Helmut Lange was on duty. The pair burst into the guard's tower, seizing an Armalite M1 rifle, and ordered Lange to pull the

CALL ME JIMMY

lever that opened the main gate. They headed down the steps to the gate, taking Lange so he could not raise the alarm. Once there, they discovered Lange had pulled the wrong lever. Ryan marched him back to the tower while Walker remained below. This time, the gate opened.

Ryan and Walker sprinted through the gates as escape sirens sounded in the prison. They had been seen by a warder coming from the Christmas party. Traffic was heavy and, while the two escapees were attempting to flag down cars, Ryan realised that a warder, George Hodson, was chasing them. He lifted the rifle and aimed it at Hodson. Witnesses heard a shot. Hodson fell to the ground. The escapees managed to commandeer a car and drive off.

The resulting police search was massive but, although there were sightings, the pair remained free for some time.

On 21 December, two days after the escape, they held up the ANZ Bank in Ormond and got away with £4000. The immediate response from the Bolte Government was to post a £5000 reward.

At a Christmas party in Elwood, a tow-truck driver called Arthur Henderson, a friend of the woman harbouring Ryan and Walker, mentioned in conversation with Walker that he thought he recognised Ronald Ryan. He didn't realise who he was talking to. Walker and Henderson left the party and, when Walker returned, he was alone. Henderson's body was discovered on Christmas Day. He had been shot in the head in a toilet block.

The pair escaped to Sydney, but on 6 January, 1966, they were recaptured following a tip-off. They were taken quietly at a phone box outside the Concord Repatriation Hospital. Walker was charged with the murder of Henderson and was lucky to be convicted of manslaughter. He was sentenced to 12 years with

RONALD RYAN'S LITTLE MATE

a further 12 for escaping. Ryan was convicted of the murder of warder Hodson, who had died soon after being shot, and sentenced to death.

Whether Ryan should be hanged divided public opinion like few other issues. Whereas more than 30 offenders routinely sentenced to death over more than a decade had had their sentences commuted, Premier Bolte was determined to see Ryan hang, for political gain as well as private conviction.

Many, including the trial judge, Sir John Starke, believed that while Ryan was guilty beyond reasonable doubt, that he should not hang, given the circumstances of the shooting. Others took the opposite view – that is, that a prisoner who kills a warder or police officer while committing a crime (escaping, in this case) should be punished with the full force of the law.

Opposition to the hanging came from all quarters – the media, religious leaders, politicians, social workers, criminologists, law reformer and those against capital punishment on principle. But their arguments and pleas did not move Bolte.

Bolte was adamant. Ryan would hang. Bolte had wanted to hang a murderer called Robert Peter Tait in 1962 for the brutal sex murder of an elderly woman in Hawthorn, but had been thwarted when Tait was declared insane, and was still smarting at the affront to his authority.

This time, apart from his consistent and genuine belief in the deterrent value of capital punishment, he also had an election to worry about, even though it was a few months later. Bolte was known to hint that nothing would concentrate the voters' minds like the prospect of a good hanging. Either way, the tough old farmer from Meredith was determined not to let another condemned killer cheat the hangman.

Bolte wanted to make an example of Ryan, who was convicted of murdering a person whose job it was to uphold overlook is accessible by several picturesque routes, giving visitors the chance to explore the surroundings and take in the area's distinctive flora and fauna.

Nelson's Dockyard

A historical treasure and UNESCO World Heritage Site, Nelson's Dockyard is situated in English Harbour on Antigua's southern shore. A must-see destination for history fans and anybody interested in learning more about the colonial history of the Caribbean, this well-preserved Georgian-era naval yard is a testimony to the island's maritime tradition.

Nelson's Dockyard was named after Admiral Horatio Nelson, who served there in the late 18th century, and was initially built in the 18th century as a British naval station. As a base for battleship maintenance and repair, the location was essential to the British Royal Navy's activities in the Caribbean.

Today, a variety of stores, eateries, and museums are housed in the dockyard and the buildings nearby that have been painstakingly restored and repurposed. Visitors get a rare chance to travel back in time while taking use of modern conveniences in this region, which is an interesting blend of historical relevance and modern convenience.

The Dockyard is a bustling center of activity in addition to being a historical landmark. Numerous sailors base themselves there, and the adjoining Falmouth Harbour organizes major international yachting competitions like Antigua Sailing Week. The Antigua and Barbuda Coast Guard is based at the Dockyard, which gives the area a modern nautical presence while maintaining its historic feel.

You can tour the Admiral's Inn, which offers a magnificent dining environment, as well as the Dockyard Museum, where displays describe the history of the location, while visiting Nelson's Dockyard. With breathtaking views of the port and rolling hills covered in greenery, the area is ideal for leisurely strolls.

A unique look at Caribbean maritime history and Antigua's colonial past may be found at Nelson's Dockyard. Because it is a location where the past is brought to life, it is a must-see

CALL ME JIMMY

public safety. Ryan's death would send a warning to criminals across the state to leave law officers alone. Bolte was a strong, forceful leader. Ryan was eventually hanged in February, 1967. Bolte won the ensuing election comfortably ...

JIMMY Smith wasn't idle while Ronald Ryan clung to the hope of a reprieve during his last year of life. Following his release from prison in May, 1966, Smith lived at a farmhouse near Anakie, about 30 minutes drive north of Geelong.

It was open, dry, grazing country backing onto the steep bushlands of the Brisbane Ranges, an area prone to cold winds in winter and fires in summer. A long driveway led off the highway to the house and there was an alarm system of sorts installed to alert Smith to unwanted visitors – one of the rubber hoses often used by garages to signal the arrival of a customer. It didn't work very well.

Police raided the farmhouse one night and found stolen items, including clothing and electrical goods valued at about $300. Smith was not at the house, but was eventually charged with receiving stolen goods and bailed to appear in court at a later date. He claimed to be self-employed, working as a refrigeration and car mechanic for farmers in the district. His gear, including oxy-acetylene equipment, was carted around in an old FJ Holden ute belonging to one of his brothers.

Newspaper reports quoted police alleging that Smith had gone to some trouble to prepare himself for a last stand, the way Ned Kelly set himself up at Glenrowan in northern Victoria before his capture and execution. Smith had rebuilt a haystack behind the house into a kind of fort with the bales as walls and strategic gaps left as loopholes from which to fire upon intruders. Beside each small window were guns and a supply of bullets.

A woman called Marion was often at the house. She was

RONALD RYAN'S LITTLE MATE

dating Jimmy's brother, Ron Smith and, with her four-year-old daughter, Lindy, was staying at the farm for the weekend when the police raided and was to recall the occasion clearly some 30 years later.

Lindy was asleep in a bedroom when armed police burst into the house, but the child didn't stay asleep for long. Marion remembers three lots of police conducting searches that night – each one went through her daughter's room, stripping the bed and emptying drawers. One broke open her daughter's piggy bank.

Both Marion and Lindy recall the haystack – Lindy because she used to play in it and Marion because she was afraid her daughter might be bitten by a snake there. Neither recalls seeing any weapons in the haystack or the house.

Smith was fond of Marion and Lindy, who were struggling on $40 a fortnight in social security payments. Smith had driven them out to the farm for the weekend when the raid happened. Lindy was sitting on her mother's knee during the trip and remembers the 'warm and expressive' eyes of the man she called uncle as he periodically glanced at her in the rear view mirror.

Lindy remembers swimming in the dam, playing hide and seek, climbing trees, exploring sheds, combing the chook houses for eggs, eating gigantic tomato sandwiches 'and, my favourite of all, being thrown up in the air and caught in my uncle's strong, safe arms time and time again'.

During the weekend, Jimmy Smith handed out presents, elegant dresses for the women and suits for the men. Lindy thought 'it was just like Christmas' and became increasingly excited as her turn approached. When it did, 'Uncle' Jimmy guided her to the monstrous wardrobe and theatrically swung open the door.

CALL ME JIMMY

'He perched me on his knee and asked me what my heart desired. After 20 minutes searching through the mountain of toys I kept returning to a boxed Snow White tea set. And, if that wasn't enough, uncle pulled out a wad of notes from his pocket and gave me $100. He smiled and explained the money was for a very special purpose – to help mummy pay for my education. He spoke as if to an adult and explained how he had never realised what a precious gift education was until it had been too late for him'.

Marion had met Ron Smith almost four years earlier, after leaving a husband who, she claims, beat her. Not that Ron turned out much better, she was to admit ruefully. 'He used to beat me all the time, give me black eyes, split lips and, once, he even broke a finger.'

Given her background, Marion had an odd taste in men. She had been educated at the Hermitage, an exclusive private girls' school in Newtown, Geelong, where the two-storey sandstone school house with its creepers and period windows was set in magnificent gardens overlooking West Geelong.

When Jimmy found out that Ron had been beating Marion he threatened to kill him if he touched her again. When Marion finally left Ron, taking her sewing machine and a suitcase with her, she and Lindy took up a bed-sitter in Chilwell. Here the houses were small and packed tightly, lining narrow streets along which workers walked a few hundred metres to the factories lining the banks of the Barwon River.

Smith visited Marion and Lindy occasionally, sometimes bringing boxes of groceries. He rarely offered money or goods straight out; but left them lying around or hidden in places where Marion would find them. Once, he left a wad of tightly rolled notes in a Weeties packet. The first she knew of it was next morning when she poured the cereal into a bowl – the wad

RONALD RYAN'S LITTLE MATE

of notes fell in the middle of her Weeties. It kept them in rent and food for a while. There are many stories that show Jimmy Smith's generosity with other people's property. Given that he rarely had a real job after he left racing, it is obvious most of the stuff he gave away must have been stolen, but there was within him a capacity to share with those less fortunate – the memories of his own childhood and its deprivations had stayed with him.

John, a friend from Jimmy Smith's early days in crime and much later serving time in a prison near Sale in Gippsland, would recall a Christmas when 'things were pretty tough financially' and John's kids looked like going without. Smith came up with the answer: they helped themselves to a heap of new bikes he had 'found down a back alley in Richmond'.

Three of the bikes were earmarked for John's three daughters, another for 'a special youngster in Geelong'. They brought the bikes back to the Housing Commission flats in Richmond where John lived and, realising they had more bikes than they needed, gave out early Christmas presents to a group of kids nearby.

The bike for John's youngest daughter was too big but Jimmy solved that problem too. He could use the bike for another 'special kid' in Geelong, he said. He took it and returned a day or two later with a shiny new three-wheeler that just happened 'to roll out the door of a Richmond bike shop'.

Jimmy Smith relished the adventure of crime. Those who knew him believe it was the challenge that inspired many of the jobs he pulled – to see if he could get away with it. He enjoyed the cat and mouse games with police, and was, effectively, 'getting up their noses', as one friend observed.

During the Anakie period, towards the end of 1966, Jimmy Smith maintained his connection to the racing world by buying a horse called Mount Martha in partnership with friend and colleague, Kenny Richards.

CALL ME JIMMY

BY October of 1966 Smith was once again under police interrogation – charged this time with receiving stolen goods, possession of explosives, bank robbery and illegal use of a motor car. These charges related to an armed robbery at the Bank of NSW in Bendigo, in the old gold mining district in north-central Victoria. Smith was quickly arraigned and bailed to appear in Bendigo court on 1 December, 1966.

The police pressure against Smith was mounting. Only days before he was due to defend the Bendigo bank charges, he was again arrested, this time in company with his brother, Ron, at Geelong, and charged with possession of explosives. Not only did he have the outcome of the Bendigo robbery trial to worry about but, whatever the result there, he would have to face further charges soon afterwards.

The Bendigo bank job was a joint venture between Smith and the Richards brothers – Albert, David and Alan – three of eight children in the Richards family. Jean Smith attended the trial and was surprised when she saw the face and ears of one of the Richards boys. They were 'all bruised', she said later. It reminded her of Jimmy's words to her after his 14-hour interrogation: 'Don't let them take me down there again, Mum'.

The four co-accused were tried together. Their counsel, under direction from the newly prominent criminal law firm Galbally & O'Bryan, tried to discredit police evidence throughout the trial. This was particularly so in Smith's case, where the balance of evidence against him related to banknotes taken in the robbery which police claimed were in his possession when he was arrested. Smith had no alibi, but insisted that the notes had come into his hands through a legitimate bank transaction in Geelong.

The notes were a mixture of old and new currency, a temporary oddity due to the fact Australia had switched to decimal currency from pounds, shilling and pence in February,

RONALD RYAN'S LITTLE MATE

1966. That alone proved little, although both new and old currency had been taken in the robbery.

What was damning for Smith was that one of the notes was mutilated and bore a stamp from the Bank of NSW indicating it was scheduled for destruction. Smith argued that he'd had ample opportunity to get rid of the note. He'd waited three hours at Russell Street police station to be questioned and, during that time, went to the toilet. He could have disposed of the note then if he had been worried about it. He doggedly maintained he came by the note honestly.

The court was not convinced entirely. Smith was acquitted on all charges with the exception of receiving stolen goods, a charge relating to the $123 (including the mutilated note) he had in his possession at the time of his arrest. He was sentenced to two years with a minimum of twelve months to be served before being eligible for parole. Smith signalled his intention to appeal and was released on bail until August, 1967, when the appeal would be heard.

So, in late December, 1966, two months before his mate Ronald Ryan was due to hang, Smith was free on bail.

AS Ronald Ryan moved closer to his appointment with the hangman in the first weeks of 1967, Jimmy Smith became increasingly agitated. He wasn't prepared to let his friend die without a fight. Ryan had exhausted the appeals process; his only hope was clemency. With Sir Henry Bolte adamant that Ryan be executed at the allotted time the chance of winning even an 11th-hour reprieve was remote. As the hours ticked past and days slipped away, it seemed only a miracle would save Ryan. Smith knew instinctively he was his friend's last and best hope. He planned a daring raid on Pentridge.

He got word to Ryan to be ready. The plan was brutally

simple – if foolhardy and dangerous. Smith was to lead a group of ex-prisoners, all friends of Ryan's, in an all-out assault on the prison. They were going to charge the main doors using explosives to get inside and, with guns blazing, work their way to Ryan's cell. The raid would be at night, when fewer staff were on duty and fewer casualties likely.

When Ryan became aware of the plan he took immediate steps to stop it. He didn't want to be burdened further by the deaths that would likely result from the raid. But he was under 24-hour guard with no opportunity to speak to Smith face-to-face. He had to get a message out to abort the plan, which Smith would believe and accept as having come from Ryan.

There was no alternative. Ryan let it be known he wanted to speak with his friend, Governor Grindlay, who had been promoted to Pentridge. As Mike Richards reconstructs the scene in his thought-provoking book, *The Hanged Man,* Grindlay was with the hangman in D Division as he tested the gallows using sandbags tied to the execution rope to stretch it, when a warder called him to the telephone.

It was the prison's Catholic chaplain, the knockabout priest Father John Brosnan, asking Grindlay to come to Ryan's cell in H Division as soon as possible.

When Grindlay got to the cell, Brosnan left to allow Ryan to speak to his old friend and former mentor alone. Ryan then told Grindlay what he had already told Brosnan, words to the effect his associates outside were going to 'spring' him that night unless someone could get a message to them.

'Why are you telling me this?' Grindlay asked.

Ryan replied: 'I have made my peace with God and I will never be as well prepared to die as I am now. I have got nothing to lose but there has been enough bloodshed and I don't want any more. If this thing goes on it could develop into a

RONALD RYAN'S LITTLE MATE

bloodbath.' Ryan then filled in the details of how for several weeks a plan had been hatched between him and three associates to spring him from prison.

Amazed, Grindlay listened to details of how the gang planned to blow a hole in the prison wall with gelignite and, using machine guns, get to Ryan's cell and release him. Ryan explained that he had received a coded message earlier that day from a visitor, a member of his family. The ringleader was Jockey Smith.

Ryan told Grindlay he had changed his mind and appealed to him to get a message to Smith and the others. He said if Grindlay took a note to a certain address, the raid would be abandoned. Worried that he might be taken hostage and used as a bargaining chip in a desperate attempt to negotiate Ryan's reprieve, Grindlay refused to take the note himself but, after consulting Brosnan, he chose the right man for the job.

He was 'Jocka' Bell, a one-time gunman who had served long stretches in jail and was well known to all parties. Ryan wrote out a message in pencil on prison notepaper, using the code of racehorses' names used earlier that day to ensure the recipient would know it was a genuine message from him.

The next problem for Brosnan was to find Bell. Having done that, he had to persuade him that it was deadly serious. Bell eventually took the note to a house in Elwood. When he returned, he no longer had any doubts that the raid had been set to happen. He said he had seen a car loaded with guns, ammunition, ropes and gelignite.

One thing seems certain: had the raid not been called off, either Ryan would have been sprung from jail or Smith and his two comrades-in-arms could have been killed in the attempt. By deciding to accept death quietly, Ronald Ryan might well have saved the life of his friend Jockey Smith.

CALL ME JIMMY

RYAN sat in his cell on death row and waited for his meeting with the man known as Mr Jones, who had officiated at hangings for 38 years, including several at Pentridge. Ryan's physical needs were met by warders who kept a 24-hour watch in case he tried to commit suicide, while his spiritual needs were cared for by Father Brosnan.

When the time came, just before 8am on Friday, February 3, Ryan walked the last few steps from the condemned cell to the scaffold with Grindlay, whose awful task it was to supervise the execution of a man who had become his friend.

That morning, some 3000 protestors gathered outside Pentridge to voice their anger at what they saw as a barbaric punishment. Mounted police rode into the crowd, attempting to disperse the protestor. Armed police, some with dogs, threaded their way through the lines of demonstrators, jostling them. Some saw the police as deliberately provocative, decoys to draw the anger that belonged inside the prison walls and inside the office of the Premier.

The crowd knew it was over when a flock of pigeons flew from the roof of D Division, startled by the crash of the trapdoor that dropped Ronald Joseph Ryan into eternity.

Ryan's still quivering body received the Last Rites from Father Brosnan and was later buried in an unmarked plot in the grounds of Pentridge, with a bag of quicklime to hasten decomposition. There was no funeral, no last farewells from a family grieving the loss of their father and husband, no headstone to mark the grave. Fourteen witnesses, members of the press and officials, filed out of the prison gates, most of them devastated by what they had seen.

One of those was journalist and broadcaster, Patrick Tennison, whose report appeared in *The Australian* newspaper the following day. This is what he wrote:

RONALD RYAN'S LITTLE MATE

THE life that was Ronald Ryan's was taken from him yesterday.

He died silently. His face white but impassive. His thin lips together, but not clenched.

You get weird mental impressions. His face was strangely like a small child who had composed himself into calm bravery just before the doctor gives a needle.

Only once did this change. The hangman readying the knot jolted his head with the rope. Ryan turned his head slightly towards him. That was all.

The hangman stepped back, the body fell from view. The rope dragged taut and swayed just slightly. The voice of the priest was heard reading his prayers.

I was one of 14 newsmen-witnesses representing the public. We were marshalled first into a long visitors' room with plastic flowers. An official warning was given: No cameras or tape recorders – 'that wouldn't be cricket'. No smoking once inside either.

Then the clock took over. At 10 minutes to eight we were led to D Block. Our bodies were counted on the way, tallied at the door.

A last impression going through the door: A lot of birds singing.

Inside small fluorescent lights helped the bits of sunglow seeping through roof windows. A rope was held back up 40 ft from a green canvas-like screen. On a catwalk above, the noose lay neatly placed on a railing. Its rope ended on the thick beam above, tied around the beam in six loops.

Two minutes to eight. The prison officials' party walked on the tier catwalk above to Ryan's cell. The hangman suddenly walked quickly under the scaffold and entered behind them. A big, dark green cap – like English soccer

CALL ME JIMMY

fans wear – pulled down low around his head. Big sun goggles over his eyes.

Forty seconds before eight. Ryan emerged. Five long paces from his cell door to the noose. Dull blue prison denims. Hands tied behind his back. A grey cloth on his head. As the hangman fixed the rope, you could see wispy grey hair under his cap on his neck. It was a redly sunburnt neck.

Ryan, white, immobile, passive, as a wide flap from the cloth on his head was dropped over his face.

The trap door opened efficiently at eight.

THE debate over Ryan's execution continued for many years and dogged Sir Henry Bolte for the remainder of his time in office. Outwardly, he showed no remorse, holding fast to his view that the state did have the moral and legal right to take life. In 1975 the Victorian Government, under the leadership of Bolte's successor, Rupert Hamer, formally abolished capital punishment and confirmed what most people already knew: that Ronald Ryan would be the last man hanged in Australia.

In January 1990, 23 years after Ryan was hanged, Jimmy Smith wrote to Ryan's daughter, Wendy, from his cell at Pentridge, where he was facing leftover Victorian charges in the hope of clearing the slate and speeding his eventual release.

He had spent more than 12 years behind bars in New South Wales by then and had lost touch with the Ryan family, but the trip back to Pentridge rekindled much of the emotion he'd felt on Ryan's death. The letter was written on lined prison issue paper in a neat, unjoined print. It was a difficult letter for Smith to write. While the quality of his expression and grammar had improved over the years, he slipped back to an earlier style as he struggled to say what was in his heart.

RONALD RYAN'S LITTLE MATE

>Edward James Smith
>A Division
>Box 114
>Coburg 3058
>Friday 26th

Dear Wendy,
I had debated since seeing your whereabouts in the paper whether to write or not ... It brought things back ... As I'd just come back to Pentridge, from Sydney, after escaping from here in 74. First I was in Jika then transfer to A which is next to H where I last seen your dad on a visit with your aunty Gloria ... the photo of the Queen as you walk in the door hanging on the wall its still there. Also a soldier which reminded me of the way it use to be run ... bloody military type punishment ... No doubt you'd recall the many weekends going to Bendigo, I was there with him. He was my mate. He got out prior to me. But ... picked me up when I was release. I stayed a few days at Cotter St Richmond with yous. I hope I am not intruding writting, I do it mainly to explain how much he wanted to see you three before he went ... And the whereabouts of his grave ... And your plight wishing both to see the grave and to get permission to exhume the body and have a proper burial and grave. His old mother tried at the time, no luck ... now Feel happier that you've got at least seeing the grave for a starter ... I lost contact with Gloria Erma Violet and also Diane E. As I was put away back here, Trying to do something for your dad, To take him before, they did Alfred Hitchcock Bolte. Bros can explain. You may already know, And Rons last wish was to see you

CALL ME JIMMY

three as you probably already know. But your mum. I guess thinking it was the right thing at the time, wouldn't allow it, Gloria tried her, She wanted to just take yous. But didn't want to cause any trouble for your mum as I always thought of her as a good woman, Who had endure a lot, And I guess one can only take so much, I just wanted to get yous and take yous out on a visit without her knowing first. One of yous was ringing the Governor Mr Grindly who would tell your dad, He was good to him, But I never got to take yous out to see him which he wanted dearly. Because we had to go into hiding. As an informer told the police we were going to free Ron before they could carry out the sentence. I say no more. You may know. Father Brosnan knows ... I was working on maintenance last time here, And had been to Rons grave many times If its the right spot which I am sure it is, There wasn't much there bar grass and weeds I do hope they clean it up before they take you there Its just a triangle block behind D division with a tin fence across it as they say unmarked. Its about 100 yards from where they took his life; Its good that Bros will be with you. I can imagine how much it will mean to you, I hope they allow you to re-bury him Which I doubt But things have changed, Or at least a headstone. If any help is needed with either financially or otherwise, There's many friends of Rons who will help. Especially down the docks I hope it all goes okay. I imagine it will be a lot off your mind. After so long; Just don't let it upset you re the grave being nothing there But that's the way it done by law. Just knowing its there is the main thing and being able to see it. When I escape I went

RONALD RYAN'S LITTLE MATE

over where his buried, and said see ya mate hope I am not back to see you here again. But although Ive gone past there I hav'nt been to it as yet this time. So just say hello for me please, Guess I followed in Rons footsteps escaping from here and guess its fate as arrested in Sydney and ringing up in a phone box too. Worse thing I done escaping. Should have learnt from Rons experience. But its always on ones mind in these places especially with your love one out there. Although I was away three years after escaping the consequences wasn't worth it ... I am alive and nearly finished it I hope, Finished here as soon as my appeal heard. Then back to Sydney to get out I hope. Sunday night spoke to the chaplin here today Peter Nordin took over from Bros, Hope to speak to Bros or see him before Thursday ... Hoping the visit to see your Dad grave is a forfillment of your wish and what you wanted. All the best to you and your family.

Regards Jimmy Smith

WENDY Ryan was moved by Jimmy's letter and remembered the times when as a child she, too, had called him Uncle. 'I felt comfortable around him and when he came to stay with us after his release, it was as if we were all members of one family,' she was to recall. 'He was a loving man who cared for so many others and his own needs came low on a long list.' Wendy replied:

Wednesday 31st Jan

Dear Jimmy,
I received your letter when I got home today and as soon as I saw the return address on the back I knew

CALL ME JIMMY

who it was from straight away. I remember when you stayed with us in Richmond and I've followed your story in the media for many years. I must admit it was a surprise to hear from you, but I'm glad that you wrote to me, as it's good to hear from a close friend of my dad's. My fiancee got one hell of a shock though as he has spent many years inside, both at Pen and Ararat, in fact he's only been out since May and will probably be back in Pen this March. But that's another story.

I've been working for years to try to get permission to see the sight of dad's grave and I'll admit that it's been a long hard slog. But I've finally won the battle and a lot of the credit belongs to Russell as he has given me the extra strength that I needed to stand up to the media coverage that we've had. It's going to be a change for him tomorrow when we walk into Pentridge and know that he can walk out with me after I've visited my dad. To be honest with you, I'm not sure how I'm going to react, as I haven't seen dad since his last court appearance. As you know, mum didn't want us to see him and it really cut me up. I went to Pen a few times before he died, but as I was on my own without mum with me, they wouldn't let me in. I tried to explain to the screws on the gate that I wouldn't stay long and that all I wanted was the chance to say goodbye to my dad, but they would not even do that.

You mentioned the spot that dad is buried and it sounds the same as the way Russell explained it to me. In fact he spoke to dad when he was in Pen in 1988 and introduced himself, that was just after we got engaged. But tomorrow it's going to be my turn to

RONALD RYAN'S LITTLE MATE

talk to him in a very long time and you have my word that I'll say 'Hi' to him from you. I've ordered 23 red roses to place on the grave, one for each year he's been gone, and I'm taking one silk rose to symbolise eternity. We've got a stone plaque made to mark the grave but we can't take it in with us tomorrow as we're being held up by a lot of Government red tape at the moment. But I'm not going to give up the fight until I can either have the grave removed or at least have it marked. Russell and I have spent every cent we had on this and we even sold our car to cover the costs, it's taken us right down the tubes but we've refused any form of financial help from the media as we don't want people to think that we're using dad's name to earn a quid. Maybe I'm too much like him in a way, as I'll help anyone that needs it but I don't like asking help when I need it most. We might be flat broke but at least we're happy and we're doing something that has never been done before. I just hope that others in my position can gain by what we're doing.

My dad was a very special man and he didn't deserve to die the way he did, I'm just glad that he had good friends like you with him at the end that stuck staunch. I know all about the plans to free him and the reason it didn't come off. I know it's a long time in coming but I'd like to thank you for trying to help. I wish I could talk to you in person as I'm sure you could tell me so much about the past. When I go in tomorrow I'm going to see the Governor and try to organise a visit with you, but if I can't do anything I hope you'll write to me again and fill me in on how dad was at the end. Mum and my sisters don't like what I'm trying to do as they just want the past forgotten, but I can't do that. I loved my dad then and I still love him today, no matter what he did or what is said that he did, I still believe in him. He's still my dad and nothing will ever change that, I'm not ashamed to be a Ryan.

It was fate that I got your letter today, the day before I go to visit dad, as I was in a very nervous state today and there was no-one I could talk to that would know what I was going through. Russell is the only one that listens and he understands what it's like inside as he first went in in 1970, but I don't like saying too much to him in case he gets worried about me.

I'm going to finish off now as I've rambled on enough. Thank you again for writing as you've been a great friend to dad in the past and I hope, a friend to me in the future. Bye for now.

All the best

Wendy Ryan

WENDY Ryan visited Jimmy Smith soon after writing the letter to him. 'As we sat and talked about dad's last days, the memory came flooding back of the kindly uncle who had spent hours playing with us all those years ago,' she was to say of the visit. 'He put my mind to rest over many things concerning my dad and it was as if we'd been in contact over the intervening years.

'My last sight of Jockey was of a lost and lonely old man, crippled with arthritis, waving goodbye as I left the prison. His words to me were full of love and understanding and his attitude was one of compassion for his fellow man. The man I knew was nothing like the media reports.'

CHAPTER 4

An early Christmas present

IN June 1967, Smith was acquitted of theft and explosives charges in Geelong only to find a couple of other matters pending. An appeal against the conviction for receiving stolen goods ($123 including a mutilated note) at Bendigo was scheduled for August, two months down the track.

And there was the explosives charge made just before his appearance in the Bendigo courts in December the previous year. Then, Smith and his brother, Ron, had their FJ ute pulled over by police in Geelong's Eastern Gardens at a popular spot known as 'tail-light alley'.

They'd been under surveillance following the armed hold-up of a Colac TAB earlier that day.

Ron Smith takes up the story.

'It was Saturday night. Jim and I were working on a car in the backyard of my house in Latrobe Terrace. The girls had gone out and we were to meet them at tail-light alley for a drink later on. So we went outside the house ready to jump in the Holden

CALL ME JIMMY

ute and we noticed two blokes sitting in a car across the road in front of the church. When we left they followed us.

'We went up Latrobe Terrace, passed the cop shop, down McCann Street, then up to tail-light alley. When we pulled up, we were intercepted by the police. They made us get out of the ute while they searched it. They didn't find anything so they took us back to the cop shop. They were detectives (name deleted) and (name deleted). They questioned Jim about a job in Colac.

'The time it happened at Colac until they picked us up was too short for anyone to do it, so they said, "What do you want, Jockey, a gun or a stick of gellie?" One of them said then, "No, he had the gun last time (possibly referring to the Foy & Bilson's robbery), give him the stick of gellie this time".

'With that, he took a parcel wrapped up in newspaper out of the cupboard and threw it at me and Jim. We didn't try and catch it; it fell on the floor. They picked it up and opened it. It had two sticks of gellie in it, a fuse and a det and could have blown us all up. They said they found it behind the seat in the ute.

'Well, they locked us up for the night. When I got out I went up to Melbourne and saw a big chief at Russell Street CIB and we had a big argument about it and I said, "I don't mind being charged with something I've done but I don't go along with this kind of bullshit. I'm not going to get life for this and if I do, when I get out, I'll personally knock those two arseholes. They're no good to society".

'Anyway, when I went to court they led no evidence on me but Jim was convicted. They said in their evidence they put their hands under the front of the seat and found the parcel up the back of the seat. But it's impossible to put your hand up the front of the seat and up the back in an FJ because in the middle of the seat there is a hump in the floor pan and you would have

AN EARLY CHRISTMAS PRESENT

to bend your arm backwards. At the trial we had photos of the seat in the ute and the seat itself, and the car was downstairs. But, they refused to look at it.'

There is no doubt that Smith used explosives, particularly in his earlier safe-cracking period. But, in this instance, Smith claimed he'd been given an early 'Christmas present' – police jargon for 'loading up' an accused person with a gun or gelignite stored at the police station.

At trial, Smith's renowned defence barrister, Frank Galbally, claimed that the gelignite had been planted. This was the main thrust of the defence case.

It ignored witnesses like the two girls the Smith brothers said they were meeting, the potential testimony of Ron Smith, who would testify to the gelignite coming from police stores, and photographic evidence which showed it was impossible to conceal gelignite behind the seat of an FJ Holden utility. It also ignored the original search of Smith's car conducted by the arresting police officers when Smith was stopped at 'tail-light alley'. Nothing had been found then.

Later, one of the arresting officers claimed Smith confessed voluntarily at Geelong police station to stashing gelignite under the front seat of the utility.

'Well, Christ ... There is a parcel of stuff under the seat,' Smith had allegedly said. 'What sort of stuff?' the policeman was recorded as asking.

'Gellie,' replied Smith, 'a man's a mug, I thought you would have had it.'

The alleged 'admission' was out of character. Smith had a reputation for saying very little in police interviews.

It was an odd trial, one where the prosecutor found himself almost advocating on Smith's behalf because his barrister, Frank Galbally, seemed content to focus the attack on one policeman. Neither Smith nor his family were pleased with

CALL ME JIMMY

Galbally's handling of the case, especially when he said, 'I propose to call the accused, Your Honour, and no other evidence'. Ron was at court and able to provide an alibi. The two girls the Smiths had arranged to meet that night – Marion, who had broken off her engagement to Ron by then and Jimmy's girlfriend, Helen – were still in the Geelong area and prepared to testify.

The ute was parked a short distance from the court with the intention, so the family thought, of it being produced in evidence. Instead, a simulation was staged using courtroom chairs to represent the front seat of the FJ ute.

The prosecutor gave Smith the opportunity to call the two girls, but Smith declined, saying, 'I will call them if I have to (but) I do not wish other people to be involved in it.' The prosecutor and the judge both noted Ron Smith's presence in the court, and the prosecutor asked Smith if 'we are going to see' the ute.

'If you want to see it,' he said bluntly.

Smith was convicted and imprisoned for five years. This was later reduced to two years. He felt cheated and urged his barristers to seek a further appeal on the basis that his witnesses and evidence were not tested at court.

Once in jail it was difficult to find the funds necessary to acquire legal representation. Galbally & O'Bryan wrote several times pointing out they could not work on Smith's behalf without a retainer being paid up front – $100 was a sum frequently mentioned. Two years after the conviction Smith's barristers seemed to have a change of heart.

A letter bearing the signatures of both Frank Galbally and Peter O'Bryan, and dated 28 May, 1969, indicated it was necessary to present Ron and the two girls as witnesses.

'As you know,' the lawyers wrote, 'we are attempting to proceed with your appeal and want you to know that we are

AN EARLY CHRISTMAS PRESENT

doing everything on your behalf. However we have struck several difficulties, one of them is the fact we have been unable to contact your brother, Ron, and have been unable to contact the two girls in question.

'We are prepared to do all in our power towards your appeal without fee because we believe that you were wrongly charged insofar as the explosive is concerned. It seems to us that quite a few people believe in your innocence on the explosive charge and believe that this was what is commonly referred to as a "frame up". However the difficulty which confronts you and ourselves is the fact that it is almost, if not absolutely impossible, to prove such a thing.'

Fine sentiments, but the horse had well and truly bolted. The appeal Smith fought so hard for never eventuated and he served both sentences in full. He was paroled on 3 May, 1972, bitter and determined to even the score with the policeman – if he ever had the chance.

Even today, many believe Smith was framed on this explosives charge and that it further poisoned his attitude. Years later, Ron Smith still nursed a grievance against one of the policemen.

Jean Smith is equally adamant her son was loaded up. 'I was stopped by a policeman in the street some time after Jimmy was charged. He would not give his name. He told me he was very sorry for me because he knew the explosives were planted – Jimmy was framed.'

A former Geelong police officer, Sergeant Jim Gardner, remembers the incident clearly and, to this day, has reservations about Smith's conviction on the gelignite charge.

Gardner, then a sergeant, was stationed at Norlane at the time and knew Smith well from the latter's earlier days in West Geelong. Before the gelignite charge, Smith was on bail for

CALL ME JIMMY

other matters and had to report to the Norlane police station daily. Gardner was to recall helping Smith resolve a problem with his bail. Smith was grateful and a trust developed between the two.

'He often sat in my office and we used to talk about how he'd really wanted to carry on life as a jockey. If only things had turned out differently, he could have been a champion jockey. He was very intelligent.'

Sergeant Gardner had a reputation locally as a straight cop. He took an interest in the little bloke who, following the explosives charge, broke down and cried. 'Jimmy spoke with me on several occasions and almost convinced me he had been fitted up. It left a nasty taste but you could do nothing about it. I had doubts.'

FOR Jimmy Smith, 1967 may well have been the point where he decided it was futile to go straight – assuming, of course, he ever had any intentions of doing so. Nobody who mattered seemed willing to listen to criminals who cried foul about the methods police used in their fight against crime; if they needed to use unorthodox tactics to secure a conviction, it seemed that society was prepared to turn a blind eye.

The next few years offered a cloistered existence for Smith. At a time when Johnny Farnham's hit single *Sadie, The Cleaning Lady* was getting airplay, Smith was wondering, perhaps, just how he had been cleaned up by the system. As an inmate, his life was ordered by the constraints of early rising, daily exercise, work in one of the trade shops or as a prison cleaner, and long periods behind bars in his cell.

By all accounts, Smith was a model prisoner. Once inside, he got on with the routine of prison life. Like many prisoners, he scanned the pages of daily newspapers for mention of his name

AN EARLY CHRISTMAS PRESENT

and the names of friends, associates and his enemies, those police officers he claimed had framed him. It was more than just a vanity thing. It was his way of keeping in touch with the world outside.

Smith still had an interest in boxing, legacy of his boyhood bouts, but now he was not so much a participant as an organiser, referee, or corner man. He was a punter.

He lived for the contest and, cut off from horse racing in Pentridge, boxing was the next best thing. Perhaps he was spurred on by the tidal wave of publicity that surged around Lionel Rose when he fluked a match against the great 'Fighting' Harada in 1968 and became a modern Australian hero by taking the world bantamweight title.

The following January, as he sweated behind the bluestone walls of the 'Bluestone College', Smith took a special interest in reports of massive fires in one of his old stamping grounds at Lara, near Geelong.

The new year of 1969 had brought in dangerously hot weather. Merciless northerly winds came out of the red centre to parch southern Australia. The country turned tinder dry and was ready to explode at a spark. When it happened at Lara, it ravaged the then small rural community, and 18 people lost their lives.

That same year *Apollo XI* landed on the moon, Australian women were granted the right to equal pay, and Harry M. Miller staged the controversial rock musical *Hair*.

WHEN Jimmy Smith walked through the gates of Pentridge in May, 1972, the first three decades of his life were behind him and he had graduated from a crime academy, wise in the black arts of robbery, theft and deception learned from willing teachers in the cells, exercise and industry yards. When he returned to Geelong, he worked as a panel beater – but not for long. He quickly embarked on a furious crime spree, showing little reason or caution. It didn't take long. By June, 1973, Smith had been arrested and charged with 'conspiracy to commit armed robbery on persons unknown', attempted theft of a motor vehicle and possession of unlicensed firearms.

One of his co-accused, nabbed for an armed robbery at the Commodore Motel in Queens Lane, Melbourne, earlier that month, claimed to have been watching *Division Four*, a locally-produced police television drama, at the time when Smith picked him up in Geelong and drove to Melbourne for the job.

The pair was arrested in St Kilda Road. A search discovered a plastic bag with ammunition for a shotgun, a .22 rifle and .357 Magnum pistol, an ignition barrel intended for use in the theft of a car, various tools and a set of Queensland licence plates.

Two months later, in the small hours of the morning, Smith was seen loitering near the Detroit Crescent shops in Corio, minutes from his mother's home, with a hacksaw in his hand. He was stopped and a scuffle broke out. A knife fell from his possession to the ground.

After calling for back-up, the arresting officers managed to handcuff Smith and take him back to Geelong police station where he was locked up. The following month, at Geelong Court, he was found guilty of six charges including loiter with intent, possession of an offensive weapon, assault by kicking and refusing to give his name and address.

On the loitering charge, he was sentenced to three months and the weapon charge earned a further seven days. He was fined between $20 and $75 on the other charges.

In March, 1974, Smith was charged with the theft of welding gear and tools to the value of $1800 from the Biland Trading Company in Werribee. Oxy-acetylene equipment was used in

AN EARLY CHRISTMAS PRESENT

this robbery, which was interrupted when a passer-by saw the intruders, phoned D24, returned to the scene and noted the licence plate of a Torana with two male and two female occupants.

On 11 May, 1974, the Ding-a-Ling and Tic Tac shops in Jackson Street, Toorak, were broken into and reproduction antique clocks valued at $8000 were stolen.

The following month, Smith was stopped by police in Glenferrie Road, Malvern. At the time, he was living at Cheltenham, a Melbourne bayside suburb. The police officers asked Smith to open a box sitting on the front seat of the vehicle he was driving. Under protest he eventually opened the box to reveal a reproduction antique telephone.

Smith and the stolen telephone were taken to Camberwell police station. He was questioned about various offences including theft of a quantity of clothing from the Woodstock Inn Gear shop in Cheltenham on 24 May, 1974. When the officer was called out of the room to take a phone call and another officer directed to keep watch over the prisoner, Smith lunged at a closed window, smashed his way through and landed on the footpath outside the police station. He was last seen travelling in a north-westerly direction along Camberwell Road. It was his first successful escape from custody, but it didn't last long. He should have learned from that, but didn't.

Smith was recaptured next day and escape from lawful custody was added to the list of charges. He was carrying a mailbag stolen from an unattended truck parked in the yard at the Geelong Post Office the previous evening. According to the record of interview, which Smith signed, it was 'an impulse thing'.

Smith made records of interview relating to all these matters and signed them. He appeared before a magistrate and was granted bail pending his trial on 12 December that year. But he decided not to wait around and absconded. These charges would remain on the books and were to dog him many years later.

IN 1974, two major crimes put Jimmy Smith squarely in the frame as an audacious armed robber. The first, on 5 August, was the hold-up of the ANZ Bank at the Prahran market in Melbourne's inner suburbs.

It was a violent robbery, and left tellers in shock. At 5.15pm on a busy Monday, just as tellers were balancing their tills for the day, three masked bandits smashed through the plate glass door and, to use the phrase newspapers did, menaced them with guns.

Although one of the robbers cut his hand on the broken glass and lost quite a bit of blood, the operation went smoothly and the bandits fled to where a fourth man was waiting in a stolen Valiant sedan with the motor running.

The hold-up netted thieves $107,000 – even today a substantial amount but, in 1974, it was a fortune. The robbery was one of the biggest in the state's history at the time, and attracted the Victoria Police's undivided attention. They swarmed within moments of the alarm, but the robbers had escaped, dumping the Valiant nearby.

It might have been a good time for a prudent person to consider retiring from a career in armed robbery, using a share of the loot to quietly set up some legitimate business. But that is not the nature of the beast.

Robbers are by nature gamblers and while they are often shrewd, they are rarely prudent. The gambler's rush of adrenalin has to get its fix. So it was that a month later, on 4 September, the same crew struck again.

This time the payout was not so grand – a mere $6733 – but

AN EARLY CHRISTMAS PRESENT

still equivalent to a year's earnings for the average worker. The target was the payroll of an after-care hospital in Collingwood, close to the home of author Frank Hardy and his beloved Collingwood Football Club.

The ferocity of the attack was obviously intended to instil such terror that the operation would not be jeopardised by a heroic employee mounting some sort of counter-attack.

As with the ANZ Bank job, a stolen Valiant sedan screamed to a halt outside the pay office and three masked men forced their way to the pay area, shouting threats, waving guns and herding staff as they went.

The three worked quickly, said little, and bolted to the waiting car, escaping along Victoria Parade. The entire operation took only minutes, and had been well planned. By the time police found the getaway car, the bandits were long gone.

Each of the robberies provided clues; blood at one and a hooded bandit calling his mate by name at the other. The police knew the robberies were the work of the same gang because there were so many similarities: the violent entries with guns waving, the screaming at staff herded to a corner, the getaway cars, and the descriptions of the perpetrators.

And there were similarities to earlier crimes where the culprits had been caught and charged. Jimmy Smith became a suspect and police began a surveillance operation. His phone line was tapped a few days later.

Smith was 32 years old and had decided a life of crime was his calling. His father once asked him what he would do when he got out of prison. His reply: 'I only know one profession'.

It was time to give New South Wales a go.

CHAPTER 5

The conspiracy

ON 9 September, 1974, Jimmy Smith boarded an Ansett flight for Sydney. He was travelling with another man, Marko Motric, a Yugoslav who, police suspected, had been Smith's accomplice in the after-care hospital robbery just five days earlier. The pair didn't know they were being watched.

Their 10.50pm arrival at Mascot airport was monitored by members of the Sydney 'shadow squad' following a request by Melbourne detectives. Police had heard Smith mention a trip to Sydney to 'get some money' and assumed he was on his way to commit a major crime there. A large-scale surveillance operation was in place by the time Smith stepped off the plane.

Smith and Motric were met by a woman called Jeannie Baxter, who was driving a blue Toyota Corolla sedan. She lapped the airport carpark a couple of times, passing an unmarked police car on at least one occasion, before heading to Victoria Street, Bellevue Hill, in Sydney's eastern suburbs, where she lived with George Archibald, a friend of Motric.

CALL ME JIMMY

Police tailed them. After a couple of hours, Smith and Motric left. This time Motric was driving and the pair made their way to the Glensynd Motel near Randwick racecourse, where Smith booked in under an assumed name. The surveillance crew waited. Smith spent some time in his room before heading to the Forbes casino.

About 2am, he returned to his room to change his leather jacket and blue flared jeans for a tracksuit and, at first light, set off at a jog to the nearby racecourse where he watched early morning track work. Later that morning, Motric collected him from the motel and the pair returned to Bellevue Hill, where they made phone calls and arranged to meet two other men, Stanley Ernest James and Brian Leslie O'Callaghan, at a motel in Bondi Junction. This time Archibald was on board.

Smith was introduced to James, who had flown in from Western Australia. All five piled into a 1967 bronze Falcon sedan that O'Callaghan had picked up on his arrival at Mascot airport that morning. The car had been left there a week or two earlier with the keys inside. O'Callaghan smashed a side window to gain entry. Glass littered the back seat.

The five men drove the 10 kilometres to Redfern railway station. It was 10.30am on a fine day and passengers were milling about. Smith and company found a park within walking distance of the station, but sat in the Falcon for a few minutes before leaving the car. Detective Senior Constable Frank Buffoni, dressed in street clothes, followed them to the entrance of the station but waited outside. He noted that Motric was carrying a black, vinyl bag.

Buffoni returned to the police vehicle and conferred with his partner, Detective Nagle, who had parked 40 to 50 metres behind the Falcon. Other members of the shadow squad were in position at various places up and down the street. Altogether, three unmarked police cars and a police motorcycle were

THE CONSPIRACY

involved. If the other policemen worked similar hours to Detective Buffoni, they would have been feeling the strain of long hours on watch. Buffoni had been on duty since 8.30 the previous evening, a shift that had already stretched to more than 12 hours straight.

The surveillance team kept a close eye on the station entrance. Like most of the buildings in Redfern, the station was old, built in the 19th Century from mottled red bricks. The high, tiled roofs with their staggered levels suggested the railway station had grown with the demands of the population.

The arched entrance looked north towards the city. To the east, congested traffic struggled through a maze of roads; to the west, tightly-packed homes lined narrow streets as haphazardly laid-out as tent-lined tracks on a goldfield, a legacy of its early colonial origins, before the sort of civic planning that made Melbourne and Adelaide comparatively well designed. .

After half an hour, O'Callaghan emerged from the station and returned to the Falcon. Archibald followed him out, but went off on foot. James and Smith slipped back to the car unobserved as heavy traffic and a truck obscured the view of the watchers. Motric was the last to arrive. The Falcon returned to Bondi Junction with three police cars and a motorcycle taking turns to tag behind.

The surveillance team was in radio contact with Detective Sergeant Brian Gardner, of the armed hold-up squad, throughout the operation and he gave the word to move in.

Police cars screeched into position in front and behind the Falcon. Within seconds, the four occupants were each staring down shotguns barrels as police officers swamped the car.

They were dragged out of the car and spread-eagled against the sides of the Falcon and one of the surveillance cars that had drawn alongside to block escape.

Two Melbourne detectives were there for the kill. They had

CALL ME JIMMY

flown to Sydney to interview Smith about the ANZ Bank and after-care hospital robberies.

Pedestrians and motorists witnessing the arrests at Bondi Junction could have been excused for thinking they were at a TV shoot for a cop show. The Falcon, stopped in the middle of the road, was surrounded by police vehicles. Traffic banked up. Police wearing bullet-proof vests screamed orders at the arrested men.

Hands on the roof! Spread your legs!

For a few moments it was pandemonium until one of the officers directed cars past the scene. No shots were fired. Pedestrians on the sidelines, enthralled by the action out in the street, weren't going to miss any of it if they could help it.

Police moved quickly to clear the area. The four were handcuffed, bundled into police cars and taken to police headquarters in Sydney.

The Falcon was driven back to CIB headquarters and searched. There was never any doubt that the NSW armed hold-up squad would find weapons in such circumstances. If the crooks had the bad manners to have left their weapons elsewhere, some could always be provided from what detectives jokingly called 'the future exhibits store'. It was just a matter of how many and what sort.

Not that they needed to in this case. According to police, they found a bag of firearms – a sawn-off .303 rifle, a .22 Ruger pistol, a .45 Colt pistol, a Walther pistol and a quantity of bullets – in the boot, along with a grey dust coat and pantyhose, a Sydney telephone directory and three tubes of plastic skin.

The weapons were sent for finger-printing. Each suspect was charged with conspiracy to rob the Eveleigh railway workshops at Redfern.

Smith, wearing overalls which he said were for protection

THE CONSPIRACY

against broken glass in the back seat of the Falcon, was interviewed by two detectives, who typed the record of interview.

He told detectives he was in Sydney to organise a party of five or six punters to place sizeable bets with either SP bookmakers or at the Canterbury races on a horse called Callyapple. He declined to say how much money was involved or for whom he was working in Melbourne.

It was an unlikely story, particularly when he admitted the horse was running in Melbourne. He claimed that during the day he'd rung his 'boss' in Melbourne and was told all betting was off for the time being because the four-year-old wasn't 'trying' after all. Callyapple did race in the Ringwood trial stakes at Sandown that day and came in third by three-quarters of a length with Harry White in the saddle.

Jimmy Smith still had a passion for racing and spent much of his time at the track. So did a lot of other criminals. The race-track, like illegal gambling houses, could launder large sums of money. So much cash changed hands in the course of a few hours that it was impossible to detect who had brought it in. Jimmy Smith was a big punter; he bet in units of $1000. It was a lot of money in the 1970s, when many people worked for less than $100 a week.

CRIME squad detectives wanted to know why Smith had gone to the Redfern railway station. He said it was to make a phone call to secure documents from somebody in Newtown on behalf of Dr Bertram Wainer.

It was a sensitive matter because Wainer was waging war against police corruption in Victoria and had already received death threats warning him to stay away from Sydney. Smith claimed that when they left Bondi Junction, he was on his way

CALL ME JIMMY

to collect the documents, but he realised he was being followed, phoned his contact and was told new arrangements would be made.

Bertram Wainer was a doctor with a social conscience. His early days were spent in the army, where he rose to the rank of lieutenant-colonel at Yeronga military hospital, a few minutes drive south of Brisbane.

He had seen active service in war zones and, in his book *It Isn't Nice*, he recalled, 'It is not a pretty sight to see a young man with his left leg blown off, his scrotum torn away and his intestines permanently attached to his belly wall. It is even worse when you are aware he did not know why'. He left the army and took up private practice in St Kilda.

Wainer became 'an angry doctor'. He was outside Pentridge the morning Ronald Ryan was executed. 'A man ... knew that in half an hour he would walk along a dark corridor, led by fellow human beings to a place where his arms and legs would be tied, a rope would be fastened around his neck, and then he would wait for a trapdoor to give way beneath his life. There would be an eternity of consciousness as he fell and then snap! ... A man had been killed at the will of a politician.'

Dr Wainer became a voice for abortion reform when a young woman arrived on his doorstep one morning, haemorrhaging badly. She had been butchered by a backyard abortionist who, as Wainer subsequently discovered, was under the protection of Victorian police.

He became involved in the trade himself – but not as a backyarder; not as one of those sham 'doctors' offering half-hour 'surgery' jobs in some sordid suburban kitchen before sending a woman, bleeding and in shock, on her way.

In 1969, an estimated 20,000 illegal abortions were performed by backyarders in unclean conditions where 'after

THE CONSPIRACY

care' equated with ensuring that the day's takings were banked, or hidden, before the close of business.

Wainer decided to change things and set about exposing police involved in the abortion racket. He offered medically safe abortions and clinical after care and so women flocked to him from all over Victoria and New South Wales.

It was a conservative time, with the state run by Bolte and morals determined by the churches. Wainer soon found himself in conflict with the Australian Medical Association; his licence to practice medicine was threatened. He persisted, setting traps for police involved in the illegal abortion trade, which resulted in him becoming one of the most controversial and reviled figures of the era. But it also forced a government inquiry.

The inquiry started on 12 January, 1970, and lasted eight days. While its findings were white-anted to the extent that they were not tabled in parliament for 18 months, it did find that several police officers had been profiting from the illegal abortion trade. Four officers, all well-known, eventually went to prison and the wheels of abortion law reform were set in motion.

While Jimmy Smith probably had little interest in the wider social and moral issues raised by the abortion debate, he knew an angle when he saw one. The criminal grapevine had telegraphed the Wainer agenda loud and clear, and Smith was willing to try anything that might muddy the waters about the true nature of his activities.

He knew that, having exposed abortion rackets in Victoria, Wainer was turning his attention to other police corruption in that state. Wainer knew of incidences of police corruption and was sceptical about some members of the force.

Smith refused to speak when he was asked about his errand for Wainer in Sydney. Police claimed this was a ruse by Smith, and that he had been at Redfern that morning with the intention of robbing the Redfern railway workshops pay office. A record of interview was made. Some of the admissions allegedly made by Smith that day require scrutiny.

According to police statements, Smith admitted he was a 'mug' for even considering the Redfern job and implicated Motric as the one who approached him to be in on '… an easy job in Sydney'. But after they had reconnoitred the railway station the suspects decided '… it was ridiculous. We were parked so far from where we had to hold them up and there were so many people around that we gave it a miss'.

Police suggested, and they said Smith corroborated, that the plan had been to take the bag of guns to the men's toilets on the railway platform, wait for the armoured van carrying the payroll, pull out the guns, put on their masks and do the job.

There was a big defect in this scenario. The pay office at the workshops was not at the station itself. It was several hundred metres away. That meant that if Smith and Co. had waited on the platform for the payroll to show up, they would have had to put on face masks and pull out guns in the station toilets, then run several hundred metres to the pay office, first through the crowd at the station and then along a narrow suburban street running alongside the yards.

Between the pay office and the station there were sheds where carriages were repaired and engines serviced. The pay office was a small building at the base of a short flight of steps leading to the street. It was opposite the Carriage Workshops Eveleigh, several rows of huge red brick buildings with gabled roofs.

If the pay office had been the target, there were complications with a getaway because there were only two exits, north and east. The road west was a dead-end, while escape south was cut off by the railway complex. Travelling north would take too long because it was honeycombed with short, narrow streets

CALL ME JIMMY

The fugitive kind ... a handcuffed and pensive Smith is taken to a waiting police car after his recapture, 1977.

CALL ME JIMMY

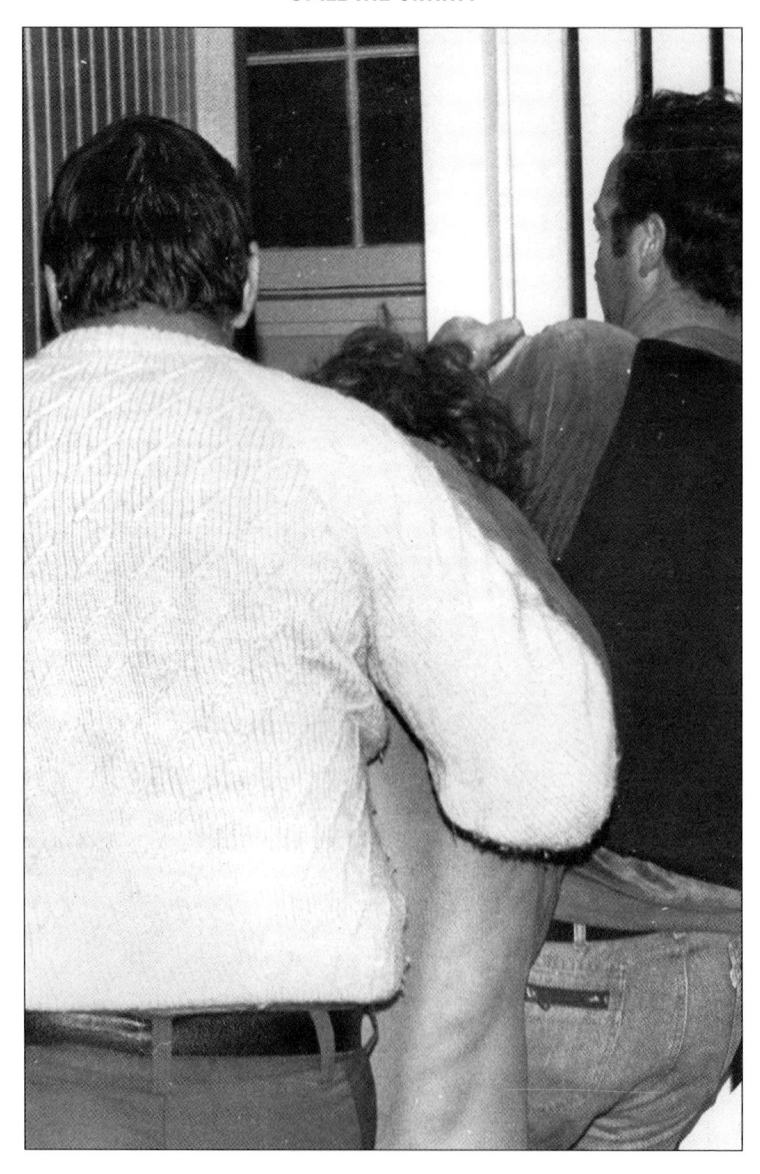

Under protest ... detectives drag a half-naked Smith into the charge room at the old Nowra police station.

CALL ME JIMMY

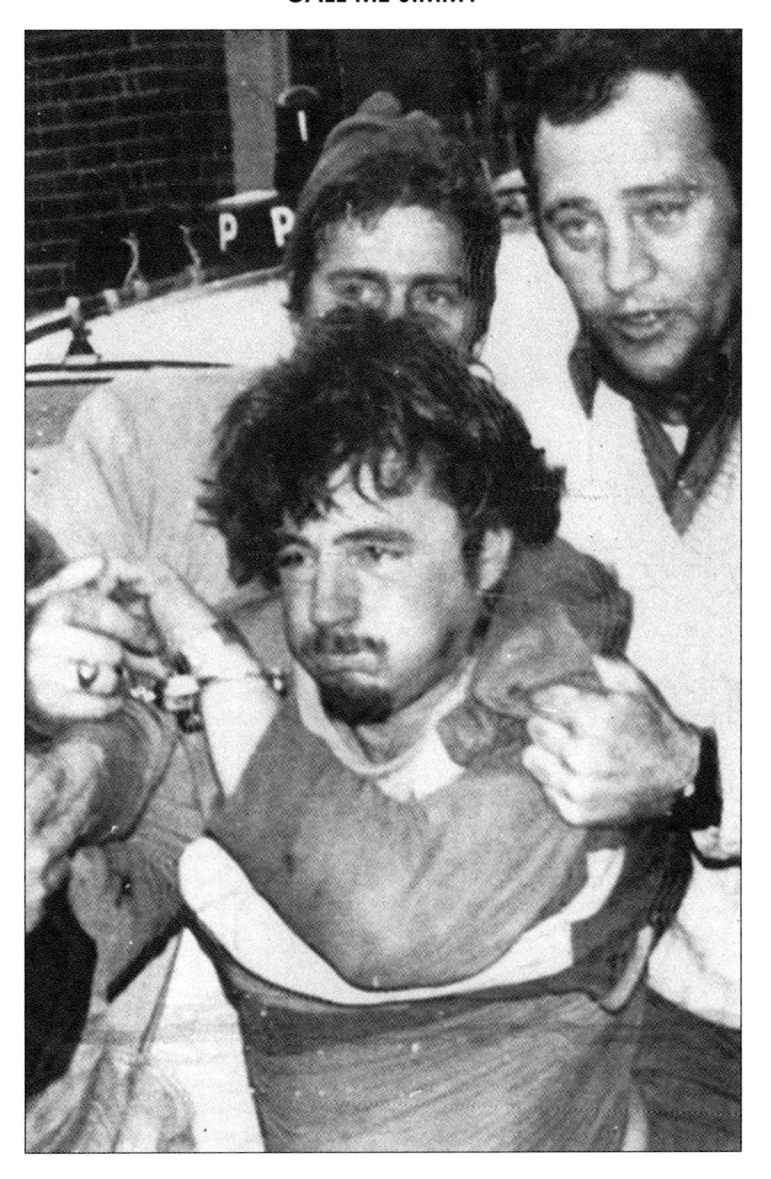

Moment of truth ... triumphant detectives frogmarch a furious Smith for the cameras after his recapture.

CALL ME JIMMY

Hands up, chin down ... Smith tries to dodge the undivided attention of the media in 1977.

CALL ME JIMMY

CALL ME JIMMY

Caught in the non-act ... Sydney detectives taking it easy after snaring 'Public Enemy No. 1'.

CALL ME JIMMY

Guns, but no money ... detectives reveal Smith's hardware after the 1977 arrest.

CALL ME JIMMY

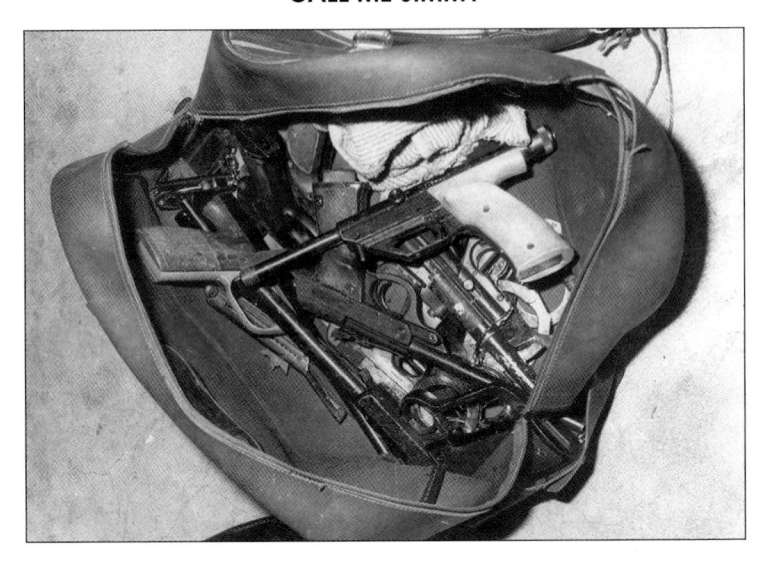

Smith had guns for every occasion ... sawn-off shotguns and rifles, handguns and target pistols.

CALL ME JIMMY

Nothing left to chance … cars being searched at Smith's hideout and the man himself handcuffed and tightly held.

CALL ME JIMMY

The getaway bike Smith borrowed briefly and (below) the telephone box where he was arrested.

CALL ME JIMMY

A view of the water from Smith's hideout.

Local crooks thought they would find a stash of cash in Smith's septic tank. They were wrong.

CALL ME JIMMY

Keystone cops ... Sydney police raided this house. Unfortunately, Smith lived next door.

Local talent ... Les Haywood (left) towed Smith from a ditch and Alan Walker (right) witnessed the bungled police raid on Smith's hideout.

CALL ME JIMMY

Working out inside ... the horse trainer rubs down a different type of beast.

CALL ME JIMMY

Weighting it out ... Smith (right, white singlet) watches

CALL ME JIMMY

fellow prisoners pump iron in a Sydney jail in the 1980s.

CALL ME JIMMY

Heavy crims ... Jockey, well above his riding weight, studies the form (top) and models a prison tracksuit (below).

THE CONSPIRACY

and a police cordon could be easily established. To escape east, the robbers would have to backtrack past the railway station before getting to the highway and escape. Along the way, they'd have to manoeuvre along the narrow street outside the station, clogged with rail users, and then face congested traffic.

Smith and the other three might have had guns on them that day. Their form suggested that they were rarely unarmed. But, given the apparent planning that had gone into Smith's other raids, it was improbable he would front at Redfern expecting to carry out a robbery with no surveillance beforehand.

Another odd aspect of the record of interview is the apparent ease with which police got Smith to talk about the planned robbery. Smith was a tough customer who, even in his earlier days, would never inform on his mates or volunteer information when he had not been caught red-handed.

Documentation on Smith from Victorian and New South Wales police departments, obtained through the Freedom of Information Act, specifically states, 'This person has been well schooled by solicitors and will tell you nothing'.

But, at the Sydney CIB in September 1974, he appeared to have had a change of heart. He was ready to tell all; he was happy to dob in himself and his mates for the crime of conspiracy, a crime that police, ordinarily, would have a hard time proving without transcripts of covertly recorded conversations between parties to the alleged conspiracy.

Police alleged Smith took them through the entire operation, describing the disguises to be used, ratting on Motric for supplying all the gear, detailing the plan to change in the toilets and burst out when the armoured van arrived, even down to expecting a haul of $160,000. It was a case of crime solved, as easily as that, without a shot fired or a dollar stolen.

The officers must have been wishing there were more

CALL ME JIMMY

criminals like Jimmy Smith; he rolled over without a whimper. Smith refused to sign the record of interview but, on its completion two hours after the interview started, the officer later claimed, he took it and Smith to a more senior officer who verified that Smith had given the information voluntarily.

It was fair to say that Sydney police didn't like Victorian robbers intruding on their patch.

SMITH'S story was very different from that of police who eventually charged him with conspiracy to rob the pay office at Redfern. He claimed the guns had not been in the boot of the Falcon and were planted there.

At CIB headquarters, Smith, Motric, O'Callaghan and James were separated, with Smith and O'Callaghan taken to the consorting squad office. Smith reckoned later that Detective Inspector Carmody, with a Victorian detective, stuck his head through one of the office doors and called out, 'Brian O'Callaghan and Jimmy Smith, what are you doing up here, boys? We'll give you your come-up here. What about a bank at Bondi for starters, how will that do?'

Smith's story was that he was taken to another section in the CIB where he alleged he again met a senior officer who, he claimed later, wiped his hands with a white towel and said, 'Hang on to his arms. This is going to hurt'. He then allegedly pressed a gun into Smith's left hand. Smith said he then abused the officer and spat at him. Smith always maintained another officer prised his hand open and forced it shut around the gun's magazine.

Back in the room where O'Callaghan was still sitting, Smith cried out, 'Be careful, there's a load on'. Smith was handcuffed to a detective's desk and left alone there for most of the day. That evening Smith and O'Callaghan were taken into another

THE CONSPIRACY

office where several detectives spoke to them while an officer was typing.

Afterwards they were walked across to Central police station where a detective allegedly whispered, 'There is a present in the property for you', and the two men were locked in the cells. Just as Smith claimed to have received an early Christmas present of explosives in 1966, there was one for him in Sydney, too. It turned out to be the record of interview, an unsigned document in which Smith supposedly confessed all.

O'CALLAGHAN suffered a similar fate, he claimed, when he found a fabricated confession in his property. O'Callaghan had a record dating back 20 years. He was an escapee from an English prison where he'd served time for theft of jewellery valued at £12,000 before walking out of jail disguised as a prison warder, a point not lost on Smith.

Four records of interview were made in which O'Callaghan confessed to the conspiracy charge and two subsequent charges relating to other armed robberies. But his signature did not appear on any of these documents and the admissions made regarding himself and Smith were so freely given and with such good cheer that a cautious reader would be somewhat sceptical.

A detective inspector's signature on the confessions meant nothing. It was standard practice to have a statement countersigned by a superior, particularly when the accused refused to sign it – as if the superior's signature lent the document some legitimacy.

The records of interview purportedly show that apart from his involvement in the Redfern conspiracy, Brian O'Callaghan confessed to his part in the armed robberies of the after-care hospital and the ANZ Bank at Prahran where, it was said, he was the getaway driver. The language used in two excerpts rang hollow. The interview relating to the robbery of the ANZ Bank was conducted by a detective in Sydney at 5.45pm on the day of the arrest at Bondi Junction.

> **Detective:** From what I have been told I believe that you were one of four men who committed this armed robbery on the ANZ Bank at Commercial Road, Prahran, on 5 August this year. Were you involved in this armed robbery?
> **O'Callaghan:** Yes, it makes no difference now. I am caught and I might as well be reasonable about it.
> **Detective:** When you say that you may as well be reasonable about it, are you inferring that you intend to tell me about that armed robbery?
> **O'Callaghan:** Look, I know you have a job to do. I don't dislike you. If I put myself in any position like this I can't be crook on anyone but myself.

O'CALLAGHAN was also questioned about an armed robbery in 1971 at Reservoir in Melbourne's northern suburbs. For this robbery, a Valiant sedan with the keys in the ignition was stolen from a used car lot and left overnight in a parking lot in Spring Street. A shotgun was concealed inside.

Next day, two men drove to the car park, hopped into the stolen car and waited. Mid-morning, two employees from a nearby factory drove into the car park carrying the payroll. As the ute passed the stolen Valiant, O'Callaghan backed out and blocked its path. He and the other man, who was dressed in female clothing and whose name O'Callaghan did not give up, jumped out and bailed up the factory workers. They then drove off and dumped the Valiant in a side street where another car was waiting. Later that day they burnt the clothes used in the robbery.

THE CONSPIRACY

O'Callaghan allegedly admitted stealing $7350 and the detective had solved another crime. O'Callaghan was uncharacteristically frank during the interview, to say the least.

Detective: I intend to ask you questions about an armed robbery that occurred in 1971.

O'Callaghan: That'll be the one in Reservoir, where we snatched the pay from the ute.

Detective: That is the one. You know something about it?

O'Callaghan: Oh yes, as a matter of fact it was getting so old I thought that you must have forgotten about it.

Detective: Not really. Did you know we were looking for you?

O'Callaghan: Yes, some coppers come running through my house in Melbourne a couple of days after. They said they were looking for me for that. I've been out of sight ever since.

Detective: Who was the other person involved?

O'Callaghan: Oh, come on now, detective be fair. If I'm charged with this your records are right. That's one more finished. That's the way you work, isn't it?

Detective: No, not really. I would like to know who the other person was.

O'Callaghan: I bet you would. I couldn't tell you. If you haven't found out in three years, you probably won't find out at all now, will you?

Detective: Are you prepared to tell me your part of the hold-up?

O'Callaghan: Well, it's a long time ago, I honestly forget about most of it. I'll do the best I can.

Detective: Well, go on.

O'Callaghan: I was the baddy in the whole bit. I was the desperate in the whole bit.

Detective: The hold-up was committed on two men who

CALL ME JIMMY

were driving a utility with a payroll for their firm. The amount was $7350. They were held up in a side street off Spring Street. Does that help you to remember at all?

O'Callaghan: Oh, I can remember all right. It's just the little things I forget, you know, like what I did with the money. (Laughed.)

Detective: You said that you were the baddy. What did you mean?

O'Callaghan: Oh, I was the silly bugger with the gun.

Detective: Whose idea was it to rob these men?

O'Callaghan: It was just something that me and my friend knew about. You must admit it was an easy go. Gee, they were asking to lose it.

Detective: Whose car did you use to do the hold-up?

O'Callaghan: I don't know that, it was one we pinched from a car yard in Heidelberg Road. I forget whose yard it was.

Detective: (A couple of questions later) You took the car on the Tuesday and the hold-up was done on the Wednesday. What did you do with the car in the interim?

O'Callaghan: When we took it, we took it especially for the job, so we drove it up to the car park where it happened and left it there overnight. See, if we went back the next day, it was there all ready for us.

Detective: I see. What happened next?

O'Callaghan: Oh, we drove up there in another car, left it a bit away and as a matter of fact we walked to the other car we had.

Detective: Just a minute, this hold-up was done with a full length shotgun. Also, your offsider was dressed in woman's clothing. How did you carry that if you were walking?

O'Callaghan: Oh, that was in the car from the day before. It was already there.

THE CONSPIRACY

Detective: All right, what happened on the day of the hold-up?
O'Callaghan: You'd have to know that it'd been looked at. They always went the same way. We got in that Valiant, put the funny gear on and waited. I was lying in the back seat. My very good friend was at the wheel and we waited. You would have laughed if you had've seen him. He had all this funny sheila's gear on.
Detective: Where did you get the clothes from?
O'Callaghan: I forget.
Detective: What were you wearing.
O'Callaghan: I'm not sure, probably overalls. Some stocking or a sleeve from a jumper. I just forget. True, I do.
Detective: How did you actually do the hold-up?
O'Callaghan: We just waited in the drive part and backed out in front of them. I jumped out of the back seat and poked the shotty in the window, simple as that.
Detective: I see in one of the witness statements that you yelled at him and said that you would blow his guts out or something similar. Did you say that?
O'Callaghan: Probably something similar, I don't know.

THIS is an interesting record of interview because, even before O'Callaghan is asked a question, he volunteers information which incriminates him in the Reservoir hold-up: 'That'll be the one at Reservoir'.

This man had a long criminal history. He was experienced in police interviews and able to create a story that might draw attention away from any involvement he might have had in a crime. To come out and say something like, 'Oh yes, as a matter of fact it was getting so old I thought you must have forgotten about it', contradicts every tenet of the criminal code, certainly of the old school where, if you didn't have an alibi, you kept your mouth shut. It is hardly plausible that O'Callaghan would so freely implicate himself when the result could only be more time in jail.

One of the questions is particularly interesting. In asking O'Callaghan if he was prepared to divulge his part in the crime and then having O'Callaghan say it was such 'a long time ago, I honestly forgot about most of it', the detective effectively dealt with the problem he would have if he did concoct the record of interview – that of providing precise details.

The wording of some of the answers – 'I was the baddy in the whole bit' or 'I was the silly bugger with the gun' or 'My very good friend was at the wheel' – doesn't tally with the language of a hardened criminal.

The surveillance team that nabbed Smith, O'Callaghan and company was part of a larger operation to catch those responsible for the theft of weapons from an Adelaide store a couple of weeks earlier.

While the four were being interviewed by police in Sydney, simultaneous raids were carried out in Geelong on homes belonging to other members of the Smith family.

Jean Smith received a visit from police, whom she recalls as being civil, as did others in the family. Ron and his wife, Evelyn, were in their pizza shop at Ocean Grove when police demanded entry and searched the premises. During the search some damage was done to a door in the shop and to walls in the living area. Nothing was found.

ONCE all the conspirators had apparently made records of interview comprehensively implicating themselves in a plan to rob the railways at Redfern, they were presented to the courts. In the presence of the magistrate, Smith said, 'I want it recorded

THE CONSPIRACY

and put in writing I believe there are records of interview that have been put into our property, that we have made no records of interview and we have made no statements to police, and if there are records of interview being put into our property, we want access to it before we go any longer, (and) that we have been denied a phone call for a solicitor.'

The magistrate ordered the police to provide to the accused any records of interview that had been placed in their property. This was done soon after they returned to their cells. Smith further protested that he had made affidavits and tape recordings to the effect that, if he was arrested, he would refuse to answer any questions unless in the presence of his solicitor and that any statement made in the presence of a solicitor would be signed.

One such affidavit, typical of his stance, read: 'I Edward James Smith – State that if the police at any time attempt to question me on any matters that I will not answer any questions whatsoever because it's my legal rights. A signed copy of this is also held by my barrister'. It was signed E. J. Smith.

At his appearance before the magistrate on 12 September, 1974, Smith was remanded in custody to 20 September, 1974, at which time he was granted bail on $20,000 surety. He couldn't find the money and remained in custody. On 20 September, the matter was remanded to 27 September after being part heard. Bail was reduced to $10,000 and again Smith was remanded, this time to 4 October.

After further evidence was heard, the matter was remanded for the fourth time to 18 October, 1974. Smith's family put together $10,000. Free on bail, Smith failed to appear on 18 October. A warrant for his arrest was issued that day.

Smith was later to say that he skipped bail because, in a telephone conversation the day before, James said that neither he nor O'Callaghan was going to appear and the result for

CALL ME JIMMY

Smith would be the loss of his bail. In a letter to the magistrate and to the media, Smith explained he didn't think he was going to get justice.

Of the four accused, Motric was the only one to appear in court and he was sentenced to 15 years' prison. Smith thought Motric was hard done by. He was a Yugoslav, relatively new to Australia, who spoke broken English and was at a disadvantage defending himself in court.

In sentencing Motric on 24 June, 1975, His Honour Judge Hicks said, 'I am forced to the conclusion that had you been in complete control of the quartet, the robbery would have gone on ... You are a useless fellow. You have not a terribly bad record, but you have no regard for the law; you apparently do not work except at gambling; you are a thoroughly undesirable member of the community. Nonetheless, I cannot on that simple ground, impose a very severe penalty, but I can and I do impose a very severe penalty for the offence you did commit.'

Smith was in Melbourne on 18 October, 1974, when he was supposed to front the conspiracy charges in Sydney. He was living in Caulfield, not far from his sister's flat in Brighton and Valerie Hill's home in Cheltenham. His time was split between the races at Caulfield and the beach at Sandringham.

On 8 December, 1974, Smith was sunbaking on the beach at Sandringham with Valerie Hill. It was a warm summer's day and he was dressed in togs. Smith was taking in the view of Port Phillip Bay when a voice said quietly, 'G'day, Jockey'. He turned around to find two police officers standing behind him.

Acting on a tip-off, Detective Senior Constable Bob Turner and Detective Sergeant Lalor had slipped down to the beach and walked along until they saw Smith in the distance. According to Detective Turner, Smith was surprised but 'came like a lamb'.

THE CONSPIRACY

He was handcuffed and taken to Sandringham police station, where he was charged with a couple of minor offences and remanded in custody to appear at Brighton Court four days later. Because he'd skipped bail and was facing more serious charges in New South Wales, he was taken directly to Pentridge.

Bob Turner, who got to the rank of chief inspector before retiring, remembered Smith as a career criminal – 'one that doesn't like permanent employment'. It was a fair point, because Smith had virtually no employment record and, seemingly, had survived on his wits as a criminal.

Turner recalled Smith's days as a safe-cutter and acknowledged his skill with the oxy-acetylene torch and explosives. 'He was a successful bank robber and enterer because he was never charged with armed robbery on a bank in Victoria' – this despite police believing he had been involved, but unable to do anything about it without sufficient evidence.

On 10 December, 1974, Smith escaped from the remand section at Pentridge. It was a farcical episode and it embarrassed prison staff.

He somehow got over a two-metre high internal fence and worked his way to the visitors' area where his girlfriend, Valerie Hill, and her sister Melanie were waiting for him. Smith, or possibly one of the women, persuaded an elderly gentleman who spoke little English to part with his visitor's pass. Smith, minus his prison jacket, put on sunglasses and, together with Melanie, simply walked out of the south gate.

Myths have grown around this escape. One version tells of Smith walking past the guard on duty at the main gate, doffing his hat and saying something along the lines of 'See ya later, Duncan', as nonchalantly as if he were knocking off work for the day.

CALL ME JIMMY

Newspapers reported next day that Smith and the two women had got past the guard, Duncan Wilcox, when he opened the gate to allow another two visitors into the prison. Almost immediately, Wilcox felt something was wrong with the threesome that had just walked out, threw his keys to another guard and went to investigate.

Smith was running down Urquhart Street outside the prison wall just as the governor of Pentridge, John Dawes, was crossing the road. Wilcox informed the governor of Smith's exit and together they hailed a passing taxi and began what some have described as a Keystone Cops chase into Sydney Road, Brunswick.

But Jockey Smith had disappeared.

CHAPTER 6

Taking a hike

THE song ends and the polished voice of the newsreader stops Jean in her tracks.

> *Police are hunting for a prisoner who escaped from Pentridge Prison earlier today. Edward James Smith, wanted on conspiracy charges in NSW and for armed robbery in Victoria, walked out of Pentridge on a visitor's pass before fleeing into neighbouring suburbs. Smith had been captured just two days ago on the beach at Sandringham and placed in the remand centre at Pentridge. Smith is described as 5 foot 6 inches tall, with long brown hair, brown eyes and of medium build. He is considered dangerous and may be armed. Anyone knowing his ...*

Jean clutches at her breast. She loves her wild son and he is breaking her heart. Give yourself up, boy. A silent prayer – one

CALL ME JIMMY

that goes unanswered. *Oh Jimmy, I love you son ... but why are you doin' this to me? Give yourself up, boy. It'll only go worse for you if you run.*

She sits and waits. She knows they'll come, and they do. *You know he's escaped, Mrs Smith. Has he tried to contact you yet?* She looks at them coldly, standing just inside the door, and then in the cluttered lounge-room, her one good leg braced against the world. She holds her own, steeling herself against any flicker in her manner that might betray her boy. She contains her bitterness – a sore not yet healed, and unlikely to be – over the way the police treated her Daniel and others in her family, dragged into the whole sorry mess only because they were related to Jimmy. Blood is thicker than water.

He knows better than to come here for help, better than to involve his mother. You can search the place if you like but you won't find nothin' of Jimmy's here.

The police leave and keep watch from a distance, just in case.

JIMMY separated from Valerie Hill and her sister, Melanie, as soon as they got away from Pentridge. He had a network of friends in Melbourne, dock workers and criminals, willing to provide safe haven while police thrashed about the more obvious known haunts looking for him.

Valerie headed home to Cheltenham and wasn't surprised to find police waiting on her doorstep. She was questioned but not arrested because, she says, the police figured she had not known Smith's intention was to escape when she arrived at Pentridge that morning.

Meanwhile, Smith was confused. Now that he'd escaped, he wasn't sure what to do next. At one stage, he entertained the idea of giving himself up and approached Dr Bertram Wainer for advice. Watchful in case the controversial abortionist was under surveillance, he made contact with the doctor through a

TAKING A HIKE

friend, arranging to meet at Wainer's house a few evenings after his escape. This meeting was brief. He decided against giving himself up. Instead, he wrote a letter to *Truth* newspaper in Melbourne outlining his reasons for escaping ... that he had been framed on the explosives charge and was being framed again on the Redfern conspiracy charge.

Smith was confident he could approach Wainer without fear of being turned in. Wainer was gathering information from the underworld to force a government inquiry into police corruption. He was sympathetic to criminals he believed were convicted through police 'verbals' or confessions obtained under duress or through informers paid by police to lie under oath. He was compiling evidence of crimes organised by police.

On 23 October, 1974, six weeks before Smith's arrest at Sandringham and escape from Pentridge, Wainer taped a conversation between a criminal, David Hinkler Keely, and Senior Sergeant Bert Gaudion, which he subsequently handed to the Solicitor-General, Daryl Dawson QC, and Assistant Commissioner of Police, Bill Crowley.

Wainer alleged Gaudion had accepted a bribe from Keely before 23 October and, as of that date, was prepared to enter into a conspiracy with Keely. Keely alleged Gaudion accepted $500 on condition Gaudion would not charge Keely with the offence of breaking, entering and stealing a quantity of clothing and would instead charge him only with receiving stolen clothing.

Wainer and others further alleged police malpractices including falsifying evidence, perjury, damage to property and assault causing serious injury In February, 1975, Victoria's Chief Secretary, John Rossiter, instructed barrister Cairns Villeneuve-Smith to make a preliminary investigation into Wainer's allegations. Following that investigation the 'Board of Inquiry into Allegations Against Members of the Victoria Police Force' was established on 18 March, 1975, with Barry Beach QC presiding.

CALL ME JIMMY

Advertisements announcing the inquiry's terms of reference were run in *The Age, The Sun* and *The Australian* newspapers four days later. They called for public input. Similar advertisements were later published in *The Herald* and *Truth*. The board of inquiry eventually sat for 227 days and took evidence from 240 witnesses, and in the process, inspected police headquarters at Russell Street and several suburban police stations.

Beach looked at 131 complaints. Of those, only 21 were fully investigated. While acknowledging Wainer as the instigator of the inquiry, Beach saw him as having 'the shortcomings of a crusader – a propensity to exaggerate, a propensity to carry on his investigations on the basis that the end justifies the means, and an insatiable desire for publicity'.

On balance, Beach's assessment might have been reasonable, as Wainer did exaggerate about the number of cases he would present to the inquiry. Initially, he claimed to know of 50 documented cases of corruption but, eventually, presented only four and participated in a further seven.

As in the abortion law campaign, Wainer had attracted many people to his cause against police corruption – both criminals and law reformers. Obviously, many of the criminals who provided information hoped to get their own back on a police force they felt had treated them harshly. In particular, it was a chance to even the score with individual officers. They saw in Wainer not only an articulate and committed advocate but, as an educated man, someone who appeared to have the credibility, integrity and polish they lacked. They might have overestimated him.

One of the matters before the Beach inquiry related to the raid on Ron and Evelyn Smith's pizza parlour in Ocean Grove on the day Jimmy Smith was arrested in Sydney and charged with conspiracy to rob the Redfern Railway Workshops. This matter

TAKING A HIKE

alleged police damage to the pizza parlour during the raid. The damage amounted to $250 and was reported in the *Geelong Advertiser* on several occasions – as was the inspection of the pizza parlour by Beach and his assistants.

During the raid, police had a search warrant to look for guns stolen from a sports goods distributor in Adelaide on the evening of 26 or 27 December, 1973. Jimmy Smith was a suspect. While Beach found the four police officers who raided the Smiths' pizza parlour had 'ample reason' to conduct a search, he criticised them for causing damage to the Smiths' property, for using intimidating tactics, for unlawful imprisonment of Colleen Paton (an employee at the pizza parlour) for unlawful seizure of property and for conspiring to lie to the inquiry.

In making adverse findings against 55 members of the Victoria Police Force, Beach singled out the armed robbery and consorting squads for special mention. He found officers in those squads had committed perjury, conspired with known criminals to fabricate evidence, assaulted witnesses during interrogation and suppressed evidence favourable to accused persons.

Beach recommended prosecution for more than 30 of the 55 officers found by the inquiry to have been involved in corrupt activities. Only 17 eventually faced committal proceedings. The police association in Victoria, led by Inspector Tom Rippon, voiced anger over the inquiry's findings and a meeting of more than 4000 officers at Festival Hall in Melbourne threatened massive police strike action. The Hamer Government was under pressure to buckle to police demands while Beach QC became the target for personal attacks from the police association.

John Jost reported in *The National Times* in March 1977 that the police association and Premier Hamer had struck an agreement. 'The agreement included this paragraph: "No police will be presented for trial upon any alleged indictable offence without a normal preliminary hearing in a magistrate's court". Implicit in this agreement was that if the magistrate's court discharged a police defendant then no further action would be taken.'

At the committal hearings, charges against 15 of 17 accused officers were dismissed. Of the remaining two, one was committed to trial for pistol whipping a suspect and the other for falsely imprisoning a woman. Neither was convicted. None of those involved in the Smith matter reached trial.

There is speculation that one reason the charges against 15 officers were dismissed relates to the nature of evidence led. It seems likely the evidence Beach was presented with at the inquiry, and on which he based his recommendations, had been watered down by the time it was heard in the magistrate's court.

Interestingly, many of the 55 officers went on to become senior members of the Victoria Police Force, up to the rank of deputy commissioner.

EVEN though several of the matters before Beach involved Jimmy Smith's close friends and family, he ultimately decided to keep running. He needed money. It is likely he had cash hidden from past jobs, but whether or not this was enough to sustain him for long is impossible to know.

He had to move quickly and to get out of Victoria so, with Valerie Hill and her daughter, Smith moved to New South Wales where his profile was less likely to draw attention despite his having skipped bail there on conspiracy charges only months earlier. He had connections and was able to stay sporadically with friends. Mostly, he was on the move, living out of caravan parks or camping, shifting frequently in an effort to obscure whatever trail he may have left behind.

TAKING A HIKE

For Valerie Hill and her daughter, it was an equally difficult time. Valerie's daughter, who was 14, had to leave school and learn about life on the run. Valerie risked detection every time she travelled back to Melbourne to see her mother and family.

Following 11 months of life on the run, Smith felt it was safe to settle down for a longer period in one place and, in November, 1975, he rented a house in Brighton-le-Sands on the western shores of Botany Bay. It was a convenient location, close to Sydney Airport, and happened to be across the bay from Long Bay Jail.

During this time, the alias of Douglas Cumming first surfaced. A NSW Department of Transport vehicle search shows that Smith, using this alias, purchased a 1973 HQ Holden sedan on 7 May, 1976, and gave as his address a street in Elizabeth Bay on the New South Wales central coast. Whether or not he kept a house at this address is unclear. The car was bought from a dealer in Kogarah, a suburb next to Brighton-le-Sands. It seems likely the Elizabeth Bay address was to lay a false trail for anyone who might have been following him.

A few months after Smith moved into Brighton-le-Sands, a confidential circular did the rounds of police stations in New South Wales and Victoria. It said Terry Keith Clark and Edward James Smith were urgently wanted over the attempted murder of Constable Jeremiah Ambrose at Kingsford, near the University of New South Wales, on 21 January, 1976. The boxed Special Circular read:

At 9.30pm on Wednesday, 21 January 1976, Constable Ambrose and Constable Love, both attached to the highway patrol, North Sydney, were patrolling in Anzac Parade, Kingsford, Sydney, when they saw a 1967 model Austin 1800 sedan, maroon in colour, registered number

CALL ME JIMMY

GTS-535 travelling north in Anzac Parade without headlights. Constable Love turned the police vehicle around and, as they drew level with the car, Constable Ambrose called on the occupants to stop. The Austin was then driven into Day Avenue where it stopped. As the police car stopped behind the Austin, the rear, nearside door was opened by the passenger, who looked back at the police car. He then closed the door and the Austin sedan was driven off, followed by the police vehicle.

After travelling several hundred metres during which the passenger of the Austin fired several shots toward the police car, the car collided with the kerb at the intersection of Harben St, Kingsford. The driver of the Austin decamped, pursued by Constable Love. Love called on the offender to stop to no avail. Offender stopped behind an electrical installation and fired a shot at Love. He then made good his escape.

Constable Ambrose alighted from the police car to apprehend the passenger in the rear of the Austin. He called on the offender to surrender and, as he did so, the rear passenger door was opened and the occupant fired several shots, hitting Ambrose in the stomach. Ambrose fell to the ground and another shot was fired at him, apparently missing and the offender decamped.

Both these men are armed and extremely dangerous and will not hesitate to shoot again. Extreme caution should be exercised in approaching vehicles suspected to contain above offenders.

TAKING A HIKE

By March 1976, Smith was Australia's Public Enemy No. 1 – he'd made the top 10 list in Victoria some months earlier. Police were determined to recapture him, following a tip off he was still living somewhere in the state.

Raids of known haunts around Melbourne and in country Victoria were synchronised to reduce any opportunity for friends to alert Smith. More than 60 detectives gathered at Russell Street headquarters around 4.30am on 12 March to be briefed before setting out on co-ordinated raids. Other detectives met elsewhere in Victoria at the same time. Despite all the planning and secrecy, the raids failed to trap Smith who, if he had been in Victoria as rumoured, had already returned to Sydney.

On 25 September, 1976, Smith decided he'd stayed put long enough. He moved out of Sydney and took a six-month lease on a fully furnished house in Bunkers Hill Road, Kangaroo Valley, about half an hour from Nowra, on the Shoalhaven River just inland from the NSW south coast.

The property was far from prying eyes and chance meetings. It was the weekend retreat of Sydney dentist, John Quick, who was overseas at the time and had arranged to rent the property through King's Real Estate agent, Ralph Cook. The agent showed the family over the property and, before leaving, was invited by Smith to bring his wife out for a barbecue some time. Cook knew Smith as Douglas Cumming, a self-employed panel beater. The rent was $40 a week and Smith paid the full six months in advance in $50 notes before leaving the agent's office.

Cook saw nothing of the Cumming family for six months. There was no need to make periodic inspections; John Quick had arranged for a neighbouring dairy farmer, Ian Vance, to keep an eye on his new tenants, giving Vance the authority to revoke their lease if the property was abused in any way.

Throughout the district Smith quickly became known as

CALL ME JIMMY

Doug Cumming, a name he later altered to Tom Cumming in a sly tribute to the two dominant horse trainers of the era, Tommy Smith and Bart Cummings.

Valerie Hill called herself Judy Cumming while her daughter was known as Debbie. They were three happy-go-lucky people with an interest in cars and horses who arrived in town complete with their very own Grandpa, who was in fact one of Smith's associates in crime, Frank Montgomery. Doug and Judy Cumming, their daughter and 'Grandpa' seemed to casual observers to be a happy, lively family popular in the area, welcome at the Friendly Inn Hotel and the local bowling club. 'Grandpa' enjoyed meeting people and was given to telling tall stories and amusing yarns.

Some locals still talk about another member of the family who often stayed with the Cumming family. They said he was Judy's brother; in fact, he was Neil Collings, an associate of Smith, and he looked like a young version of former South Australian Premier, the late Don Dunstan.

The rented house was an ideal hideout in the misty hills of Morton National Park. To get there from the township of Kangaroo Valley, the Cumming family had to cross the single lane Hampden Bridge, known locally as the oldest suspension bridge in Australia, travel three or four kilometres along the Moss Vale Road before turning right into Bunker's Hill Road and then wind their way up the mountain through horse-shoe bends and across the flood-prone Barrengarry Creek.

The last two kilometres of road were private and shut off from general traffic by a set of heavy gates. A couple of kilometres further on the road, narrow now and treacherous when it rained, ended abruptly at Smith's rented property.

The house itself was small but comfortable, a 1940s fibro bungalow next to several sheds. Surrounded by rugged

TAKING A HIKE

mountains and big paddocks, it was a world away from the brutal confines of prison life. He had found himself a home carved out of the wilderness hidden between two steep mountain ranges, a hideaway fit for a bushranger of old.

There was room for his horses and all the cars that eventually found their way along Bunker's Hill Road. So many, in fact, that Ian Vance made a point of reporting to Ralph Cook that a lot of cars were going up the hill and later coming down with different number plates attached. Little escaped Vance's eye.

As part of his duties, Vance worked on Quick's property and had reason to be around the farmhouse from time to time, occasionally early in the morning. Sometimes, a car or horse float would block access to the cattle yards or dairy and need to be shifted. Even at 5am, Smith would be aware of the farmer's needs and bolt from the house fully clothed, a knack learned from months of looking over his shoulder. Smith seemed to sense when there was an intruder to his environment. He was wary of unusual sights and sounds, alert and watchful for any telltale changes in the humdrum tenor of country life.

For all their strange car dealings, the Cumming family looked after John Quick's property. They came and went frequently, often pulling a horse float to a safe stretch of the Shoalhaven River where the horses were given a swim as part of their conditioning routine. Towing the float up Bunker's Hill Road was a strain on the family's Holden sedan and, according to Vance, the car was quickly knocked about. 'He'd tear up the road, sparks flying off the bottom of the car as he crossed the creek. I'd think he was a maniac.'

Vance remembers well the man he now knows as Jockey Smith, the fugitive. 'He was a good mate of mine, but he didn't leave anything for me in his will. He did take me in (with his alias) but I always felt there was something not quite right. He said he had a factory in Bomaderry, but it seemed like pie in the sky to me so I offered to give him work hay carting. He quickly backed off, saying his factory was nearly ready to open.'

Vance liked the man he knew as Doug Cumming, despite the fast driving, the merry-go-round of cars and his feeling that something was not quite right. He quickly made friends with his new neighbours and was grateful to Val, who occasionally brought out tea and cakes when he was refuelling his tractor at the farm.

At the time Smith sported a droopy moustache and long hair, down to his shoulders. He was stocky and Vance remembers seeing tattoos and a 'fair roll of fat' hanging over his stubby shorts. But that image was short-lived because Smith changed his appearance frequently: sometimes he had long hair and a goatee beard; other times, he wore his hair short and was clean-shaven. He altered the colour of his hair as well as the style, variously parted at the side or in the middle, and he was apparently able to shed weight quickly so he appeared relatively thin at times.

While the Cumming family rarely had outsiders to their house, they socialised with the Kangaroo Valley folk. Locals recalled how one of the Cumming family would always wait in the car outside the Friendly Inn Hotel while the others went inside to put back an ale or two. They'd take it in turns to go inside while the one waiting in the car would be periodically brought drinks from the bar.

The Cummings fitted in easily; they were accepted without question as the horse people they appeared to be. They paid cash for purchases around town and collected their mail at the Barrengarry Post Office on the outskirts of town, a postal agency in a corner of the quaint, turn-of-the-century Barrengarry Store, with its flat iron verandah and single gable

TAKING A HIKE

roof. Later, Valerie Hill had fond memories of their time in Kangaroo Valley and of the people they met there. One of her friends was Eileen Rebbeck, who was 18 at the time and worked behind the bar at the hotel. Eileen invited Judy and the family to her engagement party. 'They were good people and made friends easily. My brother, Robert, met Doug Cumming at the hotel almost as soon as he arrived in town and used to go out with their daughter.

'Doug didn't flash money around but Grandpa did. He was a nice, old man and always had lots of money. When Grandpa opened his wallet he'd say he'd had a good win at the races. He'd flash money and buy drinks for everyone in the hotel.'

Montgomery was an old man and, for all his big noting at the pub, not well. He suffered severe joint pain in both knees from osteoarthritis, cirrhosis of the liver and a hernia in the groin.

When a stranger sidled up to the bar at the Friendly Inn one day he stood out immediately. Jimmy Smith was with David Rebbeck and others when his attention to the conversation drifted. He was tuned into the movements of the stranger. Later, after Smith left and David was about to drive home, he was surprised to find the stranger sitting in the back of his car. The man never identified himself, but wanted to know about Doug Cumming and the people at the farmhouse.

Around this time, the lease expired at John Quick's property and, within a couple of weeks, the Cumming family had gathered their possessions and moved out. Ian Vance was surprised at the speed with which they left, but was pleased with the condition of the property. His part in Jimmy Smith's life was over. Well, almost, anyway. Some months later, he was called to give evidence because he was the only person who could testify to the association of those he came to know as Edward James Smith, Frank Montgomery and Neil Collings.

CALL ME JIMMY

BEFORE leaving Bunker's Hill Road, Jimmy Smith approached Ralph Cook to find another property to rent. Cook took Smith to a property in Pyree, but Smith wasn't keen on it. Why that would be was a mystery to the agent at the time, but it was possibly because Smith thought it was too open to passers-by. Smith eventually found another place through Terry Watson Real Estate in Nowra and Ralph Cook was asked to give a reference.

The Nowra property was known as the Little House. It was a compact, timber bungalow overlooking the Shoalhaven River at Long Point, about two kilometres from the North Nowra shops. The owner was from Sydney and had used the property as a retreat, a place to enjoy acres of farmland and bush, sheer cliffs and steep, wooded ground leading to the banks of the river. It was secluded; the road ended at bushland surrounding the farm and the only other way in was by boat.

There were three houses at Long Point. Smith's was the first, at the start of a steep and winding, partly-concreted track leading down to the river and the other houses. The next house was at the bottom of this track and was independently owned; it had been carved off from the rest of the property years earlier. The third house was the weekend retreat of Coorong Farm's owner and was at the end of a long track, which followed the river.

The so-called Cumming family moved in on 25 March, 1977. Judy signed the lease, but did not note her husband's name. It was at this point, most likely, that 'Doug' began introducing himself as 'Tom', a panel beater, self-employed and the operator of a rented premises in Bomaderry.

Again, Smith had chosen an isolated location with postcard scenery. Tall gums shielded the house from the wind. The bush was alive with birds: finches, wrens, parrots and the cockatoos from which the city of Nowra derived its Aboriginal name. It

TAKING A HIKE

was thick bush, the undergrowth full of tree creepers, tussocks and ferns. Below the house was a network of caves carved out of the sheer rock face, which fell 20 or so metres to where the forest and tangled undergrowth ran away to the river.

In 1977, Nowra was a sleepy farming town of around 8000 people, about two and a half hours drive south of Sydney. These days, it is a bustling rural city with a population of around 20,000, the centre of a growing tourist industry built around the network of coastal coves, river activities and the rugged mountain terrain for which the area has become known.

Jimmy Smith quickly hooked up with the Nowra racing fraternity and joined early risers at the local race track most mornings. Although he didn't have a trainer's licence he was able to put his two horses, Regency Head and Dornier, through their paces under the supervision of local trainer, Kerry Walker, who became good friends with the man he knew as 'Tom Cumming'. Both horses were registered in the name of Neil Collings but they were Smith's responsibility.

Kerry Walker, who no longer trains at Nowra, remembers Smith as 'a terrific bloke' with a sense of humour. 'Everyone liked him. Knowing the bloke as I did, the picture painted by the media doesn't fit. The so-called violence stunned me; I never saw it, not once.'

Most of those who knew Smith described him as a 'knockabout' type of bloke, a 'real character', always joking and telling stories, especially when he popped into the bowling club, the Empire Hotel or the Bridge Hotel for a drink. Some later guessed that his visits to local watering holes were part of a counter-surveillance operation on police, which included checks on strange cars at the local nick. He'd prop himself at the bar, within cooee of off-duty police officers and, while talking with someone else, would tune into the conversations of officers. He probably didn't fear detection because his appearance had altered significantly from the photos on wanted posters taken years earlier. And he used disguises.

Jimmy Smith would be at the track early, often with Grandpa in tow, to put his horses through their paces. Often, he would ride one himself, enjoying a return to the saddle. Smith's horses were not top class, but they did have some success.

Kerry Walker had commitments to other owners and Smith would help out two or three times a week by travelling the five miles to Illaroo Road Primary School to collect Walker's two daughters and take them home. The two families were close and often socialised together.

Like many a small trainer, Walker was not rolling in money and Smith sometimes helped him out. 'I used to have trouble with cars and he would loan me cars whenever I needed them,' he was to say later of Smith. 'He was that kind of guy, always willing to help. I would have trusted him with my life.'

During the six months Smith was in Nowra he and Walker raced the pair of horses about 18 times – at Canterbury, Randwick, Kembla Grange, Rose Hill, Canberra and Nowra. Walker remembers Smith's hard driving.

'The trip to Canberra was normally a three hour drive. We got back in two, coming through Exeter, Barrengarry and Cambewarra. He was a very good driver, intense, but too fast for me. One time, he was on his way to Jervis Bay and got picked up for speeding. The copper had no idea who was behind the wheel.'

Smith loved the punt, often placing upwards of $10,000 on one race. It was common enough to see him slip into the ring with a brown paper bag under his arm to dole out bets in multiples of $1000.

Walker recalled one such incident at Nowra when Smith

TAKING A HIKE

arrived at the track, tossed a paper bag to Grandpa with instructions to put the money in the race bag. When Walker looked, the bag contained about $12,000.

'He did back winners. He won three or four times in a row on a Bart Cummings' horse called Ngawyni. It was a good run and, I'm guessing, but I reckon he won around $50,000.' Of course, Smith also lost heavily, like the time he put ten grand on Dornier to win at Canberra at odds of 8-1. The horse was slow out of the starting gates and ran fourth.

The track has long been seen as a place to launder money. It's an image disputed by some bookmakers, who say there's little value in trying to 'clean' stolen money at the races because, often as not, a person is likely to get back the same notes used to place a bet. The theory is simple enough — bet using stolen notes at whatever odds in the hope of a win and a cash return in different notes. Of course, even if police nab the launderer with stolen notes in his possession, if he can show they were returned via a bet, he can claim he won it at the races, a claim easily verified by the bookie.

Jimmy Smith's bets in multiples of a thousand dollars stood out at a time when the average punter wagered $5 to $50. It was before the days when legal casinos became a surer bet. Casinos carry massive quantities of cash and the likelihood of getting back the same notes is slim. The chances of winning consistently are also slim, but that doesn't seem to worry most criminals, who have to be gamblers by nature to risk their liberty and their lives (or someone else's) every time they commit a crime.

While Smith was living at Nowra, a prominent Sydney bookmaker, Lloyd Tidmarsh, was shot dead in his Kogarah home. The bookie and his family were confronted by three masked intruders who entered through an open rear door of the

CALL ME JIMMY

Tidmarsh home late one night and demanded cash. The bandits fled but not before a neighbour managed to note part of their car's registration number.

It was a senseless murder, perhaps never intended, resulting from frustration and anger because Tidmarsh's race takings were not in the house but had already been banked for the day. The crime was committed while the victim's family cowered in their beds, afraid they would be next. Tidmarsh's daughter, Michelle, pretended to be asleep throughout the ordeal and was not approached by the killers. But she listened hard to what was being said and took note of one voice in particular, a voice she would later describe in the witness box as 'rough and gruff', a voice she would attribute to Jimmy Smith.

Tidmarsh's death aroused alarm throughout the racing fraternity. The New South Wales Bookmakers' Co-operative Society offered a $20,000 reward *'... for information leading to the arrest and conviction of the of the persons responsible ...'*

It was standing room only for many of those who attended his Requiem Mass at St Patrick's Catholic Church; everyone turned out, from racing identities to nuns to young mothers with babes-at-arms. There was even an honour guard as the coffin left the church.

The media reported everything to do with the case. For weeks after Tidmarsh's death barely a day passed when his photograph did not appear in one or other Sydney newspaper. There was enormous pressure on the police to solve the crime. They set to work, starting with the partial licence plate of the car spotted leaving the scene with its lights off.

KERRY Walker, the horse trainer, was surprised to learn Smith's real identity later but it all made sense when he put the patterns together. 'We'd come back from the races and have a

TAKING A HIKE

Chinese meal or a drink. Apart from trackwork, we socialised two or three times a week. I never saw him drunk; he wouldn't allow himself to get in that position. But he was observant; he seemed to know if someone was behind him or beside him that shouldn't have been there.'

Another of those who knew Smith as Tom Cumming was a farrier, Henry Duren. He'd met Smith soon after his arrival at Nowra and probably as a result of the way Smith drove the road to his hide-out in Kangaroo Valley. 'The first time I met him, he had trouble on the horse float. I had to straighten the U-bolts at Frank Rowen's blacksmith shop in Nowra. I was at the track a fair bit and used to shoe the horses for him. He always called around the house to have his work done.'

Like others, Duren noticed the frequent changes in Smith's hair length and colour, but felt it was nothing out of the ordinary. 'He told me he had been a jockey in Melbourne, had got too heavy and ran a panel beating shop in Sydney. He was a decent bloke. You could have knocked me over with a feather when I heard about his arrest. I was in Cambewarra that day and if I'd seen him on the road I probably would have picked him up. I was listening to the wireless all day but had no idea Tom Cumming was Jockey Smith.'

Apart from his interest in horses, Smith continued to handle cars and often had several parked in amongst the bush next to the Little House. He rented an industrial shed in Concord Way, Bomaderry, across the street from Longford's Southern Delivery, a transport business operated by Kevin Longford who, these days, operates a tourist agency in Nowra.

'We saw him coming and going over a couple of months but didn't know who he was. He'd arrive with a vehicle and horse float but everything was secretive. He'd pull up to the gates outside the shed, open them and drive in, and close them again

CALL ME JIMMY

before opening the roller door to the shed, driving in and closing it as well.' This shed was the factory Jimmy Smith had mentioned to Ian Vance months earlier.

Kevin Longford never spoke to Smith, but his wife did. 'Catherine arrived at our business early one morning and Smith was opening his gates. He said g'day and made some comment about what a fine car she was driving. It was only a P76 but a little bit special in that it was a Targa or Florian or some such thing. Anyway, the car was stolen later and I always wondered if it was him. I heard later he had cars planted around Nowra so he could make a getaway from any direction. It was nine months before our car was located, gutted by fire; I think someone came across it in the bush and torched it.'

Smith had set up at the Little House in anticipation of trouble. As well as the rumoured cars strategically located he'd put mirrors on the lounge-room wall as part of an early warning system. The lounge was at the rear, facing north and overlooking a wide stretch of the Shoalhaven River. The mirrors allowed him to sit anywhere in that room and keep an eye on the river, in the event strangers approached from that side.

The new family in the area was accepted fairly readily. Another horse float travelling back and forth was not notable, apart from the speed of the driving, because these were racing people and that was what was expected of them.

The Cummings kept to themselves. Debbie was old enough to have left school and spent time with her horses in the paddocks around the Little House while Judy split her time between the township and home where she would make the daily trek to the letter box a few hundred metres away. If she met anyone collecting their mail, she made a point of saying hello. There was no reason for anyone to think anything untoward about the Cumming family.

TAKING A HIKE

As in Kangaroo Valley, they enjoyed an occasional night out dancing. According to Gordon Smith, a local, the man he knew as Tom was 'a terrific dancer'. Gordon's sister Jenny, herself a competition ballroom dancer, thought him very polished on the dance floor.

Gordon recalls: 'We were coming home from Kembla Grange race track one day when we came across an overturned horse float. A mare called Opetta was trapped in the wreckage and the only way to free her was to use oxy-acetylene equipment. Tom was passing and saw the problem. He said, "Here, give it to me," and cut her out. The owners of the float reckoned Tom was pretty handy with the oxy equipment and he replied, "Yeah, I'm known as The Torch". He was a very accomplished horseman and very polite in front of women.'

The owner of the Little House, a Sydney woman, had no problems with her new tenants. She kept horses as well and remembers the time she phoned Judy Cumming to say Smith's two horses had broken through the fence and were mixing with horses on her property. The horses were cut and bleeding around the neck and legs from barbed wire. Judy collected the horses with the intention of taking them to the sea where the salt water would heal their wounds. She said her husband was away that night. The owner of the property speculated later it would have been around the time a bank in South Hurstville was robbed.

On 7 September, 1977, three months after Lloyd Tidmarsh was killed, the Commercial Bank in South Hurstville was robbed by armed bandits who got away with about $180,000. The bank was a suburb or two west of Botany Bay and not far from the Tidmarsh home at Kogarah.

Newspapers labelled it one of the biggest bank robberies in Australia's history. The gunmen waited at the rear of the bank and attacked from behind as the back door of the bank was

CALL ME JIMMY

opened to let in staff. Once inside, they forced staff into a corner and waited for the manager to arrive before bagging all the cash and making a getaway in a stolen car. Shots were fired.

Meanwhile, Smith was always on guard, even with visitors he knew and trusted. When Eileen Rebbeck came to dinner, Judy was the perfect hostess while Smith hardly touched a morsel. Not long into the meal he excused himself, saying he had to make an important phone call and, thereafter, joined the group fleetingly and in between other calls. To Eileen Rebbeck, he seemed uneasy, even agitated.

In any event, the stranger who had stole his way into the back seat of David Rebbeck's car and asked questions about that bloke Cumming seemed to have found out what he wanted to know. Despite Smith leaving Kangaroo Valley before a surveillance operation could be established, the link had been made and it was much easier this time to trace Smith's movements.

It might have been even easier still had Sydney detectives confided in local police once they realised Smith was in the Nowra district. One resident recalled Inspector Waldren, the officer in charge at Nowra, telling her some months later how he saw a female driver having difficulty parking one day. The driver had managed to put one wheel onto the pavement and he approached the car to offer help when he noticed a male passenger slinking down into the seat. He thought better of offering assistance because he figured the man was embarrassed enough. As it turned out, the driver was Valerie Hill and the passenger was Jimmy Smith.

Ralph Cook, the agent who leased the Kangaroo Valley property to Smith, used to nod to Smith as they passed in the streets of Nowra. He noticed the regular changes to Smith's appearance but put it down to vanity. Even the occasional addition of John Lennon glasses did nothing more than amuse

TAKING A HIKE

Cook, who had no reason to think Cumming was anyone other than he claimed to be. Until, that is, he took a phone call from another agent in town.

Frank Cornell phoned to ask Cook if he'd leased a property in Kangaroo Valley in the recent past. The name of Jockey Smith was mentioned and, although the name was unfamiliar to Cook, he told Cornell about leasing the house in Bunker's Hill Road. It was 13 September, 1977, and Cook had taken the call about 10.45am. Within minutes, three police officers led by a Sydney detective, Brian Harding, were in Cook's office and flashing photographs of a man they called Jockey Smith. Cook recognised him immediately as Doug Cumming and told police where Smith could be found and took them along to the leasing agent, Terry Watson.

From Ralph Cook's perspective, that phone call would lead to an association with Sydney detectives that gave him an insight into their surveillance methods and a feeling for the fervour with which they sought their prey.

'They didn't want to go to the Little House, but they did ask me to take them somewhere from which they could view the property. I took them to Longreach Road, on the opposite side of the river, guided them through the bush to a position almost directly opposite Smith's house and we watched as Jockey moved around the house. He was mucking around with an F100 truck. It was around midday and, during the half hour we were there, the police were able to identify Smith through binoculars.'

With Smith's location established, Cook took the detectives back to the police station where they examined maps of the area and telephoned Sydney to arrange for more police to come down. 'They wanted at least 100 police down here. Meanwhile, we looked at a map of the river to work out how a police boat could be launched and taken up river.' They were worried that

CALL ME JIMMY

any attempt to arrest Smith would be foiled if he were able to swim the river and escape through the bush on the other side.

That afternoon, two more police turned up. They wore sleek, long blue overcoats and wanted to be taken out to the observation post. Cook was again called in to guide them through the bush. He'd sold a property in that area not long before and the lie of the land was still fresh in his mind.

'These two guys were sharp shooters. As soon as I got them to the surveillance point, they pulled out their rifles and pointed them in the direction of Smith, who they could see clearly through the sights. They were keen to put a bullet in his direction. The whole way through, they were treating Smith as someone to be eliminated. They wanted me to get a plan of the house from council and I did. It was a two bedroom house and these guys were sighting against it and saying they could get a shot through the window if he was against a window. These guys were really keen to fire.'

Ralph Cook's memory of events hasn't faded. In fact, he speaks carefully, always trying to allow for any distortion which might have occurred over the years, but it's obvious a lasting impression was made as he stood on the banks of the Shoalhaven and watched two expert marksmen go about their business. 'I thought it was strange at the time, that no-one's that bad, but then I thought this is what these guys do for a living. I had no doubt if they decided then and there to shoot Smith, they could have. On the day Smith was raided, those two guys set up camp on that side of the river and waited for him to run that way.'

Cook took groups of police out to the observation post four or five times that day. As new groups turned up in Nowra, he would ferry them out so they could see the lie of the land first hand.

'We spoke about putting a boat in and Richard Clever (a local

CALL ME JIMMY

any attempt to arrest Smith would be foiled if he were able to swim the river and escape through the bush on the other side.

That afternoon, two more police turned up. They wore sleek, long blue overcoats and wanted to be taken out to the observation post. Cook was again called in to guide them through the bush. He'd sold a property in that area not long before and the lie of the land was still fresh in his mind.

'These two guys were sharp shooters. As soon as I got them to the surveillance point, they pulled out their rifles and pointed them in the direction of Smith, who they could see clearly through the sights. They were keen to put a bullet in his direction. The whole way through, they were treating Smith as someone to be eliminated. They wanted me to get a plan of the house from council and I did. It was a two bedroom house and these guys were sighting against it and saying they could get a shot through the window if he was against a window. These guys were really keen to fire.'

Ralph Cook's memory of events hasn't faded. In fact, he speaks carefully, always trying to allow for any distortion which might have occurred over the years, but it's obvious a lasting impression was made as he stood on the banks of the Shoalhaven and watched two expert marksmen go about their business. 'I thought it was strange at the time, that no-one's that bad, but then I thought this is what these guys do for a living. I had no doubt if they decided then and there to shoot Smith, they could have. On the day Smith was raided, those two guys set up camp on that side of the river and waited for him to run that way.'

Cook took groups of police out to the observation post four or five times that day. As new groups turned up in Nowra, he would ferry them out so they could see the lie of the land first hand.

'We spoke about putting a boat in and Richard Clever (a local

TAKING A HIKE

police officer) was in charge of this operation. The idea was for him to take a boat out and position it underneath where Smith was living. They thought he would swim the river and it was there to stop him. They were also talking about landing another party before the bend in the river and walking up the private road belonging to the owner of the property and approaching Smith's house from that direction.'

The idea of a river landing might have made sense if the raid was done in daylight. But, in the dark, it was a bit too ambitious. The operation was difficult – success depended on an understanding of the landscape and the river. Perhaps commandos could have done it, but most of the police on this operation were from Sydney – streetwise maybe, but with little experience in commando tactics.

Where they planned to land was feasible; it was a relatively gradual slope up from the river and, if they could make the roadway, it would be a matter simply of walking up it to Smith's house. The operation would require absolute silence, given that sound carries long distances on quiet nights, particularly over water.

Whether or not this was taken into account is open for conjecture now but that month had been exceptionally bleak in Nowra, with rain on ten of the preceding 13 days. The river had been up and down, not only with the tides but also with the run-off from the mountains feeding it. Wherever a boat landed would be boggy, possibly treacherously so, and disorientating for inexperienced officers.

Around 6.30pm Cook was called out of the Bridge Hotel to perform one more civic duty. The police dogs had arrived. 'They had a VW Kombi van with two dogs in the back. They wanted me to take them out to McMahons Road, to the intersection where it crosses over Rock Hill Road and Pitt Street. I pointed out the direction of the property and gathered they were going to stay there.' With police at this intersection, any escape by road had been cut off. The noose was tightening.

Cook was excited by his involvement in a big police raid. He was asked to phone the owner of the Little House, at her farmhouse just a kilometre away, to warn of the raid planned for the following morning.

'I spoke to a man. I told him who I was and that I was phoning on behalf of the police. I told him there may be some police walking through his paddocks in the morning, armed police, heading up the road to the Little House. I told him not to be alarmed. He said, "Alarmed! We're getting out of here". This was about 7pm.'

The man was Geoff Churcher, a Sydney restaurateur and guest of the property owner, who had returned to Sydney earlier that day. Churcher was staying at the house with his wife and two children, and two other adults, friends of their family. He had been instructed to keep absolutely quiet about the raid and, especially, not to inform the local police. Despite his apparent alarm when told of the raid, Churcher stayed at the property.

So far, Sydney police were sure Smith had no idea of their operation. It was securely planned and tightly co-ordinated. They effectively blocked escape by road, had him covered should he attempt to swim the Shoalhaven and, as the night wore on, more officers took up positions to ensure that, at the appointed hour, the Little House would be surrounded and Smith would surrender.

CHAPTER 7

Captured

DARKNESS descends over the river and the Little House. The 'roos camp for the night, leaving the bush to the possum gliders and the boobook owls keeping watch from their posts along the gravelled road. It's quiet, save for the sound of a motor carried on the wind from down river. The noise, foreign so late at night, is an urgent message for someone. A warning.

Jimmy Smith hears and heeds it. His instincts tell him all is not right. Rather than go to bed, he stays dressed and listens to the night for sounds of intrusion. He also listens to a radio. He lies on the bed twiddling the dial, with Val beside him and Debbie fast asleep in her room. The house concealed by the night, lights off, Smith moves uneasily from window to window, looking for signs of movement. Nothing. The pups snore in a corner of the lounge-room.

He returns to the radio. Picks up snatches of conversation in the static, a meaningless babble to anyone but a wanted man. Yeah, we're in position ... any sign of ... the river ... cars at the

CALL ME JIMMY

intersection ... dogs ... wait for the boats ... for chrissake, don't speak over the radio, go to the phone.

Something's afoot and doesn't he know what it is.

He stays put. No one knows who I am ... they're not lookin' for me. Until he hears the noise of the motor travelling up-river. He knows the sound of a boat from so many times on the water himself, swimming the horses in the Shoalhaven. Who'd be fool enough to navigate the river by night? With the flood tides still receding and dragging flotsam from the bush.

He slips a gun down the front of his strides just like an old-time gunfighter. This is the business he knows. He calls softly to the pups, which wake and bound towards him. Come on boys, he whispers, let's see who's out there. They pad behind, obedient and keen for adventure, their black skins shimmering from the light inside the car when the door is opened. He starts the motor and glides down the driveway with the headlights off.

Once on the road he flicks on the high beam, hoping to scan not just the gravel road but the adjoining scrub as well. Up ahead, near the bend where Val collects the mail, a diamond flickers briefly in his lights – the glint of a headlamp maybe or a chrome relic on the side of the road. No time for chances. He slows the car and a pair of bright lights come out of nowhere and blind him. Smith hits the skids and throws it into reverse. He's not waiting to see who's there. Floors the accelerator and speeds backwards towards the house – with the lights in pursuit.

He roars backwards past his driveway turn off and hits the skids again. Then tears down the drive to the house and races inside. They're out there, he screams at Val. The bastards are out there. Val doesn't know what to do. There's nothing she can do. He grabs some cash and takes off across the lawn towards the bush; a car pulls up across his driveway. I'm buggered, he thinks, trapped in this rathole where the only escape is the river

CAPTURED

*and the road, which already belongs to the coppers. Go for the river. And he crosses the road just 50 metres downwind of the police car waiting outside his drive*way.

SMITH and Val Hill tuned into the police frequency on a Realistic brand scanner some time before 4am on 14 September, 1977. They soon realised a covert police operation was in progress. They weren't sure what it was, but Smith wasn't about to sleep with police activity in the area. He was spooked when the radio operator cautioned, 'Don't speak over the radio. Go to the phone'.

Around this time a neighbour, Alan Walker, was awoken by sounds outside his front gate. A shift worker, he had come home after midnight and gone straight to bed. 'About four hours after I went to bed, I was awoken by vehicles coming down McMahons Road,' he said later. 'They stopped at my gate and I could hear a wireless going.'

Walker was curious; two police vehicles had stopped at his gate but drove off towards Smith's house. 'There was no wind that night and the noise carried. The police radio was loud and the officers at the car outside my gate, particularly a woman officer, were talking loudly.'

At that moment police in motor boats were moving rapidly along the river in preparation for a dawn raid on the Little House. Richard Clever was in the lead boat, with another officer from Nowra and four detectives from the New South Wales Crime Squad. The other boat, captained by a Nowra detective, carried a landing party of Sydney detectives.

Negotiating the river in darkness was tough, but Clever managed to find the beach, selected the afternoon before, and land his party. The second boat followed. When the detectives got out, the local officers took the boats to positions up and down stream of Smith's house to wait in case Smith tried to

CALL ME JIMMY

cross the river. Meanwhile, Smith was uneasy. He bundled his two black german shepherd pups into one of the cars and drove out to investigate. Alan Walker's property was about 200 metres from the Little House and Smith had covered less than half that distance when he picked up the police car travelling towards him in the high beam of his Holden sedan.

Meanwhile, the river landing party was in disarray. They had instructions outlining the direction, but were disorientated by darkness and unfamiliar territory. Even before the two boats had motored out of sight, the dogs at the second house on the property began barking.

The house lights came on and detectives knocked at the door to ask directions. They were either given the wrong directions or failed to heed them because, instead of travelling the steep road that led up to Smith's house, they took a left fork and followed the farm track along the river to the Coorong Farm retreat where the Churcher family was holidaying.

It was 'a total cock-up' according to local officers reflecting on it later. The river landing party surrounded the wrong house, the one occupied by the holidaying Churchers. They were met by a group of detectives supposed to make position behind Smith's house but who'd already passed by it in the night and carried out their raid on Churcher and his family, screaming 'Hit the floor!' and waving guns everywhere. It fell to Churcher to guide the crime squad to the place from which Jockey Smith had already fled.

When confronted by the police car coming his way Smith slammed the gears into reverse and sped backwards towards home. Police followed and, when Smith jumped from his car, the officers blocked the driveway and radioed for assistance. The raid was on. Smith raced inside, screaming, 'They're out there. I'm going.' And he fled for his life.

CAPTURED

HMPH, hmph, hmph, hmph ... he sucks in the cold night air. It doesn't relieve the burning in his lungs. Gotta get away. Fly, Jimmy ... and a cooling breeze brings with it the sounds of pursuit. Voices on this side of the road, on the opposite side from the Little House. Voices carrying from the river. Dogs barking. Car engines in the distance and getting closer.

A split second to decide on doubling back through the scrubby barrier of blackberry, lantana and blackboy. He crosses the road again, still downwind of the car blocking his driveway, but aware this time of voices from the steep track down to the river. He knows that whole side of the river is blocked off. So is the road. There are two options – either chance the dangerous descent to the river on his side of the road or keep to the ridge and make his way into town.

ALAN Walker was able to follow the ensuing chase by listening to the police radio in the car stationed at his front gate and, as someone who'd spent most of his life in the bush, by reading the signs of flight carried on the night air.

His memory of the incident was still vivid many years later. 'They thought he had gone over to the opposite side of the road and were looking for him there. Apparently, he doubled back, went past them in the bush and returned to his side of the road.'

The police continued their search oblivious to the signs Walker was reading from the bush.

'You could hear where the chase was going by the noises. A neighbour's dogs started barking on the opposite side of the road to the police and I knew he must have been there. Not long after that, the geese from the next property along started to cackle. Then it went quiet just as daylight was coming.'

Except for the police, who continued to roar up and down the road. The raid was bungled, with most officers hopelessly out of position and completely unfamiliar with local geography. It was all over within ten minutes and Smith was gone, leaving the police to flounder through the bush looking for excuses.

What happened next underlines the frustration they felt. Police converged on the Little House and took Valerie Hill and her daughter into custody.

The place swarmed with detectives toting guns and yelling orders. Hill's daughter began screaming, which set the two black pups barking. A detective, Brian Harding, shot one of the dogs, Spider, in the paw in view of Hill's daughter, claiming the dogs were vicious and about to attack. Incensed, Hill's daughter sprang at Harding, screaming and beating him on the chest with her fist.

Hill and her daughter were ordered to dress and told to wait in a patrol car while the premises were searched. Police hoped to find weapons and a part or all of the $180,000 stolen during the South Hurstville bank robbery. They figured Smith was the mastermind.

The contents of the house were splayed about the lounge-room and piled onto mattresses in the bedrooms. Police were preparing to rip up floorboards when the owner's son arrived and suggested there was plenty of room underneath the house for a thorough inspection without destroying anything.

The search bore fruit: a suitcase containing wigs, masks and other items of disguise; a large, green bag holding a quantity of hand guns including air pistols, automatic pistols, a revolver, a Sten gun, ammunition and several pairs of handcuffs; and a bullet-proof vest. Harding took Valerie Hill from the police car, showed her the weapons and said she would be charged with possession of illegal weapons as the legal tenant of the property. He also told her she would be questioned in relation to the South Hurstville bank robbery. Hill and her daughter were

CAPTURED

taken to the Nowra Police Station where she was cautioned and further questioned.

AS police ransack the Little House, Smith takes to the ridge above the Shoalhaven River. He evades police. He presses on, branches whipping his arms, face and legs. He's on a bush track, little used and grown over. He pads softly to avoid the crack of twigs that might telegraph his whereabouts.

His heart thumps while he stops to catch breath and listen for sounds of pursuit. The first rush had been frantic. Now, he is able to make a plan of sorts. To work through the bush to Bomaderry where he might lift a car and escape.

He moves on. The way is rough, despite the old track, and he stumbles more than once in the half-light of dawn as a protruding root or fallen limb trip him. For a while, he follows the course of the river from the safety of the ridge that overlooks it. He is thirsty but to move to the river is risky; the noise of the motor boats carries upstream and he knows that way is cut off.

AS the sky lightened, Walker, the neighbour, saw a stream of police vehicles converge on the Little House, including a white utility with a cage of iron bars covered by canvas. Members of the Special Weapons Operation Squad (SWOS) arrived. They were dressed in black. 'About 40 or 50 cars stopped in the paddock adjoining my house. There were 100 police, maybe more. They formed a line six to eight feet apart and worked their way through the bush. But they were still looking for him on the wrong side of the road.'

Had the police asked Walker, they might have tracked Smith but they 'never came to my house at all'. He did meet police later that day. On his way to work about 2pm he was stopped at a roadblock on a nearby corner.

CALL ME JIMMY

'They wanted to know where I'd come from. I was stopped again at the next intersection where McMahons Road crosses Rockhill Road. The police were everywhere and they were armed with rifles.'

Police had roadblocks all over the district; 21 local officers had been called in to help with the search. They were amazed the raid had been such a debacle. The feeling, then and later, was that if local police had been involved from the jump, Smith would not have got away. Local officers were indignant at being left out of the raid; to them, it was a slight by the Criminal Investigation Branch towards uniformed members.

During the day, helicopters were called in from the HMAS Albatross, the naval aviation base on the outskirts of Nowra. This caused controversy because naval policy excluded the use of its equipment to assist civilian authorities in situations where defence force personnel could be fired on.

Pilots from the 723 Squadron flew two Iroquois helicopters in shifts and airlifted several police, including Detective Sergeant Ken Webster, from the armed hold-up squad, and one of the officers in charge of the operation.

While helicopters scoured the countryside, members of the highway patrol and officers on general duties in marked and unmarked police cars drove the streets of Nowra and Bomaderry. There were a couple of sightings of Smith during the day, but each time he managed to elude his pursuers, including two tracker dogs which failed to pick up his scent.

Local radio station 2ST was alerted early and broadcast bulletins all day, warning residents to stay inside, to lock car doors and to keep children away from school. Police feared Smith would take hostages. Reporters and photographers from Sydney invaded Nowra. *The Daily Mirror* reshuffled its front page; the manhunt was big news, one of the biggest in New

CAPTURED

South Wales history. **HUNT FOR PUBLIC ENEMY NO 1** was the headline over a photograph of a surly-looking Smith taken some years earlier and bearing little resemblance to his current looks. The story started with a boxed warning to residents of Nowra.

**URGENT POLICE MESSAGE ...
... URGENT POLICE MESSAGE**

All school children have been instructed to stay away from school and all people in the search area have been told to remain indoors.

*'Residents of a south coast town were warned to lock themselves and their children indoors today as police with shotguns, rifles and teargas try to flush out Australia's most wanted man.
'Police fear the man, Edward James 'Jockey' Smith, 34, might try to grab hostages or shoot his way out of the town of Nowra.'*

By mid-morning, news of the manhunt featured in bulletins across the country. Nowra and Smith were on the lips of the nation.

JIMMY Smith is running hard again. Crossing open country behind new homes in North Nowra. He's panicky, still hyped from the dash across Illaroo Road where he came out from the bush just as a police car sped by. Its occupants didn't see him drop to the ground and flatten his body like a lizard.

It's midday. He's been running for seven hours. He is hungry and thirsty. He reaches Bomaderry Creek, which skirts the back

CALL ME JIMMY

of Bomaderry, the creek running parallel to the Princes Highway, which he is certain is swarming with coppers. No point trying to cross the narrow iron bridge into Nowra, the bridge overlooking the wharf where the two police boats were launched earlier that morning. No point because it'll be cut off too. The plan, if he had one, is fraying as he nears Bomaderry.

He's not thinking straight any more. Has some cockeyed notion he'll get help in Bomaderry. Find a phone box and call a friend to pick him up. Get him out of the place before the coppers even know he was there. But it's no plan for a man on the run, no serious plan.

Should've stayed in the bush. At home in the bush. No shortage of water in the bush. Might go a little hungry for a couple of days but what's that compared to capture? If he could stop long enough to make a decent plan he might think to head north, through the bush, towards Kangaroo Valley where friends might help him out. The longer he stays in the bush the harder it will be for police to find him. He's not thinking straight at all. He's not thinking that 24 hours after the chase begins, police will scale down their effort if they haven't caught him by then.

It's a mistake to head for Bomaderry, but he blunders on, crossing the creek where the water is shallow. He is tired and hungry and scared of what will happen to him if captured. He doesn't want to be captured. He doesn't want to die. And he realises why he is heading to Bomaderry ... and not deeper into the bush. He doesn't want to die. He believes he will be shot on sight if he happens across police anywhere away from public eyes. He's heading to Bomaderry because he knows he can't escape this time and he's trying to position himself somewhere with lots of people. Witnesses. Across the creek he hits the highway.

CAPTURED

THE Princes Highway exposed him to anyone going past. A local resident, Dianne Studdert, was waiting outside a veterinary surgery on the highway while her son, Mark, had gone inside to collect a bird. Her two-year-old son, John, was in the back seat of her car.

'Jockey came up to the car, opened the passenger door and asked me if I could give him a lift to Nowra. He had notes in his hand, rolled up as a wad and offered me the money. I said, "No, I'm not going to town". He hesitated and then closed the door.' At the time she was unaware the man who had just asked for a lift was Smith but, in the meantime, the vet had phoned police.

Dianne Studdert was later philosophical about meeting the man painted as notorious and dangerous.

'I don't believe he was as bad as they made out. He would have had no better hostage than me and a two-year-old if he had wanted to get away. Yet, when I told him I couldn't help him, he just closed the door and went away. The police frightened me more than Jockey Smith because they weren't dressed in uniforms and one of them came up to my car with a gun out. I believe had they caught him in the bush, they would have shot him.'

Shortly after the woman refused to help him, Smith entered the Bomaderry Tourist Information Centre across the highway. He was exposed now. It was mid-afternoon and Chris Beverly, the manager, was on duty.

'A man came into the tourist centre and stood at the brochure rack reading leaflets,' Beverly was to recall. 'It was just as the primary school across the highway was finishing for the day. Helicopters were flying overhead and a news bulletin announced his whereabouts. We always had the radio on in the centre and never really took much notice of it. It was just a background noise. When the man heard the radio, he bolted. We

CALL ME JIMMY

didn't really know it was him until then. We rang the council switchboard and asked them to inform the police. They arrived in minutes.'

Smith was desperate, sensing imminent capture. He was in open territory and the options were dying with every minute. He ran from the tourist centre, sprinted across Bunberra Street to the ambulance station, stole a bicycle from the attached residence and pedalled for his life down the street.

Charlie Francis, who worked at the ambulance station, takes up the story.

'I was good friends with Superintendent Tony Heslin, who was in charge of the ambulance station and lived next door. The bicycle Jockey stole belonged to Tony's son, Brendan. I lived further down Bunberra Street and was sitting in the lounge with my two daughters and son when my wife, Wendy, returned home from town and came inside with an armful of parcels. She'd only just got inside when the kids yelled out that a bloke had ridden into our carport on a pushbike and was looking inside Wendy's car. He must have seen her pull up and was checking to see if she left the keys in the ignition.

'The son, Garry, looked out the window and said, "Hey dad, that bloke's got Brendan's bike". Jockey hopped on the bike and rode towards the Bomaderry shops. The youngest daughter, Leanne, yelled out after him, "Hey you, bring that bike back". She was only five.'

Charlie and his son, Garry, flew to the car intent on following Smith as he pedalled down Bunberra Street. They lost sight of him after he turned into Tallyang Street, a dead-end only a few streets from the Bomaderry shops. 'I continued slowly down the road and passed a police car heading in the opposite direction. At that stage, I didn't know it was Smith. We finished up in Karowa Street and came in behind him.' Smith was

CAPTURED

dressed in jeans and a denim jacket and, as Charlie and Garry Francis drew closer, the jacket flapped back and the pair noticed a revolver in his belt. 'I told my son to say nothing because this was the bloke the police were looking for. We passed him, saw him turn into Coomea Street and into the back of the Bomaderry Hotel.'

Charlie Francis took off after the police car he'd passed moments earlier. 'I had the lights flashing and the horn blaring before I could get their attention. Finally, the police car stopped and I said, "Are you looking for a fellow in jeans, denim jacket, dark hair and beard?" and told them he'd parked his bike at the back of the hotel and gone through to the main street. They radioed for help and we returned home.'

Back home, Wendy Francis phoned the Heslins to see if Brendan knew his bike was missing. He answered the phone and was speaking with Wendy when a man appeared at the sliding doors of the residence. The man had a gun. Brendan Heslin relayed this to Wendy Francis, who told him to hang up so she could phone the station to organise some help for the young lad. But there was no need; the man disappeared as quickly as he came. He was, in fact, a detective chasing Smith.

WHO arrested Jockey Smith? The official police version of events and the one subsequently tendered in court goes like this. It is supported by headlines like: *How I Stopped 'Jockey' Shooting – Detective tells of struggle and 'Battle for life' in a phone box.*

Shortly before Smith pulled up at the phone box outside the Bomaderry Post Office, a squad of Sydney detectives drove into town acting on radio information that he had been sighted there. Detective Senior Constable Gary Beaumont from the observation squad drove the unmarked police car. According to testimony given under oath at the subsequent committal hearing, trial and appeal, these detectives saw Smith riding his bike along the footpath at the Bomaderry shops before stopping near the post office.

Beaumont did a U-turn, drove back to the shops and double-parked his car outside the phone box. With him were Detective Senior Constable Robert Godden and Detective Sergeant Dennis Gilligan, both from the armed hold-up squad, and Detective Senior Constable Ivan Lloyd, also a member of the observation squad. All were attached to the CIB in Sydney. Detective Godden was the first to leave the vehicle. It was 4.15pm. The four officers approached the phone box, service revolvers still in their shoulder holsters.

Bob Godden takes up the story. 'I approached the phone booth and saw Smith standing there with the phone in his right hand. Smith said, "This phone doesn't work also". I said, "We are the police, what is your name?" He said, "Mike Daniels, what do you want to know for?" I said, "You fit the description of a man we are looking for. Have you any identification?" He said, "My father works in the post office there, go and see him". I said, "You are Jockey Smith".

'Detective Gilligan and I went to take hold of Smith but he brought up a fully-loaded .38 Smith & Wesson revolver and thrust the barrel into the right side of my stomach. As he did this he said, "Fuck you two, back off or you're gone". I immediately pushed down on the revolver with both hands and Smith tried to fire but he was unable to do so due to my left thumb jamming the firing hammer. I shouted, "Look out, he's got a gun".

'I shouted at him, "Jockey, cut it, or you'll be shot". He hesitated for a moment and I managed to wrestle the gun from him. With the aid of Detective Gilligan, I managed to place my handcuffs on him. We forced him from the phone box and

CAPTURED

wrestled him to the footpath outside the phone box, searched him and found a .25 calibre automatic pistol, a quantity of money and a bag.

'Smith continued to struggle and he yelled out, "Fucking dogs, fucking cunts". A short time later a police vehicle arrived. Smith, still struggling, was placed in the vehicle and shouted out, "You fucking cunts, I'll shoot the lot of you, you're nothing but dogs".'

Within minutes of the arrest, police vehicles converged from all directions and pulled up outside the Bomaderry shops. Smith was taken to Nowra Police Station.

The arrest was the finale of an operation begun more than 24 hours earlier. Detective Gilligan had been on duty more than 12 hours when Smith was arrested. He'd been called into the Kogarah Police Station for a conference around 3.30am. With Detective Sergeant Roger Rogerson (later to achieve notoriety as Australia's most famous corrupt cop) and other police he had raided the Canterbury home of Neil Collings at 5am and found a black attache case containing 'a large amount of money'. For some reason the exact amount was not disclosed. From there, he returned to the armed hold-up squad office before leaving Sydney around 7.30am and driving to Nowra.

Detective Godden was fortunate when Smith threatened to shoot him. Grabbing the gun with both hands was a split second thing; the gun could have discharged even as his hand made contact. But the webbing between his thumb and forefinger managed to connect with the back of the hammer before Smith could pull on the trigger and fire.

Detective Godden went into a nearby shop and asked for a plaster strip to cover wounds to his hands, but there was little contact between any investigating police officers and the public at that time. Two witnesses were interviewed on the day but neither made written statements at the time. Several locals witnessed fragments of the arrest but it was not until about ten weeks later, and after the committal hearing had already begun, that detectives advertised in the local media for witnesses to the arrest.

The Shoalhaven & Nowra News published the following article on the front page of its 30 November, 1977, issue under the headline *Smith inquiries continue*. 'Police are anxious to interview anyone who saw the recent arrest of Pentridge Jail escapee, Edward James 'Jockey' Smith, at the Bomaderry shopping centre. Smith, 34, Australia's most wanted man …' A similar article made the front page of the *South Coast Register* the same day.

Why police failed to take statements on the day of the arrest or soon afterwards remains a mystery. Certainly, there was no shortage of officers to interview the many spectators caught in the action at the Bomaderry shops. It's conceivable there was no clear leader at the scene, no officer-in-charge, and that the order to interview witnesses was not given. But the four detectives who claimed the arrest were experienced officers used to operating according to procedure.

Perhaps they were overcome by the nature of the arrest. Perhaps, in the pandemonium that followed, they simply forgot to take statements. Perhaps they realised they needed witnesses' statements once the case got to court to dispel any impression that their version of events might have been the product of collusion.

Several witnesses came forward following the articles in local newspapers. Local schoolboys, Graeme Henry and Jeff Willsher, saw two men get out of a car and run to the phone booth. Both noticed a gun raised in the air but their recollections were 'hazy'; they might have mistaken the telephone

CAPTURED

handpiece for a gun because subsequent newspaper reports said Smith was threatening police with a gun in the phone box. Smith was pulled outside and the boys saw a gun fall to the pavement. It was kicked into the gutter by someone else. They were both aware of a second gun, indicating they had seen a larger revolver and smaller, silver pistol, but were unable to say where either gun had come from.

Willsher's memory of events seemed to be more detailed. He recalled the officer who kicked the gun into the gutter was in uniform. He recalled Smith being searched and some money found. There was another uniformed officer 'just around the other side telling everybody to get back into their shops and to move away'. This officer was armed and, as more police arrived, further detectives arrived 'with big rifles'.

The lapse in time between the event and the taking of statements meant the boys had time to compare stories and to hear, and perhaps accept as their own, the recollections of others. They also had time to digest copious newspaper reports and media coverage, all of which heavily reflected the police version of events.

George Madge was standing at the door to his shop. He saw three people struggling in the phone booth, soon joined by two others. Smith was dragged out and, once on the footpath, a gun fell to the ground. Madge believed this gun fell from Smith's hand and was kicked away by one of the men he assumed was a detective. At first, Madge thought it 'was two men fighting, although I did know the hunt was on in the area'.

Bob Brooker was in the post office serving a customer when he noticed a man ride a bike along the street, lean it against the front of the post office and go into one of the phone booths directly outside his front window.

'While I was watching him, a car drove past, stopped and

reversed back. Two men got out and one opened the door of the phone box and spoke to the man in the phone box. I could hear one man speak, I could hear voices, and one man tend to say, "Edward Smith, I place you under arrest" or words to that effect. He (Smith) replied, "I'll fucking shoot you". A struggle took place with the two men in the phone box.'

Two more men went to the phone box while a uniformed police officer sang out, 'Get down behind the counter. Get inside and shut the door'.

Like other witnesses, Brooker was not asked to make a statement on the day or soon after. More than two months elapsed before police questioned him and, when they did, he was asked to identify both Smith and the guns allegedly in Smith's possession from photographs. He did not see a gun in Smith's hand and, like other civilian witnesses, did not testify that Smith had a gun pointed in Detective Godden's stomach and was trying to fire it.

HAROLD Hessenberger was a private inquiry agent minding his own business. He was sitting in his car behind the Bomaderry Hotel, having a quiet drink, when he noticed Smith pull in. 'He was pushing a bike and had some sort of bag. He leant the bike against the pub wall and I noticed a few marks on the side of his face. He looked at me and at the car. He looked at the aerial and picked the push bike up and walked away. I seen the police patrol, the Charger, coming around the corner.'

At this point, the police officer driving the Charger left his car and spoke to Hessenberger, who followed the police car into Meroo Street. By the time he arrived there, the police officer was standing in the middle of the road in front of the telephone booth, waving his service revolver and telling everyone to lie down. Hessenberger spoke with the officer again and ran across

CAPTURED

to the phone booth and saw two men wrestling with a third man on the ground outside the booth.

'I seen one police officer get hold of Jockey Smith's hand and belt it against the footpath. The revolver sort of skidded out of his hand. I kicked the revolver out of the road with my foot, just away, towards the gutter. I got hold of Smith's leg and held on to it. By that time, one of the local policemen got there and then took hold of his other leg and the two detectives, the one with the bullet proof vest on, had hold of one of his arms and he just sort of held him there or tried to hold him there. Before that, we rolled him over.'

A policeman searched Smith and produced another gun, like 'a starting pistol', from Smith's back pocket.

According to Hessenberger, one of the officers asked, 'Are you Jockey Smith' and Smith replied, 'I'm not saying anything'. Smith was swearing and, when the van arrived, Hessenberger helped police officers put Smith in the back. He identified the local police officer who came in towards the end of the fracas as Mark Powderly, later a sergeant with the police rescue squad in Sydney.

Smith was subsequently convicted on the charge of maliciously attempting to discharge a loaded firearm with intent to do grievous bodily harm and sentenced to 14 years jail. There is no doubt he was convicted on the strength of the detectives' identical testimony claiming he had tried to shoot Detective Godden. And he didn't help himself by refusing to cooperate with his barrister when asked to provide a detailed account of his version of events.

So, did the four detectives arrest Jockey Smith? Years later, those who had been uniformed officers stationed at Nowra in September, 1977, say the arrest was made by uniformed officers and the four detectives came along after Smith was

CALL ME JIMMY

subdued. Officer Peter Lunney, to become a sergeant at Chatswood Police Station on the northern side of Sydney, was on highway patrol and recalled seeing Smith in the phone box. 'I was two metres away and told people in the shops to get inside.'

Many of his fellow officers at the time felt it was Lunney who had grabbed Smith in the phone box and disarmed him. But Lunney was vigorous in his denial of any involvement in the arrest.

Alec Field was employed by News Limited as bureau chief for the *Daily Telegraph* at that time and based in Nowra. He lived a kilometre from the Bomaderry Post Office.

With Sydney reporter, 'Bondi' Bill Jenkings, Field headed to McMahons Road where the search was in full swing. A call came over the radio about 4pm announcing the sighting of Smith in Bomaderry. Police and media formed a cavalcade down McMahons Road. Alec Field and Jenkings left the convoy as it hit Bomaderry because Field, being a local, knew a quicker way to the shops.

'We got to the post office as Smith and the police officer were struggling outside the phone box. He was arrested by a highway patrol officer in uniform. The cavalcade arrived 30 to 40 seconds later. I can recall seeing a weapon, but there were people crowded around. It was like something out of Hollywood: sirens blaring, red lights flashing.'

Whatever happened at the Bomaderry phone box that day, not one civilian witness testified to seeing Smith point a gun at Detective Godden.

In the end, the jury chose to believe the official prosection's version of events. What is beyond dispute is that the New South Wales police did apprehend Australia's most wanted man in a telephone box without injuring anyone.

The celebrations began soon after Smith was locked away at

CAPTURED

Nowra. The Sydney crew took to the local pubs. It was a big pinch and the talk of the town. Someone forgot to tell Richard Clever and the men on the boat patrols who were still anchored on the Shoalhaven River. They had been directed to wait there until further notice and wait they did until Fred Waldren did a check on the whereabouts of his men.

As it was, Officer Clever still had to front up for night shift at 11pm and guard Smith until next morning. According to police on duty that night, Smith was like a caged and frenzied animal, spitting and swearing at those who took turns to sit in the cold and exposed exercise yard to keep an eye on his cell door.

Constable Reg Norwood, later a sergeant and still stationed at Nowra, accepted the charges and also guarded Smith that night. Smith was charged with the attempted murder of Constable Ambrose and firing his weapon while fleeing, armed robbery of the Commercial Bank of Australia's South Hurstville branch, possession of gelignite, possession of various weapons including a sub-machine gun, assault on four officers at the Bomaderry phone booth, attempting to shoot officer Godden and attempted bribery.

Detective Brian Harding alleged Smith had offered him $2000 during an interview with 'plenty more to come' if he'd allow him to escape. Reg Norwood counted the money Smith had on him; it was $1700 in notes. The allegation that Smith had made an attempt to bribe his way out of jail made spectacular headlines, especially in the tabloid newspapers.

The Daily Mirror, in its final issue the day after the arrest, wrung every drop of drama from the alleged bribe with the headline: **$2000 TO LET ME GO!** underneath a smaller heading: **Jockey tries to bribe police.**

Following his involvement in the arrest, Detective Godden was awarded a commendation for 'Good Policemanship, Excellent

CALL ME JIMMY

Teamwork and Devotion to Duty'. He was to be involved in several notable police inquiries including the Granville rail disaster in 1977 and led the investigation into the NSW backpacker murders, which eventually saw the arrest and conviction of Ivan Milat. Dennis Gilligan rose to the rank of Assistant Commissioner and retired from active duty on 31 March, 1997. Gary Beaumont was still a serving officer stationed in northern NSW, while Ivan Lloyd left the service on 23 April, 1981.

CHAPTER 8

The jury

16 September, 1977
PUBLIC ENEMY No. 1 CAPTURED

JAMES "Jockey" Smith, branded Public Enemy No. 1 by police in two states, was arrested at gunpoint last night after a day of high drama. Smith, a jail escapee and suspected mastermind behind two of Australia's biggest robberies, was captured in a telephone box at Bomaderry on the south coast, after a day-long manhunt. Smith, armed with two revolvers, wrestled with police before he was subdued. Smith had been holing up in Nowra for three months using an alias. – CED CULBERT, the *Daily Telegraph*.

SMITH was marched into the Nowra Court of Petty Sessions by two Sydney detectives, his hands shackled and covering his face, a poor defence against photographers. He wore a jacket but, after a night in the cells, apart from his hair being slicked down and parted in the middle, he was dishevelled. His clothes were splattered with mud from the Bomaderry Creek crossing. It was a brief appearance. The charges, stacked one on another, were read to the court. Nowra police officer Senior Constable Mark Powderly acted as police prosecutor. Brian Cash, Smith's barrister in Melbourne (and uncle of tennis star Pat and descendent of Tasmanian bushranger Martin Cash) flew to Nowra and stayed long enough to hear charges and Smith's indictment. It took 10 minutes; Cash entered a not guilty plea. He did not apply for bail but made it plain Smith had not and would not make any comment to police.

'My client believes he has been the victim of unfair character assassination in the press. A man should be seen to be innocent until he is proven guilty. My client says he has made no admissions, written or verbal, and wishes it noted he proposes to exercise his common right as a citizen to refuse. He is not prepared to be further interviewed. If the police persist, he wishes that I be present.'

Smith was remanded to Sydney's Central Court of Petty Sessions where the hearing would continue on 23 January the following year. He was bundled into a police divisional van with officers Powderly and Garry Page and taken to Long Bay Jail. The van was escorted front and rear by members of the homicide squad armed with shotguns in case anyone tried to free Smith.

It was a fast trip to Sydney. There was no attempt to free Smith. His view of the landscape was restricted by the tiny windows of the divisional van as the entourage sped past Kiama and Wollongong on the southern coast of NSW, through mountain ranges in the Heathcote National Park near Sutherland and on into the southern suburbs of Sydney. They took him along the shores of Botany Bay, near Hurstville, and past Kingsford Smith Airport at Mascot before pulling up outside the gates of Long Bay, where Smith was greeted by

THE JURY

prison officials and the routine of prison life. He was taken immediately to Katingal Special Security Unit, a backhanded compliment for the country's most wanted man.

The following week he appeared at Central Court of Petty Sessions, in Liverpool Street, Sydney, where he was formally charged for his part in the South Hurstville bank robbery. He had been identified by a staff member who had seen one of the robbers remove a balaclava during the robbery. The bank's accountant, Daniel Taylor, had recognised Smith's photograph in the *Daily Telegraph* after his recapture at Nowra.

At this brief hearing, a further nine charges were added. These included armed robbery of the payroll from the Patrick Stevedoring Company in Ultimo in March 1976 which netted $71,640, discharging a loaded shotgun at pursuers from the South Hurstville bank robbery, theft of various motor vehicles and the charge for which he skipped bail in 1974, that of conspiracy to steal the payroll from the Redfern railway workshops.

Smith did not answer the charges in the order that the crimes occurred. Rather, he fronted the most recent charges first, so the 1974 conspiracy charge was not heard until well after he'd been processed on charges relating to his arrest, which included the alleged attempt to fire his weapon at Detective Godden, and the attempted murder of Constable Jeremiah Ambrose.

So serious were these charges that some of the lesser charges were dropped and never heard.

Joining Smith in court were Valerie Hill, 35, Neil Collings, 26, and Frank Montgomery, 54.

Hill was charged with possession of firearms at Nowra. She was also charged as an accessory before and after the South Hurstville robbery because it was alleged she drove Smith to and from that armed hold-up. Collings and Montgomery had been captured the night before the early-morning raid at Nowra

CALL ME JIMMY

and charged at the Central Court of Petty Sessions for their part in the robbery.

The *Daily Telegraph* labelled the South Hurstville bank robbery 'the biggest bank hold-up' in Australia and described it as a 'commando-style operation'. The committal hearing started on 13 October, 1977, a month after Smith's arrest. The onus was on the Crown to establish substantial evidence of guilt.

The prosecution claimed Smith was the mastermind.

Two stolen cars were used during the robbery. The first, a white Ford panel van, had been stolen three weeks before the crime and partly disguised by having a series of orange stripes painted out. Holes had been drilled into the side of the van so the bank could be kept under surveillance.

A second vehicle, a Holden sedan, was stolen from an Ashfield car yard the day before the robbery. On the day of the robbery two employees were already inside the bank when a third employee, 19-year-old Vicki Langston, arrived about 8.30am. She'd noticed the white panel van follow her down the lane and stop outside the bank's back yard. The bank door opened and, as Vicki Langston entered, an armed man in a balaclava forced his way inside and was quickly joined by two others, also masked.

The robbers demanded keys to the vault from the accountant, Daniel Taylor. The vault required two sets of keys and the intruders were told the manager, a Mr Stewart, had the other set, but had not yet arrived.

While one robber kept watch over staff, another disabled the bank's alarm system. The manager was not expected until 9am but, in the meantime, other employees arrived and were taken to the manager's office. The manager drove into the rear car park but waited in his car for the 9am news to finish. When he

THE JURY

went inside, the bandits bundled him into his office and demanded his keys. But the manager had no keys to the vault – the accountant, Taylor, had suggested this as a ruse to gain time. The second set of keys was eventually found in Taylor's brief case.

Taylor was ordered to open the vault, but, before it could be completed, an additional combination lock had to be opened by another bank employee who was quickly fetched from the manager's office. The night safe was also opened and both were cleaned out.

Before the robbers could get away, an armoured van arrived and one of the guards entered the bank. He was disarmed and taken captive. At this stage, the robbery had been in progress for about 45 minutes.

While the first security van guard had entered the bank, the second had gone to do some shopping. On his return, he glanced through the front door, saw the robbery in progress, hurried to a nearby shop and asked the proprietor to phone the police. The robbers were already reversing out of the laneway by the time he arrived there. It was 9.20am.

The guard drew his revolver and fired two rounds. The passenger in the panel van fired one round from a shotgun and the guard took cover while the van sped off, closely followed by the Holden sedan, which had been blocking traffic in the main street.

During the robbery, just a week before Smith's arrest at Bomaderry, several events occurred that eventually led police to Montgomery, Collings and Smith.

The manager, seated near the strongroom throughout the robbery, was able to describe a belt and pouch worn by one of the bandits. A similar belt and pouch was found at Smith's Nowra home following the police operation to capture Smith on

CALL ME JIMMY

14 September. At some stage during the robbery, Smith had taken off his balaclava and was seen by the accountant, Daniel Taylor.

One of the bandits inside the bank constantly referred to another of the bandits as 'Frank', Montgomery's first name, and in conversation with a member of the bank staff had mentioned that he was receiving only $98 on the dole. This person turned out to be Collings.

The weapons, a Mauser-type pistol with a silencer and two Smith & Wesson revolvers, were noted by staff; the same sorts of weapons were found at the Little House. Other items, like bags, walkie-talkies and clothing, which had been described by bank staff, were also found in the possession of the accused. And, around 9.30am, a Sydney detective, Sergeant Arndell, claimed a lucky sighting of a man resembling Frank Montgomery leaving the Holden sedan near the detective's Carlton home and driving away in a white Valiant sedan found parked near Montgomery's home in Bardwell Park on the morning of 14 September.

The sharp-eyed Arndell had been involved in the operation to locate the robbers from the beginning and, on the afternoon of the robbery, had attended the Carlton home of a woman who reported the discovery in her front garden of an assortment of articles dumped there after the robbery.

The white panel van was located at 9.40 on the morning of the robbery; the motor still hot. A packet of $2 notes amounting to $2000 fell out of the van when the driver's door, left ajar, was opened further by detectives.

There were so many untidy ends to the robbery that it was inevitable police would eventually find their way to the homes of Montgomery and Collings. Both were arrested the night before Smith was taken at Bomaderry. They had large sums of

THE JURY

money either in their possession or recently banked, together with damning items from the robbery that a smart criminal playing by the rules would have disposed of quickly.

And Collings had kept a telegram sent to him by "Tom Cumming" at Nowra together with some photographs of Jimmy Smith and his horses, Regency Head and Dornier. The link between Collings and Smith had been established.

In January, 1978, all accused were ordered to stand trial at Darlinghurst District Court. National headlines throughout the hearing focused on Smith, calling him *The Man of Many Faces* and suggesting he was a *'major security risk'*. As the media forecast, it was the end of the line for Smith.

Because Montgomery pleaded guilty to his part in the $180,000 robbery his case was heard separately. He was convicted and sentenced to 10 years. The trial involving Smith, Collings and Hill was scheduled for 18 September, 1978. In the meantime, there were other charges to defend.

Jimmy Smith was committed to stand trial in the Supreme Court of NSW on 21 January, 1978, for the attempted murder of Constable Ambrose at Kingsford. Smith had been living at Brighton-le-Sands when Ambrose was shot. Because of the publicity following Smith's every move, Justice Slattery instructed the jury be confined until a verdict was brought in. This was the first time a jury had been locked away since the 1974 NSW decision to allow judges discretionary powers with respect to juries.

The trial started on 13 March, 1978, and lasted four days. Security was tight. Police cars patrolled outside the court while, inside, plain clothes and uniformed officers searched for bombs and concealed weapons. They feared an attempt to free Smith and kept in touch through walkie-talkies. Newspapers reported that more than 100 extra police officers attended the Parramatta court. The public was not permitted into the court area until after the trial began. Everyone's identity was checked.

Smith pleaded not guilty. The verdict hinged on two crucial entries into evidence – an oral confession allegedly given by Smith at the time of his arrest in Nowra and a positive identification in court by Ambrose who testified Smith was the man who shot him. The jury took 64 minutes to bring in a guilty verdict; Jimmy Smith was sentenced to life imprisonment.

The indisputable facts in the case were: that Constable Ambrose was shot at close range; that the shooting followed a car chase; that a police vehicle with its lights flashing and siren operating had pulled up behind another vehicle; that there had been two individuals in the car being pursued; that shots were fired; and that all witnesses saw a part of the play but not all of it.

There were many discrepancies. The man who allegedly shot Constable Ambrose was described variously as being five feet two inches to five feet eight inches; aged from 22 to 36; of slim to stocky build; with shoulder-length hair, which some witnesses thought to be brown while others believed was blond; to be wearing a full beard, a partial beard, to be unshaven or clean shaven with a moustache or no moustache.

The shooting occurred at 9.30pm while the lights of the police car were trained on the fugitives' Austin sedan. The two police officers claimed it was not raining at the time, while others reported drizzle.

All the witnesses, apart from the two police officers, were some distance from the scene of the crime – five to 10 metres – and were not focused on the event 100 per cent of the time. One witness, a gate attendant on duty in the entrance box to the University of NSW, was distracted while phoning police. A mother and daughter watched from the ground floor veranda of

THE JURY

their unit at Barker Lodge, some distance east. Another witness was distracted from writing a letter by the sounds of gunfire and tuned in as the driver of the Austin escaped. He also watched the event from his home, some distance away.

The only witness who positively identified Jimmy Smith was Constable Ambrose and that was in the Central Court of Petty Sessions 22 months after the shooting and two months after Smith had been arrested in Bomaderry.

Justice Slattery was careful to point out to the jury that 'where, as in this trial, a witness is confronted with the accused in a courtroom in a situation where he was the person charged with a crime, you must have regard to the likelihood of such witnesses identifying the person charged'. He also advised the jury of the possibility that Constable Ambrose had memorised a photograph of Smith on the wall of the police station and produced that memory when identifying Smith in court.

If anybody could have identified Smith it would have been Constable Ambrose. In evidence he said the lighting at the scene was 'good' because the lights of the police car were shining directly through the rear window of the Austin. When Ambrose moved closer to the Austin he had a 'clear view of the passenger sitting' in the middle of the back seat with his face 'looking at me directly'. He moved forward to the rear door of the Austin. He aimed his gun at the passenger and said, 'Get your hands up'. This was repeated several times when Ambrose was distracted by the noise of gunshots coming from the driver of the Austin who was being pursued by Constable Love. He glanced in the direction of the gunshots and it was then the passenger shot Ambrose.

Under cross-examination from Smith's barrister, Cash, Ambrose was asked about his assailant's clothing. He replied,

CALL ME JIMMY

'I was looking directly at his face. I was not concerned with his clothing'.

The confession made by Smith at the Nowra police station after his arrest amounted to a few words and a shrug of the shoulders. It was around 9.30 that night. Three detectives, led by Detective Sergeant K. P. Ryan, testified to questioning Smith but no record of interview was made. According to Justice Slattery, Smith's alleged answers to these questions amounted to an 'oral statement' and were admitted as evidence.

Ryan: We are making enquiries concerning the shooting of Constable Ambrose at Kensington (adjoining Kingsford) on the night of 21 January, 1976. We believe that you and a person named Terence Edward Clark were responsible for shooting this constable. I am going to ask you some questions about this matter. I want you to clearly understand that you are not obliged to say anything unless you wish, as anything you do say may later be given in evidence at court. Do you understand that?

Smith: Yes. I knew you were on to us for that one.

Ryan: Do you admit that you were at Kensington on the night of 21 January, 1976?

Smith: Yes.

Ryan: Do you admit that you and the person Clark were responsible for shooting Constable Ambrose?

Smith: Yes. Just charge me with it.

Ryan: Were you the person who actually shot Constable Ambrose?

Smith: I told you once. Just charge me with it.

Ryan: Are you prepared to make a written statement or take part in a record of interview with us concerning this matter?

Smith: Just charge me. I am not telling you anything about it.

THE JURY

Ryan: Later, you will appear at Central Court of Petty Sessions. Are you agreeable to being placed in a line-up for the purpose of identification concerning the shooting of Constable Ambrose?
Smith: No.

THE interview ended there and, according to his later evidence, Detective Sergeant Ryan made a record of the conversation in his official notebook – while it was fresh in his memory. He later went back to Smith and said: 'I have made a record of our conversation in my notebook. Do you wish to read it?
Smith: No.
Ryan: You will be charged with shooting Constable Ambrose with intent to murder him. Do you understand that?
Smith made no reply and just shrugged his shoulders.

TOWARDS the close of the trial, Smith made a lengthy unsworn statement to the jury. He told the court he did not and would not make any statements to police unless in the presence of his solicitor, that he had signed statutory declarations to this effect. He referred to his arrest at the Bomaderry phone box where he 'sung out in a loud voice to any witness who was present that ... I'd be saying nothing to the police whatsoever'.

He denied being in NSW at the time of the shooting although he couldn't remember where he had been. His arrest was almost two years after the shooting. While Smith may have travelled to Melbourne at the time, there is no doubt his home had been in Brighton-le-Sands since November the year before.

In his directions to the jury, Justice Slattery likened Smith's denial of any statement to behaviour within the general community. 'People of great importance, business people, professional people, hard-headed people, all sorts of people in

CALL ME JIMMY

some situations can make admissions which they later on regret and have cause to retract from ... you would have to consider your general experience of life and, in a way, your assessment of the accused person here when he made the statement.

'You have had him under observation for practically a week. You have had the opportunity of seeing his attitude in court, his general demeanour in court, how he behaved himself, what he said and what he has done. You will have to ask yourself is he a hard-headed person who would refrain from saying anything in any given circumstance, especially to the police for whom he has a great dislike or would he be a person who, under emotional stress or strain, would become irritated and say things that he would later on regret.

'That is the type of approach you have to make towards this statement. In a sense, it is your assessment of him that has to be looked at ... he has not got to prove his case. The Crown has the onus but nevertheless you have the sworn testimony of three police officers that a certain conversation took place.'

After the jury returned with its verdict, Justice Slattery set about determining Smith's antecedents, his personal and criminal history, and to take his plea prior to sentencing. Neither was forthcoming. A short, sharp exchange took place.

Cash: I have no instructions at the moment. I cannot make a plea on sentence at this stage.
His Honour: Partly due to his own fault because he does not co-operate with people.
Smith: Apparently I co-operated with the police and I told them.
His Honour: What has he been doing since 1967? You don't know that, I suppose?
Cash: No.

CALL ME JIMMY

'Til Death Us Do Part … a wedding snap from Smith's own album.

CALL ME JIMMY

Valerie Hill … was it her former husband who shot and wounded Smith?

CALL ME JIMMY

The only statement he ever signed ... Jimmy and Valerie tie the knot in jail.

CALL ME JIMMY

Happy families ... Smith's parents Jean and Daniel (top) and his wife Valerie and her daughter.

CALL ME JIMMY

Every picture tells a story ... after visiting hours, she gets to go home and he goes back to his cell.

CALL ME JIMMY

From Val with love … a snapshot of life on the outside.

CALL ME JIMMY

Staunch to the end ... Jimmy's mother Jean Smith.

CALL ME JIMMY

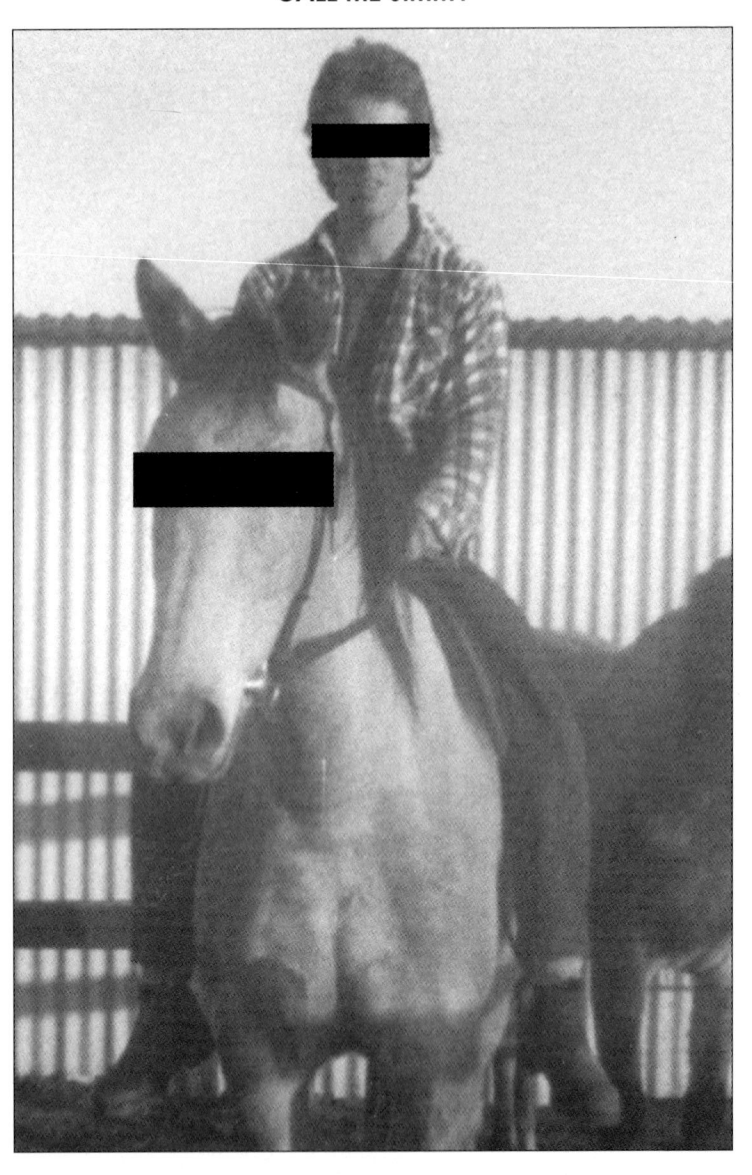

A favourite relative on a favourite horse. Identities have been obscured to protect the innocent.

CALL ME JIMMY

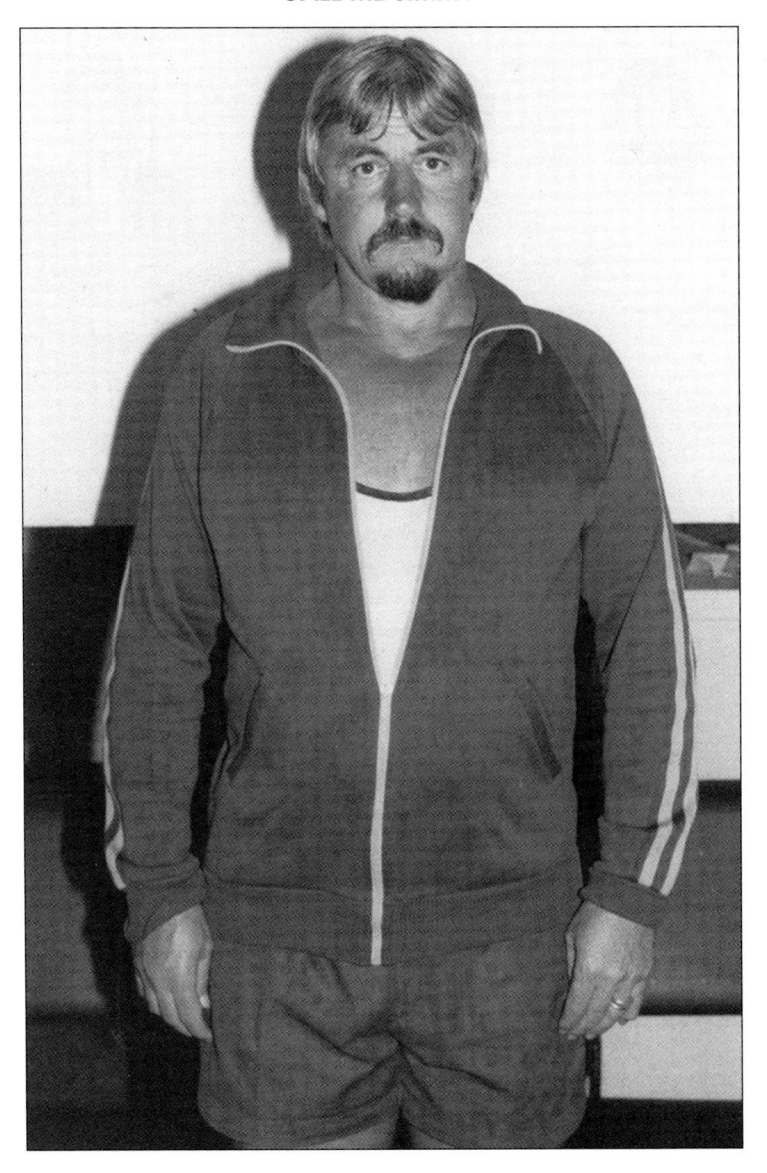

Little big man ... portrait of the armed robber as a middle-aged prisoner.

CALL ME JIMMY

Scallywags I have known ... Smith and some of his friends behind bars.

CALL ME JIMMY

Bricked in ... Smith and an unnamed inmate catch a few rays on a prison-issue blanket.

CALL ME JIMMY

More of Smith's mates in prison … hardmen, scallywags and knockabouts.

CALL ME JIMMY

All dressed down and nowhere to go ... a contact visit between "Louey" and an unnamed friend.

CALL ME JIMMY

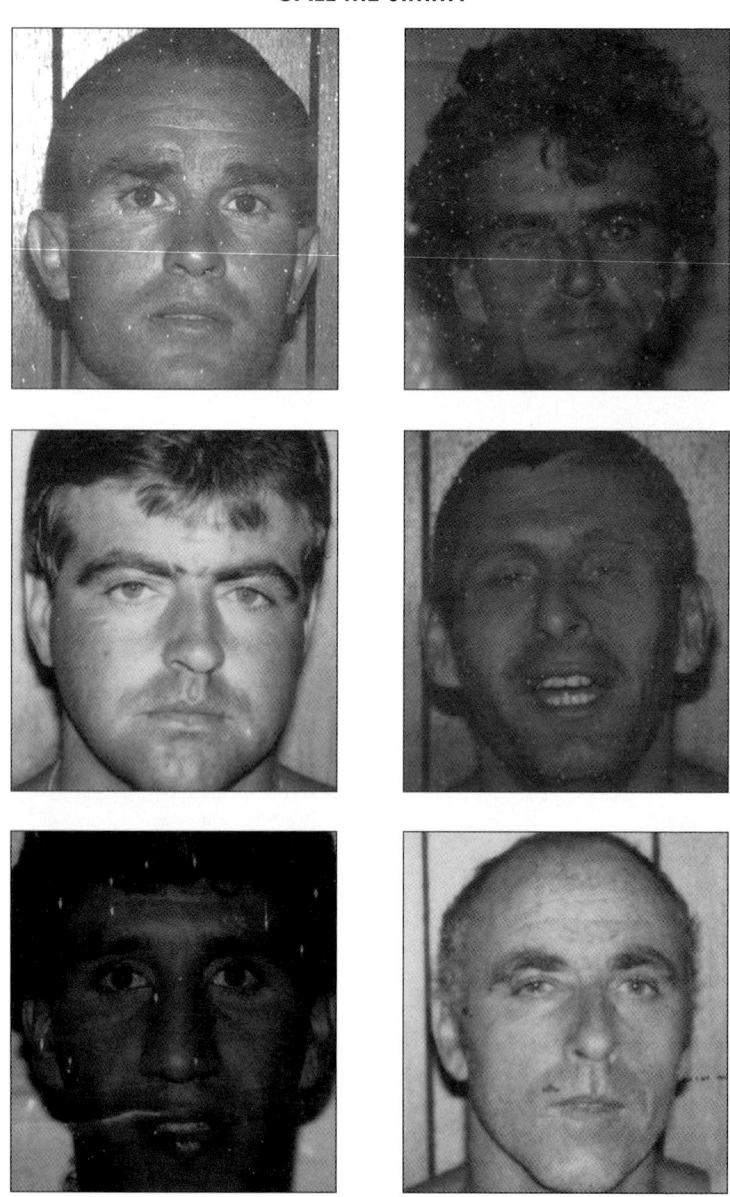

Mugshots of mates inside.

CALL ME JIMMY

The safe house that wasn't ... Daylesford, December 1992.

The end of the road ... the spot where Smith was shot dead in Creswick, Victoria.

CALL ME JIMMY

Senior Constable Ian Harris ... a good cop who faced a desperate man and shot him.

THE JURY

IN sentencing Smith to life, Justice Slattery commented, 'You have expressed your strong dislike of the police in your statement and with that dislike one can well understand that you did participate in the shooting of this unfortunate constable. It was the act of a desperate man who was cornered'.

Melbourne newspapers were far more sedate than their counterparts in Sydney when reporting the trial. However, Jimmy Smith was big news and the story competed strongly with the disappearance of former Italian Premier Aldo Moro, who had been kidnapped as a retaliatory measure against the trial of Red Brigades' leaders. Such was the enthusiasm to report on and read about crime and the mystique of the criminal world.

Twelve months later, Jimmy Smith appealed the verdict and Chief Justice Street, Justice Lee and Justice Lusher quashed the conviction. It was 'unsafe or dangerous' to allow the conviction to stand.

Chief Justice Street, in referring to photographs Constable Ambrose was shown shortly after he was shot, said, 'It does not appear expressly that a photograph of the appellant was included amongst these, but it would seem to be a reasonable inference that it was'.

He went on to say that Ambrose had not recognised any photographs of Smith 'although the appellant's photograph as a wanted man had been displayed in police stations and seen by Constable Ambrose over quite a period of time prior to the first face-to-face meeting of the two men'.

The Chief Justice also seemed to doubt the oral statement sworn to by Detective Sergeant Ryan. 'The confession in the few brief answers said to have been made by the appellant to the investigating police was in the teeth of the appellant's attitude throughout (the trial) and on all other occasions, namely, that he would say nothing and that he would not furnish the police with any information. It is inconsistent with this attitude … that he should have made these incautious admissions in answering these few questions asked of him by the police witness. The doubt that must inevitably follow … is deepened by the departure from the established practice of having any confession instantly brought before the senior police officer present, who is not concerned with the investigation.'

The Crown sought a new trial, but Justice Street declined. 'This conviction has not been set aside by reason of any error of law or in the course of the proceedings. It has been set aside because of the paucity of evidence available to be called by the Crown.'

It never attracted the sensational headlines of his past appearances, but various newspapers did report the quashing of Smith's conviction the following day.

ON 25 March, 1976, at Ultimo near the revamped Darling Harbour, armed robbers snatched a $76,000 payroll in a daring early morning raid on the Patrick Stevedoring Company.

Moments after the TNT armoured van delivered the company's pay, two masked bandits burst into the pay office and ordered staff to open up.

A shotgun blast shattered the pay office window and staff, including the van driver, were told to 'hit the floor' and surrender their weapons. It was lightning fast. Two pay tins were grabbed and the bandits were gone.

The connection to Jimmy Smith was made following his arrest at Bomaderry and the search of his home at North Nowra. Amongst his possessions, it was alleged, were a Colt pistol and a Smith & Wesson revolver, the latter being the property of the TNT Security Company, that had been taken during the robbery. Further, police also located at Smith's home a

THE JURY

Remington 870 shotgun with a missing magazine cap. Such a cap was found at Patrick Stevedoring after the raid.

The hearing began on 20 April, 1978. Smith, still a resident at Katingal, was unrepresented. Magistrate Brown found there was a case to answer and accordingly committed Smith to stand trial on 1 May, 1978. But the biggest charge of all was still to come.

At 4pm on the last day of the committal hearing into Patrick Stevedoring charges, several police officers entered the courtroom and took custody of Smith. He was charged with the murder of Lloyd Tidmarsh, the bookmaker.

That morning the Sydney *Sun* had devoted a full front page to the impending charges of a Long Bay inmate. A half-page headline proclaimed **Bookie Murder – Jail Lead.** Next day the *Daily Telegraph* also gave front page to the story under the headline **Jockey Smith accused – Tidmarsh Murder.** It included two photographs: one of Tidmarsh, another of Smith being led out of a building with the words 'Charge Room' highlighted on the wall behind him. He was flanked by several police officers. His hands were manacled and formed the prayer position. He looked stunned.

The murder charge took precedence over the armed robbery charge – for which Smith was ultimately never tried because, in 1984, the Attorney-General decided not to prosecute in the Patrick Stevedoring case. Once the murder charge was read out, Christopher Wynyard for Smith requested the accused's name be suppressed on the basis of 'unprecedented publicity'. This request was denied.

Throughout the Tidmarsh committal hearing in the Sydney Coroner's Court, Smith frequently clashed with presiding magistrate Len Nash. Every move was reported. The Melbourne *Sun* led with **'Jockey' on kill charge** and later reported **'Jockey' has a clash with SM**. Police moved for an adjournment in the hearing and Smith said, 'Just a minute, what's going on here? I've had no conference with any barrister over this matter'.

Magistrate Nash replied, 'Mr Smith, sit down and be quiet'. And later, 'Mr Smith, I'm not used to people being rude to me', to which Smith replied, 'I'm going to get railroaded again, am I?' A short adjournment followed. Smith reappeared holding a cardboard banner which read, 'I want justice. Stop police verbal'. Around this time, Wynyard withdrew from the case and Peter Livesey took over.

On one occasion Smith had to be carried into court by police; he sat before Nash handcuffed and sobbing. His barrister complained to the court that his client had been manhandled and assaulted by police. He refused to co-operate because police had not told him where they were taking him.

'They bashed me,' Smith alleged. Police prosecutor, Sergeant McGoldrick, said the claims were unfounded. Smith was ordered from court and Nash instructed police to inform Smith where he was going, what courts he would appear in and why.

Following an adjournment of a month or so, Jimmy Smith and the magistrate were at it again. This time, the ruckus was caused when police took trial papers from Smith before he entered the courtroom. Accompanied by four detectives, Smith shouted, 'My papers. The police have taken them from me. They just came into the cell and took them and tore them up'.

Smith was upset and led from the court shouting, 'Talk about justice. I'm getting no fucking justice here'. When he returned, Nash explained the papers had been taken at his direction. Smith had been forbidden to bring anything to court in line with stringent security measures that, again, included the presence of additional police and a careful sweep of the court, seats and benches.

THE JURY

The National Times described it as an 'unusual precautionary measure', adding 'So was the presence of an armed detective who sat near Nash on the bench'.

The Tidmarsh case saw Nash clash with others in the courtroom. At one point police complained that Valerie Hill and two other women had made some comment about a witness. They were evicted. Hill left quietly, but the two women with her stood their ground and argued with Nash. He threatened to charge them and they were forcibly evicted by police.

Smith's counsel, Peter Livesey, attempted to remonstrate with the magistrate over the ruling as Smith turned to him and asked, 'Is he (Nash) fair dinkum?'

On another occasion, protestors outside the court pasted posters to the walls of the building and demonstrated over the handling of Smith's case. The posters read: **Jim Smith is being framed by the police and convicted by the press**.

Nash labelled Livesey a 'puppet' being used by Smith. 'He (Smith) is pulling the strings. That is not my understanding of what instructions to a barrister should be. You should be able to ask a question without Mr Smith putting it into your mouth.'

The tension between the two increased as the hearing progressed as Livesey sought to represent his client by attacking police evidence and what he suggested were fabrications. When Smith called out that Detective Constable Brian Harding was inventing evidence, Nash had him removed from the courtroom.

He again berated Livesey and told him to 'instruct your client in his conduct'. He said, 'I must condemn you, too, Mr Livesey'. When the maligned barrister attempted to have Nash revoke his condemnation, the magistrate refused.

Throughout all of this, Smith maintained his stance with police and refused to speak with them unless a solicitor was present. Tight security for every appearance overshadowed Smith's claims of foul play. The security was justified, according to police. They had wind of an underworld reward of three-quarters of $750,000 to anyone who could 'spring' Smith.

However far-fetched that was, it created an effective distraction for the media and the court. The hearing took evidence from 49 witnesses for the prosecution and a further 34 for the defence. In March, 1980, Smith was indicted to stand trial. The committal hearing had sat for 48 days spread over two years.

During the various committal hearings, Smith remained at Katingal. He was roused early, and transported to and from the courts daily by prison van. The van did the rounds of prisons and those prisoners collected first might spend hours in the hot, cramped conditions before arriving at court. Prisoners were packed in tightly. There was no water.

Katingal housed convicted felons. Despite being a remanded inmate when he first went to Katingal (he became a convicted felon when found guilty of attempting to murder Constable Ambrose) Smith was immediately placed in isolation in Upper Red Wing. He'd been classified as an 'intractable' based on his notoriety and his escape from Pentridge.

Katingal, like 'The Circle' at Parramatta Jail and the intractables' unit at Grafton Jail, was a difficult place to prepare a proper defence. It was a state of the art 'electronic zoo', as one critic dubbed such high security units, and renowned for the sophistication of its cruelty to inmates.

It offered the ultimate in human deprivation and fell well outside human rights' conventions. By contrast, Grafton and Parramatta Jails were simply renowned for their normal, old-fashioned 19th century brutality.

At Grafton Jail, new inmates routinely received the 'Reception Biff' where they ran the gauntlet of warders' batons

THE JURY

as they entered the prison – a practice that continued from 1943 until 1976. The philosophy was simple – bash new inmates on arrival at the prison as a tangible example of what they could expect if they stepped out of line. Prisoners daren't look a warder in the eye for fear of further bashings.

'The Circle' at Parramatta was also notorious for a novel form of cruelty. Prisoners were caged in their cells 23 hours a day with their only exercise being a brief walk around and around a tiny internal circular enclosure fronting the cells. They were like donkeys pounding endlessly around a flour mill.

A former inmate and friend to Smith did time at all three prisons. Bernie Matthews was at Katingal from November 1975, two months after the unit opened, until its closure in June 1978. As the longest serving inmate at Katingal, Matthews saw men like Smith come in with some spirit and leave emotionally battered by the place.

Matthews likened Katingal to an exclusive club 'where entry was permitted only after being subjected to the physical and psychological brutality of the system at that time'.

Inmates had a special bond, 'higher than mateship, something akin to brotherhood'. It was a bond shared by men 'who did hard time' in places like Grafton and Katingal. 'Jimbo was no different because he'd been brutalised by H-Division in Pentridge.'

In December, 1977, four months after Smith arrived at Katingal and only two years after the high-tech security block opened, the ventilation system packed up.

It was a hot summer. Prisoners were denied exercise. Riots erupted in the cell blocks. Jimmy Smith, Marko Motric and others were eventually allowed into the exercise yards and barricaded themselves there. They were tear-gassed. They were trying to negotiate a 30-point charter of improved conditions,

CALL ME JIMMY

but the best they could get was clean clothing and a hot meal when making court appearances. They had tried to bargain for limits to times spent in the windowless cells, more family visits, welfare inspections and rehabilitation courses.

In January, 1978, around the time Smith was committed to stand trial on the Ambrose charge, trouble flared again at Katingal when inmates were locked down following the escape of Russell 'Mad Dog' Cox from the supposedly escape-proof fortress. Cox was serving time for offences that included kidnapping, armed hold-up and malicious wounding.

Two months after Smith was convicted on the Ambrose charge there was an audacious attempt to free inmates at Katingal. It was 31 May, 1978. Bernie Matthews takes up the story:

'An attempt was made to cut open the cell blocks on the yellow side. Katingal cell blocks were colour-coded red, green, blue and yellow so the prison guards would not become disorientated working inside the place. Katingal had 40 cells, 20 cells each side with exercise yards adjoining each block. Each cell block contained five cells, a workshop and TV recreation room, a shower and a walkway approximately 22 steps in length from the door to the exercise yard to the cell block entry door.

'A central control panel was operated by screws, in the centre and at the end of their walkway where they could observe cell blocks. Each cell block was either upper or lower ... and entry could only be gained by two automatic doors.

'Everything was closed in. It was akin to living inside a submarine with the longest distance you could walk in a straight line being 22 steps. Prisoners became completely disorientated because you did not know if you were above or below ground.'

For Jimmy Smith, the internal surveillance became a huge

impediment to his defence when even confidential and privileged meetings with his legal representatives were monitored and taped.

In late May, 1978, Barrister Christopher Wynyard applied for these restrictions to be lifted and, although he won the right to have monitoring devices switched off during lawyer-client meetings, they were not removed. The suspicion that bugging devices were still used was enough to impede free-flowing exchanges between inmates and their legal representatives. That, combined with the difficulties of meeting his client, frustrated Wynyard's efforts to defend Smith and he retired from the Tidmarsh case.

Matthews continues: 'At the time of the break-in, Jimbo was in lower green cell block with Warwick James, Mark Motric and Ray Denning. On the night of the break-in, Jimmy Murray knocked me up about 1am by tapping on the cell wall.

'I looked out the spy glass in my cell door and saw a shower of sparks dropping from the exercise yard roof. I tapped on the wall to wake the rest of the guys in my cell block. They cut through the roof of the exercise yard and began lowering the oxy bottles down off the roof into the yard. One dropped and made a loud noise. No-one came.

'They started cutting through the main entry door leading into the exercise yard from the downstairs cell blocks. The oxy made a loud bang. But they kept working.

'A screw came to the observation deck and looked in. Murray or myself had no way of warning the guys out in the yard. All we could do was watch.

'The screw walked along the observation deck to the observation window at the end that looked out into the exercise yard. He saw a shower of sparks, but didn't know what it was. The guys in the yard saw him at the window, climbed the rope to the roof and bolted. The screw shit himself and hit the alarm button. Next minute, all hell broke loose.

'And that's the story to the Katingal break-in. As far as who was involved and who wasn't involved, I cannot comment on that. I know Steve (Steven Sellers alias Steven Jorgic) got pinched over it and eventually beat the charge, but that's about it. Suffice to say it is safe to assume that every prisoner in green and yellow cell blocks would have had the opportunity to escape that night if the break-in had been successful.'

It was widely reported the attempt would have succeeded except that an elderly woman, living near the prison, noticed the escape bid in progress and phoned the police.

The perpetrators got to within five feet of the master switch to the cell doors. According to *The Age* they left behind detonators, fuses, ammunition, bolt cutters, hacksaw blades, a ladder, three sticks of gelignite, a hydraulic press, several loaded pistols, a magnum rifle and a shotgun.

The headline in the *Daily Mirror* was an eye grabber; it occupied three-quarters of the front page: **Mass Jail Escape Foiled!** The same newspaper followed the story as charges were laid and kept the public up-to-date on the **'Jockey' Smith Escape Plot.**

Bernie Matthews was an armed robber and escapee who went to prison at 20 and came out at 31. In his own words, he later 'flirted with a career in journalism' and, to date, has had several freelance articles published in the likes of the *Courier-Mail*, the *Sun-Herald* and *Penthouse*. He has also lectured on prisons to legal students at Sydney University. But a criminal past is difficult to shed and, in 1996, he found himself doing time in a Queensland prison after a bank robbery in Brisbane.

Following the Nagle Report into NSW prisons in 1978, then *Daily Mirror* journalist Michael Munro was granted an

THE JURY

interview with Smith. He described the 10 centimetre thick steel roller door that separated the waiting room from the visiting room. And the silence. 'The terrible silence that's frightening in the "concrete cage".' And the loneliness and the lack of anything to do to pass time. During the interview, Smith spoke through wire mesh either side of the plate glass window. He was edgy, nervous, switching 'from one side of his seat to the other every 15 seconds'.

'I was in this place for about five months while I was only on remand,' Smith told Munro.

'That's wrong. I should be in the remand centre like anyone else. I've been waiting on a pair of glasses I've ordered because I can hardly read any more. I could never spend my life here. I'd go absolutely mad first.'

A couple of inmates were on the way to insanity while another two had made the transition and were certified. 'I'm already a bit like that,' Smith continued. 'Sometimes I just have to scream out in my cell or abuse one of the guards. It all mounts up inside and there is nothing to do, to see. No one to talk to – just bars and concrete.'

When Justice Nagle directed that Katingal be closed in early 1978 and Premier Neville Wran effected the order, the immediate response from the Prison Officers' Association was to threaten strike action and a refusal to accept Katingal prisoners in any other jails.

Bernie Matthews recalls: 'Inside Katingal, there were numerous riots and disturbances that had gradually escalated due to the close confinement and the sensory deprivation caused by the place.' Controversy continued. Protesters banded together with trade union officials to form The Close Katingal Campaign.

Even as late as 1989, Katingal was still a problem for the

CALL ME JIMMY

NSW Government. It had been closed for more than 10 years by then, but there were still calls to re-open it as a modern, high-security jail, which drew protests.

Karen Harbutt, in *The Australian,* described Katingal as a 'nightmare', a place 'where inmates were once starved of natural light and air, fed from trays passed through a metal slot in their cell walls and where they had no control over the flushing of their toilets'.

By the time Smith left Katingal in June, 1978, he had been committed to stand trial in January for his part in the South Hurstville bank robbery; convicted of shooting officer Ambrose and sentenced in March that year to life, a conviction which was quashed 12 months later; had his trial aborted on the Patrick Stevedoring Company robbery charges; gone part way in committal proceedings on charges relating to the murder of Lloyd Tidmarsh; and was still to front the courts for threatening to shoot officer Godden and for conspiracy to rob the Redfern railway workshops.

In August, 1978, with the South Hurstville bank robbery trial underway, Smith complained to Judge Torrington that media speculation about him would prejudice any future jury. Smith asked to have his charges heard separately.

Judge Torrington responded: 'I have seen a large number of ... newspaper clippings from the Sydney press – the *Sydney Morning Herald,* the *Daily Telegraph*, the Sydney *Sun*, the *Sydney Mirror* and *The Australian*. Some of the headlines are quite lurid. Some of them would raise, in the minds of any persons seeing such headlines, a strong feeling that the accused is probably guilty. That is unfortunate, but the press has its freedom'. He went on to criticise 'the Willesee show' where one of the accused, Valerie Hill, was asked to comment about Smith's trial.

THE JURY

Judge Torrington's view of 'the Willesee show' made headlines the next day – with the unfortunate side effect of attracting even more attention to Jimmy Smith. Under the headline **Willesee Interview Improper,** Sydney's most popular tabloid newspaper, the *Daily Telegraph*, took the opportunity to report on Smith's claims of prejudicial media attention. He was damned whatever his approach to the media.

On 7 November, 1978, with the South Hurstville bank robbery trial rolling along in dribs and drabs, a newspaper article prejudiced proceedings. The trial had been going, on and off, for 34 days. About half the witnesses had been heard.

The *Telegraph* article featured the escape of 'Mad Dog' Cox from Katingal and linked him to Smith by saying they had been cell mates. The article was sparked by another escape from another unit of Long Bay Jail while the South Hurstville trial was in progress. The escapee was Eric Harold Heuston who, the article said, was 'old friends' with Cox.

A similar story was aired on radio 2SM. Judge Leslie was forced to abort the hearing midway and to discharge the jury.

In his address to the jury he said Smith had made several applications to have his case heard separately but had been refused. 'The accused Smith had received a great deal of media publicity at the time of his arrest, in the course of which the nickname Jockey had been associated with him. But, because I had no power to suppress the use of the appellation under which Smith was known, I requested the press ... not use the nickname in relation to him until the nickname appeared in evidence, as it has not done to this date, and I further requested ... the press not use the nickname in headlines at all.'

Judge Leslie specifically targeted the *Daily Telegraph*, saying the reference to Edward 'Jockey' Smith in the article dealing with Heuston's escape was 'pure speculation' that 'clearly seeks to establish a link between the aforementioned escaper (Russell Cox) and one of the accused in this trial'.

Judge Leslie went on to savage the media. 'None of the news media in the course of this trial,' he said, 'have shown any interest whatsoever in the publication of factual reports of the proceedings, and I remark that the use of the appellation to which I have referred so far as newspapers are concerned has been on each occasion, other than in the course of the original publicity, by one group of newspapers. It seems to me the height of irresponsibility for the news media to draw attention during the course of a trial to the notoriety of that accused person, particularly when that notoriety has originally, at least in large part, been created by the media by the original treatment of the story of Smith's arrest.'

By the time a new trial could be scheduled and a new jury empanelled, Smith had won his argument to have his charges heard separately from the others. It was impossible to find an impartial jury with media speculation about the trial. Equally, Judge Leslie believed 'the very association of the other two accused with Smith makes it impossible that they should have a fair trial'.

So powerful were Judge Leslie's words that the NSW Attorney-General, Mr Walker, weighed in immediately and further censured the media for what he saw as a 'worrying trend'. He was reported to be 'considering strong action' against sections of the news media, including charges relating to contempt of court.

While Walker referred indirectly to the accused, his words were hollow because Jimmy Smith's greatest trial-by-media was yet to come. At one stage, around 100 separate media reports within an 11-month period had highlighted either Smith's career or his criminal proceedings.

THE JURY

Despite winning the right to have South Hurstville robbery charges against Smith heard separately, the Crown never returned to the case. Smith spent the next few years entangled in the legal system and, in 1984, the NSW Department of the Attorney-General and of Justice decided not to proceed with the case that saw Valerie Hill and Frank Montgomery convicted. It is fair to assume the Crown saw no point in pursuing the case because Smith, by then, had already been sentenced to a life term on other charges and, even if convicted, the likely outcome would only be another prison term to be served concurrently.

The first of the other charges Smith faced went back to the 1974 allegations of a conspiracy in company with Marko Motric, Brian Leslie O'Callaghan and Stanley Ernest James, to rob the pay office at the Redfern railway workshops. He had been indicted to stand trial in January 1978 but that trial was delayed until mid-1981 while he answered more serious charges in a higher court.

SMITH'S experiences with the New South Wales legal system and the media caused a whiff of controversy that rankled some people. Following the *Sydney Morning Herald's* reference to Smith as **Public Enemy No 1**, Roger Court, the Director of the Criminal Law Review Division of the NSW Attorney-General's and Justice Department, accused the newspaper of using the term as a means of increasing sales. He challenged the paper to show 'public interest' and to explain 'specifically what that "public interest" is said to be'.

Court's letter prompted an editor's note explaining the term had been used by defence counsel and reported as part of counsel's case to have a suppression order placed on Smith's name.

In fairness to the *Sydney Morning Herald*, the reference had not been employed in any grandstanding way but incorporated far into the body of the text. That paper also complemented Roger Court's letter with a leading article raising the issue of reporting an accused person's name prior to any conviction – an article that found the weight of argument against suppression.

'Let us say we had not named the accused in the Tidmarsh case. Would not the city have been full of rumours by now as to whom it might be? Might not malicious people be paying off old scores by spreading names? Then there are those who like to appear well-informed when they are not. Would half a dozen – a dozen – 20 – people have to live with suspicion for weeks or months, where now suspicion is focused on one.'

FRANK 'Grandpa' Montgomery, who many described as a 'great old man, a real joker', died from cirrhosis while the trial against Collings and Hill was in progress. His drinking had caught up with him before the law had time to do likewise. While his death left two to face the jury, eventually that would be whittled away to one.

During the afternoon of 27 February, 1979, Valerie Hill and Neil Collings were in their cells waiting for the jury's verdict. Staff at the centre had allowed Hill to join him there for a while because, Hill says, 'It was our day for the jury to come in'. But Collings never got to hear the jury verdict. Around 3pm he was found alone and dead in his cell.

Neil Collings was married and father of a young child. The day after his death, the *Sydney Morning Herald* reported Collings had '... collapsed and died in the cells of the Darlinghurst Courts and was taken by police car to nearby St Vincent's Hospital. Judge Redapple recalled the jury shortly afterwards and reported that Collings had suffered a cardiac arrest and despite immediate treatment had failed to respond'.

THE JURY

Judge Redapple discharged the jury without a verdict on the charges against Collings. The jury of 10 men and one woman (one juror had been discharged as a result of jury tampering) then retired to consider its verdict on the charges against Hill.

On its return 15 minutes later, the jury announced 36-year-old Hill guilty for her part in the South Hurstville bank robbery. She was sentenced to 4½ years with a two-year non-parole period. Although Judge Redapple was quoted as saying Hill 'was completely under the domination' of Smith, he found she stood to gain, however indirectly, from her involvement in the crime.

Hill's conviction was a curious result. She had been found guilty for her alleged involvement before and after the committing of a crime while Smith, her link to the $180,000 robbery, had not yet stood trial.

Hill offered an alibi that relied on the diary kept by a young strapper, Helen Beverley Ward, though it was never admitted into evidence. It noted that on 7 September, 1977, the day of the robbery, Smith, Hill's daughter, Ward and another two people from Nowra, Warren Hoffman and Peter Contino, had swum Regency Head and another horse called Rudmar in the Shoalhaven River early that morning and, later, Ward had been drinking with Valerie Hill at the Empire Hotel in Nowra. This version of events suggested that Hill and Smith could not be in two places at once.

According to Ward's statement, 'Tom Cumming' (Smith) rowed the boat while she or the man named Peter held the horse's lead rope. The swim had taken about an hour – from 6am to 7am. If this was accurate, it was important because, Nowra being a good two-hour drive from South Hurstville, it would have been impossible for Smith to have off-loaded Regency Head, prepared himself for the robbery and got himself to the bank by 8.30am. Furthermore, if taken at face value, the claimed alibi meant that Hill would have been a Houdini to have driven Smith to Sutherland, on the Nowra side of Kogarah Bay to Hurstville, in time for him to set up for the robbery and for her to drive back to the Empire Hotel by mid-morning and drink with Ward until 1pm.

Not everyone was overwhelmed by the strapper's diary. In summing up, Judge Redapple instructed the jury by concluding that: 'If you are satisfied by other evidence in the case that Edward James Smith did in fact assist or take part in the commission of the armed robbery at the bank, then Miss Ward's evidence that he was at Nowra at 7am is obviously untrue and you may think that … tends also to make the alibi evidence in respect of Hill unacceptable.

'It is a matter for you, of course. However, if you are left in doubt as to whether Edward James Smith was one of the robbers then, since he is the only link with Hill, as I have directed you, she is entitled for that reason to be acquitted since in those circumstances it is not proved beyond reasonable doubt.'

Unfortunately for Hill, the jury was in no doubt. In July 1979, she was taken to Mulawa Training and Detention Centre for Women at Silverwater Prison.

THE coronial inquest into the death of Neil Collings got underway in late July, 1979. For the 18 months before his death, Collings had been in Long Bay Jail. He often saw prison doctors and was also treated by specialist physicians and psychiatrists. He was an epileptic and needed medication three times a day.

On the day he died he received his first dose at 8.30am and his second at 11am. The third was due at around 3pm but was never administered. The medication was controlled by the jail

THE JURY

recorder, who doled out the day's dosage to the officer in charge of the cells. It was held in a small plain envelope, which noted the patient's name, medication and administering times. Collings was taking Dilantin for the control of epilepsy and Valium for anxiety.

Senior Constable Vincent Stoker was on duty at Darlinghurst police cells at the time. During a regular inspection of the cells he found Collings slumped forward, hands supporting his head and quite still, with vomit down either side of his pants. 'I said "Are you all right, Neil?" When I saw he never made any movement or answer, I immediately opened the door, went over to him and shook him, and he slumped down on his left hand side.' Stoker felt for a pulse but found none. He put Collings' legs on the bench and went for assistance.

Seconds later, Stoker was followed back to the cell by other officers, who loosened Collings' clothing and did mouth-to-mouth along with heart massage. A police vehicle arrived and Collings was carried out, face up, and placed in the back seat for the short trip to hospital. He was already dead.

Officially, Collings died from 'asphyxia due to aspiration of vomitus' – he choked to death on his food. Dr Dennis Gomez conducted the post-mortem in full view of family representatives, police and a physician engaged by the family.

Under oath, he gave evidence it was likely Collings vomited while having an epileptic fit, which resulted in the plugging of his airways. He came to this conclusion based on the patient's previous medical history, but acknowledged any number of causes could have resulted in a similar death including a coughing fit while eating, which could allow a chunk of food to become lodged in the trachea.

Counsel representing Collings' family – the barrister Peter Livesey – had other ideas. Acting on instructions, he probed

CALL ME JIMMY

alternative causes and made several references to alcohol in the blood and cyanide poisoning. It was clear he thought Collings' death might have been caused by someone who entered his cell. While he made frequent reference to a particular police officer, no one on duty that day recalled seeing that officer in the cells.

That officer, a member of the armed hold-up squad, was represented by counsel at the inquest. He was the officer who arrested and charged Valerie Hill at Nowra. He had also interviewed Smith in the Nowra cells and subsequently charged him with the attempted bribe.

The possibility of any link between Collings' death and the policeman was never established because the inquest was aborted when the coroner was forced to discharge the jury. He did so following an application from the policeman's barrister, who had sat back for some time, listening to Livesey suggesting the idea of cyanide poisoning but without producing any evidence.

Finally, the policeman's barrister challenged the roundabout accusation. 'If my learned friend (Livesey) is to allege the administration of cyanide he is alleging crime, serious crime. Without evidence, that is the grossest misconduct and I say that whether my learned friend alleges crime against an individual or crime against a group, if the evidence is in my learned friend's hands, and it must be for his conduct to be proper, I would have submitted Your Worship, with respect, that he had a certain duty in relation to that. He has in front of the press made an accusation, that cyanide is an accusation. People don't read the facts, that my learned friend was unable to produce one shred of evidence to support that accusation.'

Livesey attempted to salvage his position by suggesting cyanide could not be detected in the body after 24 hours. Unfortunately, the autopsy was carried out 44 hours after

THE JURY

Collings' death. But, the following morning, the policeman's barrister arrived in court prepared. During the night he had discovered cyanide remains in the body for much longer than 24 hours and had brought along an expert to testify to that fact.

Livesey's ship was taking on water quickly and his opponent, perhaps sensing victory, grew more vitriolic. 'You cannot put a leading question unless you have instructions. You cannot have instructions without evidence. There is a responsibility on counsel, however junior – however junior – to come to these courts and conduct oneself properly.' The ship was listing.

Further attacks on Livesey proved equally damaging. He had been probing away about alcohol while examining witnesses, but the coroner readily agreed with the assertion that everyone has small traces of alcohol in their systems, even teetotallers.

More importantly, after death, there is often a build-up of alcohol within the system as fats turn to sugars and ferment. When asked to name the doctor who had informed him of the dissipation time of cyanide within the body, Livesey refused.

He tried one last attempt to salvage his case. The other side had claimed 'that I have no evidence of (a) the presence, (b) the administration or (c) the existence of cyanide. I do state that the medical advice I received was, to the best of my understanding, correct.'

The jury was discharged and, although the hearing was unfinished, it was not rescheduled but left as a date to be fixed. A second coronial inquest into the death of Neil Collings never eventuated.

WHILE Smith was fighting the harsh conditions at Katingal, John Grant, in the *Daily Mirror* on 17 January, 1978, broke news of Smith's desire to wed Valerie Hill under the headline **Public Enemy No 1 Pleads: Let Me Wed In Jail.** Grant told readers, 'Smith and Hill, both 35, spoke of their "never to end" love for each other during an exclusive interview – the first time a journalist has entered Katingal'.

He continued, 'Hill said she was to have had Smith's child but lost the baby early in the pregnancy while in Silverwater Women's Prison'. At the time this article went to press Valerie Hill was free on $20,000 bail and awaiting her day in court.

The marriage was celebrated two years later, almost to the day, on 20 January, 1980. By then Hill was an inmate at the Mulawa Training and Detention Centre.

The ceremony took place in the Metropolitan Remand Centre at Long Bay Jail, where Smith was serving time after Katingal closed. Smith's barrister, Peter Livesey, was best man while the Reverend Ted Noffs, from the Wayside Chapel in Kings Cross, officiated.

The ceremony took about half an hour with the couple allowed a further 15 minutes together before Smith was whisked back to the cells.

Smith, heavily guarded, wore a brown pin-striped suit with flared trousers and a white carnation in the breast pocket. His greying hair, slicked down and parted in the middle, was showing signs of thinning. He sported a moustache and small goatee beard.

Valerie Hill was driven to Long Bay by prison officers from Mulawa, where she was about halfway through her sentence following her conviction as an accessory to the South Hurstville bank robbery.

Photographs of the wedding show her as a slim woman in the prime of life. She wore a full-length cream dress with cream flowers in her blond hair and on her wrists and carried a bouquet of white and pink flowers.

The room was bare except for a couple of tables, one to sign

THE JURY

the marriage documents, the other to cut the cake. Valerie looked wistful while Jimmy Smith stood straight, his face pallid and lips drawn together. He looked tired.

Whatever his emotional state that day, Smith kept one document, a parchment-style prose piece called *Spectrum of Love* by Walter Rinder. It was a gift from Valerie who wrote, 'To You Jim Darling, 20.1.80', and below 'My Total Love To You On Our Wedding Day. Totally Yours, Valerie'.

Valerie persuaded the governor of Mulawa to allow her a few hours freedom to attend a wedding reception. 'I begged the governor to allow us to go to a motel that night and he just laughed his head off,' she said.

'I pleaded with him to have the day off. He did give in and I was able to party on to five.'

Prison staff drove her to the home of a friend where others joined in the celebrations. There was plenty to eat and drink and, on her return to the prison that evening, Valerie Smith found the governor less than pleased with her condition.

'I got punished for drinking,' says Valerie. 'Next day I had to clean the cars of those officers who took me there.' Confetti had been thrown in the cars, but the governor had approved it and 'nothing else happened'.

The newlyweds had little option but to continue their contact via the mail and very occasional visits. Valerie saw her husband once every three months for about an hour. She was driven to Long Bay by staff at Mulawa.

Smith, aided by the Prisoners' Action Group, repeatedly called for inmates to be allowed conjugal visits from their partners. But Corrective Services Minister at the time, Rex Jackson, later to be disgraced, refused to bend and a spokesperson for his department was reported in the *Truth* of 15 May, 1982, as saying, 'Smith and Valerie expected to be married while they were both in jail. They cannot consummate their marriage as there is no such relationship allowed between prisoners'.

Truth reported the issue had come to the attention of the Builders Labourers' Federation, led until its demise by the tough old militant, Norm Gallagher.

The union was considering the possibility of bans 'on the partly-built, $35 million Parklea maximum security jail'. Prison activists wanted facilities for conjugal visits to be incorporated into the new prison. It was not on the government's agenda.

CHAPTER 9

Out for the count

ON 29 September, 1980, Jimmy Smith appeared before His Honour Judge Thorley in the District Court of New South Wales. He was charged with 'maliciously attempting to discharge loaded firearms, to wit a .38 Smith and Wesson revolver, at Robert George Godden with intent thereby to do grievous bodily harm'.

Smith represented himself, pleading not guilty. He immediately complained that he'd been thwarted in the preparation of his defence. 'Because of the publicity given to me over the last three years, a matter of 300 articles, I don't consider I have any chance of ever getting a fair trial in this state. I have been locked in virtual solitary confinement for the last two months – for the last three weeks, I should say. I have made a number of applications to see witnesses. I haven't seen them. I am under medical treatment at the moment and I have asked to see the doctors and I haven't seen them.'

Judge Thorley dealt with the last two matters – access to

CALL ME JIMMY

witnesses and medical treatment. He arranged for Smith to meet Valerie at the Darlinghurst cells the following day. She had been transferred to Mulawa Training and Detention Centre at Silverwater, on the Parramatta side of Sydney. He also agreed to provide further help when Smith decided on the witnesses he would require in his defence.

Smith told the judge he had been locked away 24 hours a day in solitary confinement for three weeks at the infamous Parramatta 'Circle', that he'd become 'mentally disturbed' and had 'asked to see a psychologist or psychiatrist'.

When asked to explain the reason for this, Smith replied, 'I haven't been charged with no offences. I believe, I have asked the governor. He said I am under a S.22 order to be held there for three months. The situation seems to arise each time I have a trial to front'.

Judge Thorley made inquiries and was told later that day there were three reasons for Smith's isolation while in jail – safety of prison officers, security of the prison and preservation of good order and discipline within the prison. On the matter of publicity he said, 'I am afraid there is nothing I can do about that'.

Smith objected to the Crown's opening address when he was referred to as '… you are Jockey Smith' and stated he wished to make an application in the absence of the jury. The jury filed out.

> **Smith**: This is a blatant attempt by the police, by the court to prejudice the trial … The whole purpose of it is to inform the jury who this person is. If they haven't already heard about it or heard that name, they will know about it now. It is through using this name, there is no way I will get a fair trial.
>
> **His Honour**: If the evidence does not live up to the opening of the Crown counsel, you may be sure I will discharge the jury.

OUT FOR THE COUNT

Smith: It is a name that is . . . not used by anybody else. It is used by the police and the media.
His Honour: That is what he is saying, those words were used by the police.
Smith: Once it is mentioned, that is the end of the section as far as I am concerned.

WHEN the jury returned, Judge Thorley explained that they would be sometimes asked to leave the court so Smith and he could discuss matters of law. At this point the first witness, Detective Sergeant Brian Harding of the armed hold-up squad, was sworn in and examined.

On cross-examining the witness, Smith spent some time establishing that the gun allegedly used in a struggle with Godden had been tested for fingerprints with a negative result. Smith moved from there to the witness's credibility, in a futile attempt to have Harding acknowledge he had distorted the facts. He suggested Harding had shot one of the two dogs at the Little House in an attempt to intimidate Valerie Hill and her daughter.

Smith was a courtroom veteran who had represented himself many times, often devoting enormous energy and time to developing an argument. But, in terms of courtroom guile, he was crude; his attacks tended to be blunt, head-on and accusatory.

Rather than show incidences where a witness had lied or provide contradictory testimony, he formed questions which he saw as statements of fact but which witnesses, particularly those like police who were used to the courtroom, could easily deny.

Smith: Of course, you would not intimidate anybody to find out a person's whereabouts?
Harding: No, I have not. I have never done that.
Smith: Have you ever been accused of it?

Harding: Of intimidating someone? I think you will have to go a bit further than that. I don't believe I have ever intimidated anyone.
His Honour: He is asking you have you ever been accused of it.
Harding: I don't think I have ever been accused in that form of intimidating persons.
Smith: Do you seriously stand in that box and say that you have never been accused of intimidating persons since you have been in the police force?
Harding: I am saying to you to the best of my recollection in my service it is the first time that question in that form has been put to me.
Smith: Have you ever been accused of fabricating evidence?
Harding: Yes, you have.
Smith: You are under investigation now for fabricating evidence, are you not?
Harding: By whom?
Smith: By the Internal Affairs Department.
Harding: No.
Smith: You don't know nothing about it?
Harding: You will have to go a bit further than what you are now.
Smith: You are also charged with conspiracy to pervert the course of justice?
Harding: Yes, that is a result of a summons taken out by you, which is for hearing in February of next year.

SMITH was a 'bush lawyer' who spent his nights poring over weighty legal texts. Why he chose to represent himself is unclear. There is some mention in a previous court appearance that he did not trust lawyers, that he knew his circumstances better than anyone. It's possible he felt let down by lawyers in the past. Another thought is that he was a shrewd tactician who knew he could probably get away with more in a courtroom than a barrister could: harassment and badgering of witnesses, poorly framed questions within the legal context, innuendo and suggestion.

In choosing to represent himself, he not only saved a lot of money, but prevailed upon the sympathies of the court and was, on occasion, offered support from the bench. During this trial barrister Peter Livesey was in court and watching from the sidelines, perhaps offering discreet advice.

But, in the end, defending himself may have been a tactic that backfired. Not only did Smith alienate the bench with his sustained and repetitive questioning, but the jury was able to view him in all his moods. Also, jury members saw that he knew about things like fingerprinting and gun powder residue on weapons – much more than an ordinary innocent citizen.

Witnesses rolled through the court – Detective Senior Constable Robert Godden, Detective Sergeant Dennis Gilligan, Detective Senior Constable Ivan Lloyd, Detective Senior Constable Gary Beaumont, Robert Alan Brooker, George Redvers Madge, Harold Walter Hessenberger, Jeffrey James Willsher and Graeme Keith Henry. These were the witnesses for the prosecution who claimed to have seen Smith in possession of a gun at the Bomaderry phone booth.

There were a handful of other witnesses for the prosecution who testified in relation to the movements of the .38 Smith and Wesson revolver once it was in police possession, to the original ownership of that revolver and to fingerprinting results.

According to police testimony, Smith was arrested and handcuffed in a phone box outside the post office at Bomaderry.

CALL ME JIMMY

While there are new, open-air phone boxes outside the post office today, those on the site in 1977 had four walls and a door. The interior of each booth measured an imperial two feet eight and a half inches wide by two feet ten and a half inches long. The ceiling stopped at seven feet.

Smith argued that two men inside such a booth would be cramped and unable to carry on a struggle, especially as one of the men, Detective Godden, was a big man of 190cm and more than 100kg. Furthermore, argued Smith, it was impossible to raise a gun from the vicinity of his waist and to bring it above his head so a struggle for the gun could take place as Godden testified.

AFTER the Crown's case was out, Smith elected to make a statement from the dock. Judge Thorley said: 'After you have finished your statement, you will then be entitled to call any witnesses that you want. Do you have any witnesses that you wish to call after that?'

Smith said he had subpoenaed Melbourne barrister Brian Cash. Judge Thorley called Cash. He did not appear. Smith asked to subpoena the 1977 diaries of detectives Gilligan, Godden, McKinnon and Sheather – the latter two had respectively testified about the gun while it was in police property and fingerprinting sections. He also asked for a series of photographs of his dogs taken from his premises at Nowra, and a photograph of himself taken on his arrival at Long Bay in September 1977.

Judge Thorley instructed the prosecutor to assist, where possible, in the execution of these subpoenas and, when the jury returned, pointed out, 'Whilst I am not appearing for the accused, it is my obligation to provide such assistance as I can to him in the preparation of his case and that I am endeavouring to do'.

OUT FOR THE COUNT

Seven days after the trial began, it was the accused's turn to present his case. Smith opened with an unsworn statement to the jury.

'Ladies and gentlemen, I will tell the whole truth and nothing but the truth, so help me God.

'On 14 September, 1977, in the early hours of the morning, round about four o'clock or thereabouts, I got up to go to the motor auctions which I generally do of a Wednesday or Friday, in Sydney ... The night before, I had me wife take $4000 out of the safe ... I said goodbye to me wife and I left them premises ... and, upon driving up the trackway to the front gate of them premises, I noticed a number of police vehicles. I immediately put me car into reverse and reversed back up the driveway, closely followed by a police Land Rover.

'Later on that afternoon, on me way to Bomaderry, I was near a vet's premises on the main road at Bomaderry, where I spoke to a woman, asked her could she give me a ride into town

'I offered to pay her and she said, "No, I wasn't going that way". I went across the road to the ambulance station and I got a pushbike and I was on my way ... I went in behind the Bomaderry Hotel and ... I rode the bike down the street and placed it against the post office window of the post office. I went into the telephone box ... to ring a barrister.

'The next minute the door of the phone box swung out and a detective I now know to be Detective Godden stepped into the box. He had the revolver in his hand. He stepped into the box and said, 'Edward Smith, you are under arrest'. The box is pretty cramped by that time. He said, "If you move, I'll fuckin' shoot you".

'I didn't know what to think at the time. I thought I was going to be shot ... I had the phone in me right hand and as he is opening the door he more or less spoke and stepped in at the same time. I dropped the phone and I don't know what made me do it, just natural reflexes, I went to push me way out, grabbed, sort of grabbed hold of the gun, and pushed me way out and he sort of raised his arm with the gun to get it out of me way and I just grabbed hold of his arm and tried to push me way out of the box.

'At that time there was another man I now know to be Detective Gilligan. I was worried about the gun in the phone box and I wanted to get out in the street where people could see me and I pushed – I don't know whether I was pushed or pulled, but I still had hold of the detective's arm with me hands.

'He had the gun still in his hand, trying to get it out of me way and I pushed me way out of the phone box and I heard – I don't know whether it was Detective Godden or Gilligan say, "Cut it out or you'll be shot" and I felt something in the side of me. It couldn't have been from Detective Godden because I had hold of his hand and he was struggling with me and the next minute I gone out in the street and we ended up on the footpath and I still had hold of his arm and the next minute there was another man there. I don't know where he come from. Now I believe it was Mr Hessenberger.

'They are all jumping over me sort of and I don't know where the gun has gone, but it's gone out of his hand somewhere. All I was worried about was hanging onto his arm and getting out in the street where witnesses could see me and they kept holding me hands ... and they pulled me trousers halfway down and search me and while that was taking place one of them – I don't know who it was – said, "Are you Jockey Smith?" and I said, "I'm saying nothing. I won't be saying anything" or words to that effect. I'll be holding out.

'Then I was searched and I had the money in me back pocket and I had a small chrome-plated pistol in me back pocket ... I

OUT FOR THE COUNT

used to leave it in the console of me car for me wife when we were out up the bush track and when I jumped out that morning, I took it with me.

'After they had searched me I was handcuffed on the footpath and then I was carried into a panel van ... I know it had a sort of mattress in the back there and I kept yelling out, "The bastards, they're trying to shoot me" because I was in fear of being shot because I knew that anything could happen to me in the van.

'Even while I was on the footpath there was a hand going over me mouth and I got hit about the head. I believe it was Detective Gilligan. I can't say for sure, but I believe it was him. They kept trying to shut me up so I kept singing out so people would see what was going on, so there would be witnesses.

'I was taken back to the police station. I was taken out of the van and I was held in front by Detective Gilligan, Detective Bowen and Detective Lloyd and other police. I was held there, handcuffed. They had hold of me arms and the photographs were being taken of me. I couldn't cover me face up or anything. They just held me while people photographed me.

'I was taken into the police station where I was placed on the floor of the police station ... still handcuffed. I was taken into a back room there ... I don't know whether it was an hour or two hours later – but I was put through the property book.

'I was searched before I was put through. They took a further $200 out of me back pocket and then I was placed in the cells and later on that night I was taken out of them cells and I was fingerprinted.

'When I was fingerprinted I was given a Biro to sign me fingerprints and I put alongside me initials, I put 'NS' meaning 'No Statements' in case the police allege I have made statements to them.

CALL ME JIMMY

'The following morning me barrister arrived. He asked what I was charged with. I told him I didn't know what I was charged with. He had to find out what I was charged with.

'I instructed him to go into court and tell the court I am not guilty of the charges and he told me that there had been a number of articles already printed in the papers regarding the matter and me.

'I asked him to complain about that and also have it put on record that I am not guilty and that I had made no admissions to the police regarding anything at all, nor would I be interviewed unless I had a legal adviser, either him or a Mr Seymour, present and the prosecutor said something about admissions and I jumped up and I said, "I have made no admissions whatsoever".

'At no time at that phone box did I have a gun in me hand. At no time in the phone box was I handcuffed. The gun that was involved in the struggle was the police officer's gun. I will go into that later on. All I have got to say to you now is to tell you what happened to me that morning and what happened to me that day and what happened to me at the phone box.

'You can see the size of detective Godden. You can imagine how much room was in the box when he stepped in there and all I was worried about was getting out of that phone box and hanging on to his arm and the charges against me have been fabricated by the police and I don't want to go into it at this stage. I will go into it later on.

'That's all I've got to say to you, ladies and gentlemen, my version of what took place at the phone box that day.

'I think I've covered it all. That's all. I'll leave it at that and I'll go into the matter further when I am summing up. I don't want to take too long with it now. I've just explained me side of what happened to me on that day.'

OUT FOR THE COUNT

FOLLOWING this, Judge Thorley asked Smith if he had any witnesses to call. He replied, 'I don't think I need to call any witnesses at all'. Once the jury retired for the day, His Honour referred once again to the subpoenas of exhibits Smith wished to present to the jury and arrangements were made for their delivery to the court.

The discussion then turned to the arrangements for summing up and, when Smith learned the prosecutor would be making a final address to the jury, he told the court, 'If I knew that was the case I wouldn't have made the dock statement ... I would have went further with me dock statement. If I had known that I would have been engaging a barrister or QC, if I had known the Crown was going to sum up ... I am devastated. I was under the opinion that by ethics the Crown didn't sum up'.

Judge Thorley noted Smith's protest and permitted him to re-open his dock statement the next morning.

What is most intriguing about this trial is that Jimmy Smith, acting alone and locked away, wasn't in a position to call witnesses.

The charge related entirely to those few seconds inside and outside the phone box at Bomaderry. The Crown's case relied on evidence from four police officers and a handful of civilians who witnessed fragments of the arrest.

At best, he could cross-examine those witnesses, which he did in an often long-winded and belligerent manner, but he could call no witnesses of his own to rebut prosecution testimony.

Judge Thorley completed his summing-up. The jury was locked away at 10.15am and returned at 7.12pm to hear part of the evidence given by one of the two teenage witnesses, Jeffrey Willsher, and the post-master, Bob Brooker. At 10.03 next morning, the jury again asked for guidance. The judge read out

CALL ME JIMMY

a lengthy section from Detective Godden's testimony. The jury took more than 30 hours to reach a verdict. Guilty.

The accused prisoner now became a convicted prisoner. Before sentence was passed, Smith made a statement. 'It was what I expected. I don't expect to get justice in this state at all because of the publicity that has surrounded me since this arrest. I have had about as much chance in this state as the alcoholics and that is nil, and I am not surprised.

'People like yourself, judges of justice and magistrates, aid and abet this type of evidence. I pleaded not guilty and I still state I am not guilty of this crime, and that is it. You have heard the evidence and everybody else has heard the evidence. You yourself and persons of intelligence believe what has took place in this court. It is what I expected because I have been crucified by the press in this state and I do not expect nothing else. I am not getting tried because of what is happening in the court, I am getting tried because of what has been printed in the papers. As I said right from the start, I have got no hope of getting justice in this state.'

The Sydney *Sun* devoted half its front page to the headline **Life Jail: Outbursts at Judge.** The report spilled to page two, saying that Smith shouted 'forced verdict' and 'Why don't you tell more lies, you bludgers?' as he was led from court.

He was sentenced to life on 23 October, 1980, the maximum sentence for such an offence. His first and previous conviction in New South Wales was for the attempted murder of Constable Jeremiah Ambrose, but this conviction had been quashed on appeal as unsafe the previous year.

He faced many committal proceedings during the 19 months between the successful appeal of his first conviction and the recording of a second conviction – the Patrick Stevedoring robbery, the Tidmarsh murder, the South Hurstville bank robbery and the Redfern conspiracy. In August the following year, an appeal against both the conviction and the severity of the sentences was dismissed when justices Street, Reynolds and Maxwell concluded Judge Thorley had been the model of 'fairness, coolness and balance'.

In June, 1991, under new sentencing laws, the sentence was set at 25 years with a 15-year 'bottom'. Smith would serve a minimum 15 years before being eligible for parole. He protested that it was more severe than most murderers received.

ON 4 May, 1981, Smith was back in court defending the 1974 charges alleging a conspiracy to rob the Eveleigh Railway Workshops at Redfern. His co-conspirators, Marko Motric, Brian Leslie O'Callaghan and Stanley Ernest James, had been tried and found guilty.

While in the process of selecting a jury, Judge Alf Goran noted there was 'something special' about this trial. He was referring to a group of Smith's friends who were passing leaflets to potential jurors entering the courthouse. Judge Goran had received one of the leaflets and, while not divulging its content, made the point any potential juror who felt in any way influenced by the leaflet would be excused from jury service. In due course, a jury was empanelled and the trial started.

Smith cried foul over pre-trial publicity which he claimed was 'a tactic used by police' to have accused people convicted. 'You see,' Smith told Judge Goran, 'most of the stuff that is printed in the newspapers ... they seem to have no trouble ... getting almost word for word what is printed in the police diaries, even before a man has stood trial.'

When Smith suggested it was a tactic His Honour would 'be well aware of' Judge Goran replied, 'Well, I am not. It is the first time I have heard it, first time I have heard of any suggestion of police assisting news media to get this material for the purpose of publishing pre-trial information about any accused. I am not aware of it. I am not disputing it, please understand that, but I am not aware of it. Perhaps I am an innocent in this matter, Mr Smith.'

Smith was not convinced. 'Your Honour, in your time at the Bar and your time at the Bench, I thought you would be aware.' When Judge Goran said he did not read newspapers Smith replied, 'I do not blame your Honour for not reading them but, unfortunately, I have been up against them.'

Judge Goran was sympathetic to Smith's dilemma. 'I can certainly see your problem and I think it is a shame that you can't be like other people who are less well-known and thus tried without continual reference to you in regard to other matters ... I do not know how it can be avoided. The next question is can you get a fair trial with this jury in the face of it.'

Later, Judge Goran tried to help Smith with his cross-examination. 'I can see what you are doing in your cross-examination and I am letting you go ahead, as you have noticed, but there comes a time – if I may speak as one advocate to another – there comes a time when you can put a jury to sleep or weary a jury, and then it is time to say "Is it worthwhile pursuing it this time or pursuing it for a second time or keeping a man in the box for as long as this", because the jury will tend to get tired and they will say "What is it all about?" and you will have missed your point.'

On 27 May, 1981, the 18th day of the trial, Smith made a plea to Judge Goran in the absence of the jury.

'Your Honour, I have been without sleep most of the night. I have not had a shower. I have got no clothes. I have got half my papers with me. I have been shifted from one jail to the other overnight and I do not know what is going on, Your Honour ...

OUT FOR THE COUNT

It is the third occasion now and the third time this has happened during trials that I am shifted from one place to the other – it is a disgrace ... I have been given no reason why it happened ... and I believe there has been several comments made regarding the matter by the media.

'I have had every obstacle put in my way during this trial. I have been denied access to a barrister by the police department or the people in charge of the cells here. I can't even have a pen to take my notes when I am going backwards and forwards to court and it just goes on and on.

'I do not know what can be done about it or what is going to happen about it but I have just got to have it recorded.'

JUDGE Goran reminded Smith he'd declined a solicitor and, in so doing, had prevented his own access to a barrister. About the trial taking so long to get to court, the judge pointed out that, for three years following the initial arrest, Smith had been on the run. He also alluded to other charges Smith was fronting which made it impossible for the current charge to be heard until now.

However, on the matter of sleep, he offered to adjourn so Smith might be 'fit to continue'. Publicity attendant to the trial posed a more difficult problem. 'I have no power, of course, to order news media not to print any references to you ... you have said that you would not be so naive, that is your expression, as to imagine that a trial concerning yourself would go on without the jury becoming aware of some of the things, at any rate, that you are supposed to have done on previous occasions and that is most unfortunate and it may, indeed, without strong measures taken by the bench with the jury, prejudice your fair trial.

'Last week I raised the question myself as to whether this trial should continue and I have not concluded the matter by giving a decision.'

CALL ME JIMMY

Much time in this trial was devoted to legal argument in the absence of the jury. Much of it related to the media. Judge Goran, as he promised, adjourned the matter until the following Monday, at which time Smith raised another media incident which he felt prejudiced his trial. This time Judge Goran had heard the same report. He referred to a news broadcast on radio station 2CH aired four days earlier. A transcript was read to the court.

Tight security once again surrounded the District Court as Smith was guarded by about a dozen police. Each person entering the court, including reporters, was body searched. Smith is serving a life sentence for the attempted murder of a policeman in 1977. He is currently being tried on a charge of armed robbery in 1974. In this case, he is defending himself. Judge Goran adjourned the matter today after Smith told him that he had little sleep last night and did not have all his papers.

Smith said he was moved from a Parramatta jail without any notice last night and this left him unprepared for today. Smith also said that certain members of the media had broadcast his transfer and this may have damaged his trial. Smith claimed it was impossible to get a fair trial.

In reply, Judge Goran referred to the Yorkshire Ripper trial in London and said that when some accused appear in the box they are already well known to the jury through the media. The judge said that this may be one of those cases.
– Brady Halls reporting

AS a result of this broadcast and similar reports on other radio stations, Judge Goran again considered discharging the jury. After argument from the prosecutor, who hoped to keep the trial alive, the judge heard Smith's views. 'It is a fair statement of your position, Mr Smith, that you feel you will not get a fair trial from this jury and at the same time you will be so disadvantaged by the jury being discharged that you feel tempted to take the risk with this jury.' He decided against discharging the jury but said he would certainly do so 'if there is a recurrence of such incidents'.

The issue of a mistrial arose again on 29 June. The trial had been in progress 38 days. Two articles, one in the Sydney *Sun* and the other in the *Sydney Morning Herald*, drew the attention of both the judge and the judged.

The *Sun* article was headed **Jockey Smith's Longest Run.** Aside from the mention of Smith's nickname and the 'facetious' double meaning in the headline, Judge Goran was unimpressed that a comment of his, made privately during a court recess, appeared in a newspaper.

According to the article, Judge Goran had said he 'must be fated to preside over long trials'.

'I did one for 14 weeks,' the article reported him as saying. 'It's like getting on a plane. You have to be prepared for a long flight. You have to keep your sense of humour.'

If nothing else, the appearance of this report did spark off some light-hearted banter between the bandit and the bench.

His Honour: Judges sometimes say this person is putting on a good show or I wish he would shut up. But you do not expect it to be reported in the paper because they don't say it in court. They say all sorts of things. They are human beings. They say it about barristers and their brother judges sometimes. They say it in confidence. But some reporter has got hold of it and has done something which is considered a breach of the code amongst journalists and has put it in the paper and that saddens me because it means you can never trust a newspaper reporter down here.

CALL ME JIMMY

Smith: It is not only damaging because of the nickname. It goes to the length of the trial, the longest run. I do not know what they mean by it. It is certainly not my longest trial.
His Honour: Certainly not. It is not the longest one in the state. There was one which took six months.
Smith: The Yugoslav one took six months. I might be wrong.
His Honour: Nine months? Well, that's long enough to do other things.
Smith: And that alone is misquoted to say it is the longest trial ever held.
His Honour: It is also said it cost you one million dollars. I do not think you have cost us one million dollars yet, Mr Smith.
Smith: I don't doubt that. It would be close to that.
His Honour: You might be worth a million, but I do not think you have cost us a million.

DEIDRE Macken described Jimmy Smith as 'an unlikely looking lawyer' in *The Age* on Saturday, 27 June, 1981: 'Standing in the dock in wide pin-stripe pants, fawn track top and white T-shirt'. Even the headline, **Mr Smith challenges his learned friend,** suggested, albeit tongue-in-cheek, a grudging respect for Smith's courtroom efforts.

The article referred to Smith standing in the defendant's box 'surrounded by three policemen' while another policeman dozed, the jury 'shifted fitfully' and Judge Goran 'looked on patiently as Mr Smith shuffled through a maze of legal files'. He waited fully five minutes before clearing his throat and 'asking in a rough, nasal voice that belied a carefully honed question: "At the time of the charge, the defendant was, at no time, told what the charge was, was he?" '

OUT FOR THE COUNT

She described Smith as a careful cross-examiner, meticulous with detail and cagey when trying to elicit admissions. 'He goes through seemingly unrelated events and then, shuffling files into neat piles, asks a question which may bring an admission favourable to his case.'

He addressed the Crown prosecutor, as 'My learned friend' and adopted the courtroom 'jargon of lawyers'. At the time Macken wrote her report, Smith was cross-examining a Melbourne policeman, Detective Sergeant Robert Scarff.

When the prosecution had put its case, Smith said he wished to call as evidence tapes made by Dr Bertram Wainer that exposed police corruption in Victoria and other states.

Judge Goran disallowed this, saying it was irrelevant to the present conspiracy charge, that his court was not another forum for the Beach Inquiry and that he would not allow his court to be used as a platform for what he termed Smith's 'campaign' against police.

Smith took a cheeky stab at dismissal by reminding the judge the jury was entitled to acquit at any time after the Crown had finished its case. Judge Goran obliged Smith by asking the jury if it wished to take that option. The jury foreman declined and Smith started the case for the defence by making an unsworn statement from the dock. He took the jury through the events of his arrival in Sydney to back a horse, his mission to run an errand for Wainer and his subsequent arrest.

After 53 days, Judge Goran made his summing-up to the jury. It was long and detailed, occupying some 55 pages of transcript. The jury retired at 2.50pm. It took less than two hours for jury members to arrive at a verdict of guilty. The next day, his antecedents were read to the court and Judge Goran gave Smith the opportunity to address the bench. A summary of his main points indicated the passion with which he approached this task.

CALL ME JIMMY

Prisoner: 'I said I was not guilty and I still maintain I am not guilty. I'm not surprised by the verdict because what Your Honour had to say to the jury was one of the most one-sided addresses I have ever heard a judge give to a jury and I'm not surprised by the verdict because of what has been written in the newspapers in this state and certainly while the trial has been going on, and no mention was made of it in your summing-up.

'I'm prepared to take any specific test, such as a lie detector ... regarding this matter and so are the other three accused. I'm not worried about the Bible, I have seen that demonstrated on many occasions and there is one way to find out the truth in this day and age and that is to do it scientifically ... I don't ask for any mercy. I don't ask for nothing because I maintain my innocence.

'I've done everything possible to stop myself getting verballed in this way but even since my arrest this time the police continually allege that I am still confessing ... why don't they use tape-recorders, because the judges would find out, the juries would find out, everybody would find out, that they don't fall over backwards and confess ... I am not frightened to say what I think and what I believe in ... I was entitled to stand in this dock unknown to the jury. That wasn't the case.'

TO support his claim of innocence and his willingness to 'undertake any test' Smith submitted to a lie detector test on 5 October, 1981, just days before his appeal was to be heard. The five questions asked focused on the weapons Smith was supposed to have in his possession at the time of his arrest and claims he made a record of interview when arrested.

It's doubtful the polygraph test proved anything and, besides, lie detector tests are not accepted in New South Wales and cannot be submitted as supporting evidence to any claim of innocence. Smith, already serving life, was sentenced to another 14 years with a non-parole period set at 10 years. He appealed the conviction and the severity of the sentence. This was heard in October, 1982, but dismissed; he was to serve the sentence in full. On 22 June, 1984, Smith tried to take his case to the High Court, but his application for leave to appeal was denied on 26 September, 1985.

ALMOST three years after Smith's conviction on the Godden charge, Ian Barker, QC, weighed the likelihood of an appeal succeeding in the High Court. He looked at three issues – Judge Thorley's refusal to allow Smith a McKenzie Advisor, Judge Thorley's failure to tell the jury that Smith's dock statement was, in fact, a sworn statement, and discrepancies in evidence between the various witnesses.

On the first issue, Barker found there was no compulsion in law for Judge Thorley to agree to a McKenzie Advisor and that he had acted quite properly in refusing the request. With respect to Smith's claim he had made a sworn statement from the dock, Barker pointed out that a sworn statement is one officiated by the court and that there was 'no such animal' in law as a sworn statement from the dock.

Smith did say the words of an oath prior to commencing his address to the jury but, in so doing, did not comply with the conditions of oath-making in the legal sense.

Finally, Barker deduced there 'were serious inconsistencies in the Crown's case. An example was the police claim that Smith was handcuffed in the telephone booth. This was contradicted by three civilian witnesses, who saw him handcuffed after he had been taken from the phone booth. Regarding a conversation between Detective Godden and Smith in the phone booth, allegedly before Detective Godden realised who

CALL ME JIMMY

Smith was, a witness had testified 'that this conversation did not take place'. During the trial, one of the detectives claimed the .38 revolver was placed on the phone booth shelf but another witness, Hessenberger, said he 'kicked one or another of the guns into the gutter'. The police said they approached the phone booth at a normal pace while two civilians 'gave evidence that they approached quickly'.

A discrepancy in Detective Harding's evidence about the time of submitting the guns for fingerprinting was picked up. Harding testified the guns taken from Smith were fingerprinted almost immediately after Smith's arrest. Detective Sheather's evidence disclosed this was not possible as the guns were handed over by the detectives about 6.30pm on the day of Smith's arrest, and locked by him in a cell.

Barker said, 'This inconsistency supports Mr Smith's argument that the guns were a police "plant", that the arresting officers were in a conspiracy to "frame" Mr Smith. It may be consistent with this argument that the detectives had a conference together on the night of the same day of the arrest and that police detectives used Detective Godden's notebook when making their statements; that the fingerprinting was negative, and that both guns were on issue to the police (but that the .38 revolver had a longer barrel than the police issue). The evidence may raise a doubt ... but does little to demonstrate the alleged conspiracy.

'The police witnesses may have been lying. It is not unknown for police officers to give false evidence and to conspire together for that purpose. But, in the end, their credibility was a matter for the jury. I do not believe it could be successfully argued that the state of evidence is such that the verdict should be set aside, in the absence of serious error or irregularity. In my opinion, an application to the High Court would fail.'

Despite Barker's report, Smith did try to appeal to the High

OUT FOR THE COUNT

Court. Although the appeal was disallowed, it was a close thing, with two of the five judges dissenting against the finding of Chief Justice Gibbs and recommending special leave to appeal be granted. But a miss was as good (or bad) as a mile: Smith had run out of last chances.

SMITH was not alone in the battle against police and the media. He took advice from Peter Livesey on presenting his case within the courtroom while, outside, others tried to swing publicity in his favour.

Brett Collins was one of his supporters. Today the successful operator of a Sydney printing business, Brett Collins was, in 1981, the administrator of Glebe House, a halfway house for former prisoners. He was also Smith's friend, having served time with him in the infamous 'Circle' at Parramatta and also in Katingal.

Collins had been convicted of armed robbery in 1971 on the strength of confessional evidence and an unsigned record of interview. When he got out of jail in June, 1980, he started a campaign to expose the police 'verbal'. He was one of those handing out pamphlets, referred to by Judge Goran, when Smith's conspiracy trial started.

In June 1981, Collins was charged and convicted with contempt of court for distributing pamphlets outside a court building. Sir Laurence Street found Collins had 'deliberately attempted to influence jurors'.

A month later, just moments before entering the Supreme Court of New South Wales where three judges would sit in sentence, Collins was at it again – this time spruiking his own case outside the court.

Judges were less than impressed, but accepted more than 20 affidavits supporting Collins' application for leniency. These

CALL ME JIMMY

included a letter from Don Chipp, leader and founder of the Australian Democrats. Collins had admitted distributing pamphlets many times to jails, and outside police stations and courts.

It was an organised counter-attack by members of the Prisoners' Action Group, along with other organisations like Women Behind Bars, who were sympathetic to the plight of inmates and angered by the scale of police corruption.

CHAPTER 10

The bookie murder

THREE twitchy men try to make themselves comfortable in a station wagon. They are waiting. They make nervy small talk about what each will do with his share of the money. The street is quiet. Every other parked car is empty except the station wagon. It is so quiet they sweat on a passerby hearing their whisperings.

They're about to move when a car pulls up outside the house. It stops a while and they watch the young couple smooching in the front seat. They lie low – to see what develops. A girl gets out of the car and lingers at the open door a moment before crossing the street into a house.

CALL ME JIMMY

MURDER
$20,000 Reward

AT about 11pm on 13 June, 1977, three men wearing balaclava-type masks entered a house in Harslett Crescent, Kogarah. Shortly afterwards the occupier, Lloyd Joseph Tidmarsh, was fatally shot. The intruders drove away in a vehicle described as a 1969 Holden station sedan, white or light coloured.

A reward of twenty thousand dollars ($20,000) will be paid by the New South Wales Bookmakers Co-operative Society for information leading to the arrest and conviction of the persons responsible for the death of Lloyd Joseph Tidmarsh. This reward will remain in force for a period of 12 months from 1 July, 1977. Any person or persons able to furnish information in respect of this matter should immediately telephone:

- **Police headquarters telephone exchange 20966, or the emergency number 000**
- **The Duty Officer, Criminal Investigation Branch, 20966, extension 31162.**

LLOYD Joseph Tidmarsh, Sydney bookmaker, was shot dead on 13 June, 1977. The following day his 17-year-old daughter, Michelle Tidmarsh, gave this statement to police at Kogarah police station.

'LAST night at about 9.20pm, I came home from my boyfriend's place at 2a Kings Road, Brighton. My boyfriend, Stephen Goode, drove me home in his car and when we stopped outside my house I noticed a number of strange cars parked in the street. However, the football was on at Jubilee Oval and this is very common when the football is on.

THE BOOKIE MURDER

'I said goodnight to Steve at his car in the street and went into the house on my own. I did not notice anything unusual at this time. When I got inside I said goodnight to my mother who was sitting in the back room watching TV and I also saw my father sitting at his desk doing his books ...

'Sometime later, I cannot say what time exactly, I was woken up by strange voices as well as my father's voice, who has a loud voice all the time. I heard one of the strange voices which came from the back of the house say, "Where is the safe, we know you have got one?". I heard my father say, "I have not got a safe, mate. I have not got any money at all".

'At this point my attention was drawn to my mother's room where I heard another strange voice near my mother's door say, "Just be quiet, lady, and no one will get hurt". I heard my mother say to this second male voice, "Please don't hurt any of us. Don't hurt my husband". This second male voice said, "Don't move. Stay there in bed. Don't yell. Just stay there in bed". He also said, "Is there anybody else in the house?" My mother did not answer and then this man repeated the question again and this time my mother said, "Yes, my daughter is asleep in her room". This man said, "Where is that?" My mother said, "Up the hall near the front door". I then became aware of a third strange voice who spoke to the second one ...

'My bedroom door was open and I saw a man walk past my door, then (he) walked to my door and looked in. He did not say anything to me because my light was off and it was dark and I don't think he saw me in bed. I did not move. I stayed in bed. This man walked away and went to my mother's room again and I heard the third male voice say to my mother, "Is the safe in here, in the bedroom?" My mother said, "No, there is nothing in here, it's not in here". Then the third man walked away and went to the back of the house and the second man stayed, I think, near my mother's bedroom door.

CALL ME JIMMY

'I heard a rough voice, that is the first voice I had heard, say something which I could not understand, and then I heard my brother's voice, and he seemed to say something like, "I don't know where it is". Then I heard a dull thud and then I heard dad say, "Don't touch him, he's only a kid. He can't tell you anything".

'The first voice I heard became louder and so did my father's, and I heard my father say, "Don't be so stupid. Didn't you know that bookies are having a bad trot at the moment?" The first man's voice said something back to my father, which I could not understand, then Dad's voice became very loud and said, "I told you, I have not got any money and get your hands off him".

There was a strange silence for a few seconds and then I heard a gunshot. And I heard Dad yell. Then Mum screamed from her room and then the man, that is, the second voice I heard, he ran down the hall and into the kitchen.

'From Mum's room there was another strange silence for a moment. And then I heard sort of running footsteps into the back room onto the bare floorboards. Then I heard two more gunshots in quick succession, and maybe one more shot, but I can't be sure of that because mum was screaming out loud and also my brother was yelling. Right through all this taking place I remained in bed. I heard almost everything that happened and only saw the second man at my doorway who had something very dark over his head and looked like he had gloves on, but I did not see if he was carrying anything in his hands.

"I heard running footsteps through the back room and then the back door, that is the fly screen door banged shut. I got out of bed and met my mother in the hallway and I saw my dad lying in the kitchen on the floor near the fridge on his back and I saw blood on his face and he had his left arm across his stomach and was very still. Both my mother and I ran to the

THE BOOKIE MURDER

front door and out onto the front veranda. I had not seen Michael at this time. I think he was still in his room. Both mum and I were on the front lawn.

'Then I heard a car start up and I looked and saw a Holden station sedan, either white or light-coloured, pull out from the gutter on our side of the street and drive off towards the Princes Highway. It did not have any lights on and drove off fast, but not real fast. It took time to pick up speed and there were three people in the front and I could not see anybody in the back seat or the far back end.

'I cannot describe the car any better than it was a Holden station sedan, about a 1968 or '69 model. As it drove away I called out to Mum to get down. Mum got down and I stepped back into the doorway and I asked Mum if she got the number, but she did not because the car lights were turned off.

'Both Mum and I went back inside and Dad was still on the floor and had not moved. I saw Michael trying to get up off the floor between the kitchen and his room, in the doorway. He was holding his head. Then mum told me to go and get Mr Baker so I did. Mum went to my grandmother's house at the back of our house to get her. When I got back with Mr Baker, I saw Michael at the telephone and some time later the police and ambulance arrived. The only description of the men I can give is of the one who stood in my doorway, and I can only say that he was slim build and short ... I cannot describe the other two men because I did not see them.'

NINE months later, on 23 March 1978, Michelle Tidmarsh gave another statement to police, this time at homicide squad offices in Sydney.

'ABOUT 11.30am today I saw Detective Smith at my school,

CALL ME JIMMY

Catholic Teacher's College, Mount Street, North Sydney. I accompanied Detective Smith to the Central Court of Petty Sessions and there saw Detective Sergeant Conwell and had a conversation with him. Sergeant Conwell said to me, "I want you to go and sit in the back of the court and if you see any person or hear the voice of any person who was in your home on the night of 13th June, 1977, will you tell me". I said, "All right".

'I then went and sat in the back of Court No. 3 about midday and remained in that court until about 12.15pm. Whilst I was in that court I heard a number of people talk and I saw a large number of people. I heard a man, who was referred to as Smith by the magistrate, speak on a number of occasions and I recognised his voice as being the voice of one of the men who was in my home the night my father was shot.

'That man's voice was the voice of the man who I heard arguing with my father about the whereabouts of the safe and where the money was in our house. On that night I know there were three intruders in my home, but I only saw two. I am not sure whether he was one of the men I saw, but his voice is definitely that of one of the men that was in my home shortly before my father was shot.'

JIMMY Smith was cross-examining a detective in Sydney's Central Court, where he was defending charges alleging armed robbery of the Patrick Stevedoring Company, when prosecutor, Sergeant Noel Whalen, interrupted the proceedings to say police wished to bring fresh charges against Smith.

It was 3.55pm on 27 April, 1978, four days after Michelle Tidmarsh identified his voice in the same court. Under the name Edward James Smith, he was formally charged with Tidmarsh's murder, assault and armed robbery of a wallet,

THE BOOKIE MURDER

personal papers and money belonging to Tidmarsh, and theft of a station sedan belonging to Muir Motors in Ashfield.

The posting of a reward by Sydney bookmakers was not the only sign that Lloyd Tidmarsh's death had shocked the community. He had been popular, not just on the racetrack, but in the local community.

The Requiem Mass at St Patrick's Roman Catholic Church was standing room only. The *Sydney Morning Herald* reported the attendance of more than 50 well-known bookmakers together with 'women in slacks and men in cardigans, and young mothers with babies in their arms, and nuns, and detectives in smart suits that looked, as always, a size too small for them'.

Tidmarsh had been a family man, a fair and honest bookie who enjoyed a spot of Irish dancing, a man who voluntarily served in the clothing shop each Friday at the parish school. As his body was taken from the church it passed by two guards of honour – one of prominent bookmakers and the other of local schoolboys clutching rosary beads.

His profile was such that the media reported anything to do with his murder. Articles in the *Daily Mirror* referred to **The senseless murder of Lloyd Tidmarsh.** The Sydney *Sun* wanted to know **Did you see murder car?** Channel 9's *A Current Affair* ran a story claiming the identity of at least one of the murderers had been given to its reporters and the information would be passed on to police.

Possible clues were widely publicised, including the finding of human hairs at the scene of the crime which were to be tested in the hope they might provide leads to the murderer's genetic make-up and looks. The Tidmarsh family's appeal for the public to help provided dramatic human interest.

CALL ME JIMMY

WHEN Smith was put on trial for Lloyd Tidmarsh's murder, extraordinary security measures were taken, as they had been at the committal. The trial started on 7 February, 1983, and ran for 81 days until a guilty verdict on all three charges was brought in the following July.

It was thought to be the longest murder trial in NSW history. The committal hearing and trial combined took some 5000 pages of transcript. Smith got life imprisonment for murder, 16 years for armed robbery and five years for larceny of a motor vehicle. Smith appealed and, in a report on the trial, Justice O'Brien gave a lengthy summary of evidence submitted by the Crown and the appellant Smith.

The case for the prosecution was that Tidmarsh, 51, was a well-known 'paddock' bookmaker who handled large bets. His close friend and 'penciller' was John Linnane, who lived in the same street. They'd worked together more than 20 years. After the races Linnane would put the cash in a leather bag to which Tidmarsh held the key. They would drop the bag into a bank night deposit on the way home.

Tidmarsh would carry a small amount of cash in his wallet. He did have a safe at home but rarely stored money there. The safe was in a linen closet in the hall.

On the day he was murdered, Tidmarsh had fielded at Randwick. It was a Monday – the Queen's Birthday weekend. As usual, he deposited the day's takings in the night safe and arrived home around 5.30pm. That evening he worked in his office at the rear of the house after everyone had gone to bed. The back door was unlocked. Around 10.15pm, three men entered the house through the back door. Mrs Tidmarsh was awakened by the slam of the flywire door. Michelle and her brother, Michael, awoke to loud voices. Michael was forced to join his father.

THE BOOKIE MURDER

According to police statements, the first thing Michael saw on entering the sunroom, which doubled as his father's office, was a man carrying a gun standing over his father, who was lying on the floor, face down. He was forced to lie next to his father.

After a while, his father got up and kicked a heater towards the man who had been standing over him. A shot was fired. His father walked towards the kitchen. Michael began to rise also, but was knocked unconscious by a lump of wood. He didn't wake until the murderers had fled. Lloyd Tidmarsh was shot four times. One of the bullets, from a .38 Walther self-loading pistol, pierced his heart.

The intruders were masked throughout the ordeal – they left behind a beanie, a stocking mask, a pair of gloves, and a blue canvas bag containing a length of timber, a torch and other items. Part of the registration number of the getaway car was noted by a neighbour. Other witnesses noted the colour and type of the getaway car.

Early next day various documents belonging to Tidmarsh were found near the Bexley North railway station. The documents themselves gave no hint of who'd thrown them there, but the location was important. The car from which the documents were thrown was travelling in the direction of Kogarah to Canterbury. Neil Collings lived in Canterbury and Frank Montgomery lived at Marrickville, a neighbouring suburb. Both men had previously been linked to Jimmy Smith. A short cut from Kogarah to Canterbury was through Bexley North.

Spent cartridge cases left at the scene were sent to the Scientific Investigation Unit. There was a delay in identifying the cartridges because the unit was also involved in investigating the death of Griffith drug crusader Donald McKay. But a description of the likely murder weapon emerged.

An examination of the vacuumed contents of the blue bag left at the scene was done at the Lidcombe Forensic Science Laboratory using a stereoscopic microscope capable of detecting welding spatter down to the smallest particle not visible to the naked eye. Welding spatter was detected along with some hairs, two lengths of brown acrylic thread, two lengths of blue cotton thread, vegetable matter and dirt. The welding spatter was distinctive and sent to a metallurgist for specialist treatment. The hairs were sent to a biologist and the threads to a specialist in textiles.

The piece of timber used to hit Michael Tidmarsh and left at the scene was similar to off-cuts left by builders at the 'factory' shed Smith rented in Bomaderry. This was given in evidence by the owner. Smith had been the first tenant. Police had inspected the shed for other timber offcuts but found none.

Smith had left a white HQ Holden station wagon at a Bomaderry garage on 13 September, 1977, three months after the murder. It was in for a grease and oil change, and he gave the name of D. Collings. The car was never collected because he was arrested the following day at Bomaderry.

Eight days later, the garage notified the police, who found the car smelt of horses and was quite dirty. In the boot, they found hessian, a horse blanket and bridle, and a whip. All showed evidence of welding spatter. On closer examination back at the police motor squad, it was discovered the number plates on the vehicle had been changed, the engine and chassis numbers filed off and changed, and the car had been stolen.

A blue boiler suit and khaki overalls were found in the Holden and it was vacuumed. Photographs found at the Little House following the dawn raid clearly showed Smith wearing the boiler suit in one and the khaki overalls in another.

Holes in the actual boiler suit matched holes found in the same article of clothing in the photograph. Welding spatter

THE BOOKIE MURDER

made the holes. That welding spatter corresponded with welding spatter found in the blue bag – both were distinctive and had been the result of a special process known as Arcair gouging, which employs compressed air to blow away the molten metal caused by the arc welder and the use of steel wool in the process.

It was a process generally unused in the car repair business, the likes of which Smith claimed to be running at Bomaderry. It was a process that efficiently removed chassis numbers from engine blocks. The hairs found in the blue canvas bag were a mixture of human and horse hair. The horse hair was of special interest because it matched similar samples taken from the boot of the Holden and from two horses, Dornier and Regency Head. Similarly, the threads found in the bag were similar to those found in the boot of the car, so much so that the specialist was prepared to swear it was beyond reasonable doubt.

ON the first day of the Patrick Stevedoring hearing, two detective sergeants, Worsley and Duff, spoke to Smith in his cell and asked him questions about the stolen car. According to their testimony, Smith admitted stealing the car. They began asking questions about the Tidmarsh murder and, in their words, Smith shouted, 'Screws, get them out of here'. When Worsley gave notice of his intention to charge him with the Tidmarsh murder, Smith replied, 'You prove it. Go your hardest. Screws, get them out of here'.

Once in custody, Smith refused to be involved in an identification parade. On advice from the senior Crown prosecutor, detectives arranged for members of the Tidmarsh family to attend the court where Smith was conducting his own defence and where he could be heard speaking. Michelle Tidmarsh identified Smith's voice.

CALL ME JIMMY

BEFORE outlining the defence case, Justice O'Brien alluded to Smith's opening address to the jury in which he promised to provide witnesses 'from all different walks of life to prove my case beyond a reasonable doubt' including barristers, housewives, stable hands, police officers, prisoners, a bank officer and magistrates.

Of these witnesses, the judge said, 'The substantive witnesses he called were Montgomery, Lattouf, Visser, his wife and her daughter. None of them were from any exalted walk of life. They were each of them singularly unimpressive as witnesses.'

Two others mentioned as capable of supporting him, Hoffman and Ward, were not called because, it was said, they could not be found. He called a stable hand, Scott Reagan, who effectively denied his alibi for 13 June, 1977.

He called no bank manager to say anything. He called Mr Brown SM and Mr Wynyard of Counsel to give some limited evidence of what happened in court on 23 and 27 March, 1978. He called Mr Walburn, an inquiry agent, to say he could not find Hoffman or Helen Ward. And that was his case. Its credibility depended upon the credibility of the appellant himself as a witness and his associates Montgomery, Lattouf, Visser, his wife and her daughter.

As for the stolen Holden HQ station wagon, Smith claimed he had come by the car quite innocently. He had bought it without number plates a week after the theft by Collings. Smith had collected the vehicle at Collings' address in Canterbury in the presence of his wife and her daughter and a man named Joseph Lattouf. Smith acknowledged he attached number plates but had not tampered with the engine and chassis numbers.

But, during the course of the trial, Smith acknowledged he did operate as an unregistered car trader. Justice O'Brien's report indicated he had been in the automotive trade for 30

THE BOOKIE MURDER

years and, in that time, kept no records nor furnished a tax return. Under examination in the courtroom, 'his regular practice in that business ultimately became established'. During 1976 and 1977, Smith had been in the business of recycling white HQ Holden station wagons. It was a specialist line. The vehicles were unregistered. Engine and chassis numbers were cut off and replaced and new compliance plates attached.

It was, Smith had told Justice O'Brien, a cost-cutting measure – 'it saves money and time ... it saves registration, saves getting the thing serviced, checked, put over the pits, getting your pink form ... (and) sales tax'.

The scam relied on a good supply of undamaged vehicles. One way was to take cars from people in lieu of gambling debts. It also relied on finding a similar vehicle, damaged but registered. The identity of one was swapped for the other. Justice O'Brien concluded the undamaged and unregistered vehicles Smith had picked up in Sydney were, indeed, stolen.

Smith had an alibi to account for the night the car was stolen – he was in the Berry Hotel, a few kilometres on the Wollongong side of Nowra, playing pool with Hoffman, Ward, Reagan and his step-daughter.

A similar alibi was presented to account for his whereabouts on the night Lloyd Tidmarsh was murdered – this time they had all been at his house in McMahons Road, Nowra. There had been two others present for part of the time, Steven Sellers and his girlfriend, Sky Blue.

The credibility of these witnesses was challenged under cross-examination and, according to Justice O'Brien, Smith, 'claimed that they, including his wife, were innocent associates of his who had been convicted of offences such as armed robbery by the corrupt practices of police in Victoria and New South Wales in the fabrication of false evidence against them'.

CALL ME JIMMY

IT appears Smith did himself harm in court by offering far too much information about the business of 'backyard' car trading, even down to how a thief might duplicate keys for a stolen car.

The Holden taken from Muir's yard, without keys, became the focus of this issue and Smith unwisely speculated on how keys for such a vehicle might be obtained when the originals were safely locked away. Knowing the keys were kept under the sun visor, the Crown suggested an impression of them might have been made in soap or plasticine and keys made from that impression.

Smith couldn't resist biting. He replied, 'I think you have been watching too many movies... There are a lot simpler ways than that'. He was then asked to suggest such a way – and he did. Experts in any field often find it hard not to air their knowledge, and Smith was no different.

There's a saying that anyone who represents himself in court has a fool for a client. Smith defended himself. When evidence was produced relating to the length of two by two timber, the beanie and the stocking mask, Smith did not say categorically they were not his. He had to admit that, at some time, he did have similar bits of timber because his landlord had already testified that several pieces were on site when Smith took over the lease.

But, with the beanie and the stocking mask, he examined them and concluded he had owned items similar to these but that police had taken them from his home at North Nowra following the dawn raid. He even tried on the beanie in court, which must have impressed the jury no end. His answers were evasive, Justice O'Brien concluded, 'rather betraying a consciousness that he was familiar with them all'.

IN July, 1983, Smith was found guilty of murdering Lloyd

THE BOOKIE MURDER

Tidmarsh and was sentenced to life, as well as 16 years for robbing Tidmarsh's home and a further five years for theft of the car. All sentences were made concurrent and added to sentences he was already serving – life imprisonment for attempting to shoot officer Godden and 14 years for his part in the conspiracy to rob the Redfern railway workshops. All up, they amounted to two life sentences plus 35 years in jail.

Three years later, in April, 1986, Smith's appeal against all three convictions was considered by justices Street, Lee and Maxwell. The appeal was based on 21 grounds, many of which were similar in nature and were critical of His Honour's directions to the jury.

As Chief Justice Street made clear from the outset, two grounds were sufficient for him to arrive at a decision.

Ground 12: His Honour's directions on the evidence relating to the identification of the voice and relating to visual identification of the vehicle by inference from the finding of spatter, hair, etc, did not in the circumstances adequately direct the jury's attention to the weaknesses of that evidence and the arguments of the accused.

Ground 16: His Honour's directions on the nature of aural evidence was erroneous and, in addition, tended to concentrate the jury wrongly on the accused's voice at committal rather than the voice heard by the Miss Tidmarsh on the 13 June, 1977.

JUSTICE Street believed Smith's connection to the murder and robbery 'was wholly circumstantial apart from evidence of a witness present at the scene of the crime who later identified the appellant by his voice, and an alleged admission to the police by the appellant of the theft of the car'.

His Honour refused to accept the admission and went on to discuss the potential value of the welding spatter, horse hairs, cotton threads, the carry bag and so on. 'It can be said with confidence,' he said, 'that one would not hesitate on just those facts to conclude the remarkable coincidence of the finding in the appellant's car of metal spatter, horse hairs, vegetable matter and threads tallying in all material respects with those found in the blue bag, it is strongly suggestive that the appellant was at the Tidmarsh house on the night in question.'

However, His Honour immediately made the point that 'any prima facie conclusion' needed to account for the alibi and for his claim the car was purchased after Tidmarsh's death. It was conceivable the incriminating details were already in the car when Smith purchased it and subsequently 'impregnated his overalls and other property quite innocently'.

Justice Street then turned to the voice identification of Smith. He referred to Michelle Tidmarsh's appearance at Central Court where Smith was defending himself on the Patrick Stevedoring charges.

'The proceedings to which she was listening involved a charge of armed robbery against the appellant in which a stolen vehicle figured, and she acknowledged at the trial that she was aware that it was a case of robbery or hold-up.' She was able to identify Smith's voice from those in the courtroom – the magistrate, the prosecutor, Smith and two witnesses – as the same 'rough, gruff sounding voice' she'd heard that night. She recognised the manner of speaking and the voice itself.

Justice Street found the evidence of voice identification was admissible and found no fault with Justice O'Brien's summation to the jury – in the main. He disagreed that the voice was sufficiently distinctive after listening to a tape made at Central Court when Michelle Tidmarsh (by this time Mrs Michelle Brennan) was in the process of identifying Smith. This same tape had been played to the jury and the suggestion was that the constant reference to a unique, distinctive voice inevitably led the jury to consider, on hearing the tape and listening to Smith conduct his trial, they were indeed listening to a unique and distinctive voice.

Justice Street noted 'an uneducated voice, that the appellant dropped some g's, his grammar was not good – "was you referring to", "what you seen". It could be called rough, but I would not have said gruff.

'I noted he had a nasal twang which lengthened the vowel sound in " 'ow long" and "now". I noted the nasal influence suggested a slight elevation in the pitch of the voice which might be described as "whiney" or "whingey", that he sometimes spoke quickly at the beginning of a sentence and more loudly than during or at the end of a sentence, giving to the voice perhaps an element of authoritativeness or, if you like, assertiveness.

'But, my overwhelming impression was that although of course the voice had its own characteristics, which could be said to make it distinctive, the level of distinctiveness was not as Mrs Brennan's evidence or the summing-up seemed to suggest'.

Even so, His Honour was careful to point out Michelle Brennan believed her identification of Smith's voice was correct.

Furthermore, the description of the distinctive qualities of the voice shifted as the committal hearing and the trial progressed. What started out as a 'rough, loud' voice became a 'whiney, whingey' voice at the trial and this was further confused by Justice O'Brien's own rendition of 'aggressive' and 'argumentative'.

'I cannot help but feel the jury, having listened to the appellant's voice for so long – 74 days – may well have come to the conclusion on that account alone that they would never forget it and Mrs Brennan could therefore readily be believed in her identification.' Eventually, Justice Street concluded that 'a more positive direction was required', including 'a direction bringing plainly to the jury's attention that the case was one in which neither the forensic evidence standing alone, nor Mrs Brennan's voice identification evidence standing alone, could be relied upon as sufficient to establish the guilt of the accused beyond reasonable doubt'.

Inevitably, there was insufficient evidence to connect the accused to the car on the night of the murder.

Justice Street also referred to 'a running battle' between Smith and Justice O'Brien during the trial and allowed for the possibility 'the appellant's conduct in court made a most unfavourable impression on the jury'.

He added, 'His Honour, on many, many occasions, saw the need to curb the appellant's excesses by the use of blunt, straightforward language and even accusation'.

The Court of Criminal Appeal found there had been a miscarriage in the trial and ordered there to be a new trial on all three counts.

An application requesting a 'No Bill' was lodged on Smith's behalf on 27 August, 1986, four months after the Court of Criminal Appeal ordered a retrial on the Tidmarsh murder charges. The application, by Legal Aid lawyer A. K. Murray, contended the evidence 'against my client was wholly circumstantial apart from the voice identification of Michelle Brennan (nee Tidmarsh) and an alleged admission to Detective Sergeant Duff and Detective Sergeant Worsley by my client.

'I would submit in the context of a retrial it would be difficult, if not impossible, to test the evidence of Michelle Brennan nee Tidmarsh – specifically, her belief and the accuracy of her belief as to the voice identification. Bearing in mind her exposure to such voice during the course of the trial'.

THE BOOKIE MURDER

Murray further argued that Jimmy Smith was unrepresented at his trial and the two detective sergeants were 'not subjected to cross-examination' by legal representatives.

Since the direction for a retrial, Detective Sergeant Worsley had died and any opportunity to cross-examine him had been lost. 'Also, the corroborating detective of this vehemently denied alleged confession has been dismissed from the New South Wales Police Force for various acts of misconduct whilst he was a serving member.'

Here, Murray was referring to James William 'Bill' Duff, who made his name in the homicide squad after joining the force in 1965, and aligning himself with the notorious police hero-turned-crook Roger Rogerson.

Duff was one of the 'old school' (as in crooked) detectives, but like Rogerson and others he was considered clever and good at getting results. One way or another, Duff solved murders and his superiors weren't prepared to ask too many questions in case they didn't like the answers.

Duff regularly drank with the late Sydney crime boss Lennie McPherson and Melbourne-born hitman Christopher Dale 'Rentakill' Flannery, himself later 'hit' in circumstances that have never been officially established.

Duff used to claim that he used these underworld contacts to gather information, but many suspected it was a two-way street. In the 1980s he was implicated in a plot to import heroin from Papua New Guinea. And in 1997 he would be jailed for drug trafficking. All of which, in retrospect, adds weight to Smith's insistence that police fabricated his alleged confession.

His counsel, Murray, argued that because the offence occurred nine years earlier, the difficulties involved in rounding up all the witnesses would cripple any fair defence of the charges.

CALL ME JIMMY

Nine months later, while an inmate at Maitland Jail, Smith received a letter from the NSW Department of the Attorney-General. The No Bill had been granted. The Attorney-General had decided not to proceed to a new trial on any of the three charges connected to the Tidmarsh murder. This reduced his sentence to life on the Godden matter and 14 years for the Redfern conspiracy.

Despite the No Bill, it would be reckless to claim Smith was innocent. Some might argue that the length of time that had passed worked in Smith's favour and that he was undeservedly lucky. Lloyd Tidmarsh's widow and children might well have felt cheated by the system, as would those who investigated the crime.

Had there been a new trial there was no guarantee the result would have changed. The same 'circumstantial' evidence would have suggested Smith's guilt and there was the possibility the prosecution would have developed arguments against the defence view that Michelle Brennan's voice identification of Smith was invalid.

The prosecution's greatest hurdle would be to convince a jury that it was fair for the murdered bookie's daughter to try to identify Smith's voice in a courtroom in which he was the accused.

As far as she knew, Smith was the only one in that court on trial, the only one likely to be a criminal by demeanour and by reputation, and so the only person present she would identify if she was going to identify anyone.

In the end, it posed an insurmountable difficulty for the prosecution and was compounded by the death of one of the investigating officers and the dismissal for misconduct of the other, Bill Duff. The prosecution's case had been considerably weakened over time.

THE BOOKIE MURDER

Despite Smith's constant protests that he would 'receive no justice' in New South Wales, the Tidmarsh case points to a system that often works in favour of the accused. He was, after all, given the benefit of the doubt. Which is more than Lloyd Tidmarsh got from his killers.

MORE than two years after her father's murder, Michelle Brennan joined the NSW Police Force. According to newspaper reports, she was motivated by the admiration and appreciation of detectives investigating her father's death.

A month after the granting of the No Bill to Smith one newspaper, the *Newcastle Herald*, featured a photograph of her aiming her service pistol. The headline read: **Terrified girl now an ace cop.**

Michelle Brennan was stationed at Newcastle, the paper reported, and 'is one of Newcastle's leading plain clothes police officers'.

The story rehashed the memories of her time in the witness box and went on to describe her present life.

'Det. Brennan is the only female on the Newcastle SWOS team which is the black-clad, para-military type commando unit that is in constant training for the event of a terrorist attack, a gun siege, an aircraft hijack or a major jail break.

'She is in the middle of it, dropping from helicopters, firing short arms and sophisticated guns, competing against other services in rifle-shooting competitions, disarming attackers with knives and other weapons and practising, over and over again, for the one day she and her fellow officers will be called out in a real crisis.'

CHAPTER 11

Doing time

SMITH put on weight in prison, but it wasn't all flab. Many of the photographs in his collection show him with friends lifting weights, towelling off those who'd just worked out, acting as a corner man in boxing tournaments and, on occasion, just sitting against a wall doing time. He had a reputation as a 'tough little bloke' other prisoners could depend on – like the time he jumped on the back of an inmate twice his size who was bashing a weaker man. Inside jail, Smith had respect.

There is little evidence of any work he might have undertaken inside. Most of his time was devoted to committals, trials and appeals in the first 10 years. He often shifted prisons leaving him little spare time to get involved in prison rehabilitation or work programs. Because of his reputation as an escapee and knowledge of trade tools and oxy-acetylene equipment, it was unlikely he would be allowed near the trade shops. Nevertheless, towards the end of his prison stay, he did work as a cleaner and storeman, and prison reports indicated he did a good job.

CALL ME JIMMY

Valerie visited him regularly. When away on trips to Queensland she wrote messages of love on postcards featuring women on the beach. These he cherished, carefully filing each into a bound folder to read time and again – his only contact with a world he'd left behind.

Smith followed the media keenly. He not only collected articles about himself, but was interested in the fates of friends and foes. In March, 1981, he kept an article from the *Sydney Sun-Herald* detailing the resolutions of a law conference attended by 300 delegates to Sydney University. It focused on how to catch 'crooked cops' and noted many of the techniques used by Bertram Wainer in Victoria.

One delegate, Mark Dimelow, a member of the Campaign Against Legal Malpractices (CALM), called for an end to police 'verballing' and recommended, as had Smith so many times himself, the introduction of tape recorded interviews and interviews conducted in the presence of an independent witness.

In March 1980, *Insurgence*, an underground newspaper aimed at judicial and prison reform, published a cartoon titled **Police Verbal Blues** with the warning: *You need not say anything unless you wish to, as anything we think of will be taken down and used as evidence against you.*

That issue devoted the front page to an advertisement titled: **WANTED for Verballing.** It included photographs of four police officers involved in charges against Jimmy Smith – Detective Sergeant Worsley and Detective Constable Duff of the homicide squad, Detective Sergeant Gilligan of the armed hold-up squad and Detective Senior Constable Bowen from the consorting squad. The mug shots of the latter two officers had been cut from a 1977 photograph where the officers were either side of a handcuffed and dishevelled Smith.

Below the photographs was printed: REWARD 10 cents per concocted confession, 20 cents per proven bashing (Limit

DOING TIME

$1,000,000), $100 per sacking. An article from the *National Times* in June 1981 featured Sydney nightclubs. The story highlighted the Roosevelt Club in Kings Cross and included a memorable photograph of the notorious nightclub boss, Abe Saffron, hand to head in the thinker position, at a table framed by the outstretched and stockinged leg of a can-can dancer.

ANOTHER article published the same month and kept by Smith featured France's 'sewer rat' thieves, who got away with $12 million in what the *Daily Telegraph* claimed was 'the world's biggest theft'.

The leader of the gang, Albert Spaggiari, and his cronies had tunnelled into the vaults of the Societe Generale Bank in Paris from sewers. They used high-powered thermal lances to carve through concrete walls and escaped with gold, cash and gems from the bank's 190 safety deposit boxes. It was the second time the gang had struck the same bank; the first raid had scored $10 million from the bank's Nice branch.

It is likely the daring and sophisticated robbery caught Smith's imagination. The gang had even installed its own air-conditioning system to make a better working environment while they cut through the walls of the bank before escaping by boat along a sewer and into the Seine. It was a first-class operation – wine bottles and chicken bones littered the gang's retreat. Spaggiari became a French folk hero.

One of Smith's old haunts, the Melbourne docks, was making national headlines as Billy 'The Texan' Longley testified to the Royal Commission into the activities of the Ship Painters and Dockers' Union.

Longley was in Pentridge, serving a life sentence for the 1973 murder of Pat Shannon, secretary of the union. The commission, headed by Francis Costigan QC, investigated widespread corrupt practices in the union including 'ghosting', payment for non-existent workers or work not done, and large amounts of payola to members of the union. Of special concern to the commission was the number of workers with criminal records, including the 11-man executive.

The union was riddled with internal fighting while the likes of Jack 'Puttynose' Nicholls, who was found mysteriously shot through the head on the Hume Highway near Wangaratta in June, 1981, and Doug Sproule battled for control in the 1970s.

The commission probed a history of violence that included unsolved murders and unexplained disappearances of workers. One union gunman, Jimmy Bazley, survived two attempts on his life by shooters who attacked him at his home. And the dashing armed robber Raymond Patrick Bennett, one of Smith's close friends, was shot dead in Melbourne City Court in front of unarmed detectives while Smith was fronting court in Sydney on the Tidmarsh murder charge.

IN July, 1981, an article in the *National Times* was of particular interest to Smith. It dealt with the acquittal of a man who, police alleged, had confessed to trafficking in heroin. In his finding Justice O'Mallaly had said, 'A conviction obtained by the aid of unlawful or unfair acts may be obtained at too high a price … I think someone once said … that you need a Beach Inquiry every five years'.

Maybe he was right and maybe Jimmy Smith could detect a subtle change in attitude towards the admittance in court of the 'verbal' and unsigned statements. Members of CALM were actively spraying the message on suburban fences and hoardings – 'Stop Police Verbals' – and it was registering with the judiciary.

Perhaps Smith felt some empathy for Harry M. Miller who spent time at Long Bay Jail for his involvement in the

DOING TIME

Computicket fraud. The *Sun-Herald* billed Miller as 'Long Bay's star boarder' in May 1982 and reported that the showbiz entrepreneur wanted his 'private secretary to visit him daily with his correspondence and business papers'.

The superintendent rejected the request, but warders reckoned Miller knew how to smile. 'He's got the right way to smile at the officers – the old professional long-termer's smile.'

Smith kept abreast of the latest technology in security systems. He kept an article from the *Sydney Morning Herald* in November, 1982, about closed-circuit TV. He also cut out a report from the Sydney *Sun* about bullet-proof T-shirts and cars with built-in machinegun ports.

Another clipping told of a Do-It-Yourself manual for making explosives and ammunition. He kept an advertisement for a 'scrambler' device for mobile telephones while the *Sunday Telegraph* in June 1987 might have set him thinking about getaways from his past. The headline was **Cheap cars? Never again!**

Smith always had some battle on his hands. In December, 1985, while at Maitland Jail, he took action through the State Ombudsman to have an illegal phone bug removed from his wife's home in Bondi. It was capable of recording conversations as well as the phone numbers of people who called. The complaint eventually found its way to the Stewart Royal Commission into telephone interceptions and the identities of the police who placed the bug were discovered. The officers involved had already been given immunity for testifying to the commission and no further action was taken against them.

BY 1987, Smith's future was sealed. He'd worked through most of the charges against him in New South Wales and exhausted the appeal system. There was no point in prosecuting him on any outstanding charges because he'd already served so much time in jail, with the prospect of many more years before him, and so it was unlikely any further convictions would prolong his current sentences. However, there were matters in Victoria to be settled. He applied for transfer back to his home state.

It was a process he'd begun as early as 1979 when Virginia Bell, of the Redfern Legal Centre, wrote to the Victorian Attorney-General on his behalf to establish the nature of any outstanding warrants against him in that state. He was on remand at Parramatta awaiting trial on armed robbery charges and, at that time, was part heard on committal proceedings with respect to the Tidmarsh murder.

The news from Melbourne was not encouraging. There were 10 outstanding warrants, all relating to the period between 1973 and 1974. These included robbery and attempted robbery, theft of a motor vehicle, burglaries at Werribee, Toorak and Cheltenham, handling stolen goods, escape from lawful custody at Camberwell in June, 1974, and the escape charge relating to his brazen walk-out from Pentridge in December, 1974.

Virginia Bell who, years later, assisted Justice Wood in the Wood Royal Commission, petitioned the possibility of Smith 'calling in' his Victorian warrants 'to enable him to serve those sentences imposed on him in Victoria whilst he is awaiting the outcome of his charges in NSW'. While the Victorian charges were relatively minor compared with the road ahead in New South Wales, it was eventually determined he should front the Melbourne courts.

But, between 1979 and 1986, the issue lapsed. Smith was so busy defending charges in Sydney it wasn't practical to organise an interstate transfer to answer charges in Victoria. In January, 1987, Legal Aid lawyer A. K. Murray canvassed the Director of Public Prosecutions in Victoria about Smith's request to remain in Sydney. Smith quickly established a rapport with Murray, who wrote to thank him 'for your kind thoughts and card at Christmas'. Many of those in the legal profession who represented Smith in some way spoke well of him.

By April, 1987, Smith had engaged Melbourne law firm Bernard J. Sutherland & Associates, which sought documents from his former barrister Brian Cash. The NSW Legal Aid Commission continued to work on his behalf and to provide instructions.

A. K. Murray was attempting to organise a nolle prosequi (no prosecution) on his Victorian charges while corresponding with the Release on Licence Board to determine the outcome of Smith's petition to be released for the 'purposes of extradition to Victoria'. His involvement in the legal process had slowed considerably, but there remained a steady flow to maintain his interest. Added to that were medical problems, particularly arthritis.

The upshot of his petition for interstate transfer was a stay of six months to allow the Release on Licence Board 'to assess his performance over a longer period'. The board recognised Smith had beaten the Tidmarsh murder charge, but noted he was serving a life sentence and 14 years respectively for attempting to shoot Detective Godden at Bomaderry and for conspiracy to rob the railway workshops at Redfern.

The board noted, 'The offender's attitude with regard to the offences remains unchanged; strongly protesting his innocence. He finds it difficult to accept his situation, which is further compounded for him by the fact that he is serving a life sentence for an offence where no death resulted. Mr Smith's prison behaviour whilst in Metropolitan Reception Prison is considered satisfactory despite being convicted of possessing non-prescribed property (needle and syringe) on 25 March,

CALL ME JIMMY

1987, for which he was admonished and discharged. He tends to keep a low profile and is rarely seen by senior custodial staff'.

With the prospect that Smith might be released on licence at some future stage, at least one police officer began to show renewed interests in his movements. On 25 January, 1988, a phone request was made by a Newcastle consorting squad officer, Detective McBride, asking to be informed of any application for release on licence submitted by Smith.

At the time, Smith had two applications in the system for interstate transfer to Melbourne, one on compassionate grounds to be with his family, the other on legal grounds to answer charges there.

In August, permission was granted with a determination that Smith could apply to stay in Victoria on compassionate grounds once his legal appearances had been finalised. But the transfer was delayed due to bureaucratic error.

In February, 1989, a Melbourne journalist reported on the impending transfer in an article titled **'Jockey' in home stretch.** It appeared in the *Sunday Press*, run with two prominent photographs showing Smith, the prisoner, as a 'tubby 45-year-old' and contrasting that against 'his earlier days as a hardened crim'. It described Smith as 'one of the most feared criminals in Australia' and went on to say 'mere mention of his name has sent shudders through the underworld'.

But not, apparently, 'through Russell Street police HQ'. It was a colourful article but, despite the sensationalism, the reporter pointed out that Smith was 'past his crime prime', noting that, 'If the Jockey does get his break to start afresh, he will not be the same man who was feared by the underworld in the 1960s and '70s. According to jail sources, Smith has mellowed.'

There were some factual inaccuracies in the article, which

reflected much of the reporting about criminals and the underworld. The claim that Smith had served 12 years of a life sentence 'for the attempted murder of a policeman' was wrong. In fact, he was convicted of 'maliciously attempting to discharge a loaded firearm with intent to do grievous bodily harm'. About Smith's Pentridge escape, the *Sunday Press* claimed Smith had 'conned a woman visitor's pass'. Wrong again: the dupe was an elderly gentleman.

The article also reported that 'Smith and two accomplices burst into the home of Sydney bookmaker Lloyd Tidmarsh. During the robbery Tidmarsh was shot dead'. By the time the article appeared Smith's connection to the Tidmarsh murder had well and truly been laid to rest, at least legally, in what was to become an historic precedent relating to the evidence of voice recognition. (The precedent is known as R v E J Smith and is widely used in law schools today.)

The reporter sent two copies of the article to Valerie Smith at her request. In a covering note he said, 'Story was altered from original by sub-editors. They cut out the fact that murder charge was quashed. Sorry about that'.

Smith wrote a four-page letter to the reporter the following year and explained how circumstances had been distorted by the media. He also outlined his belief that police information was leaked to the media in a deliberate attempt to sway jurors and judges before his court appearances.

He directed one blunt criticism at the reporter: 'Some 14 months ago you done a story on me. And I believe again just recently, which amounts to contempt of court and prejudicial to me obtaining a fair trial. I feel because of the story 14 months ago made the authorities leave me in NSW and waste 14 months before bringing me down. It was incorrect. I presume the DPP (Department of Public Prosecution) or police informed you of the move. It gives my criminal background and states I am doing a life sentence for attempted murder of a policeman which I am not.'

Another reason for the delay in transferring Smith to Victoria came in a letter to Bernard Sutherland on 9 March, 1989. It was from John Coldrey, QC, Director of Public Prosecutions in Victoria.

'As you are aware,' he said, 'although Smith's transfer to Victoria has been approved by both the Victorian and New South Wales Attorneys-General, his actual transfer has not taken place because it is hoped that arrangements for Smith's court hearings can be made prior to his transfer.'

In the interim, Smith received notification that charges of armed robbery, attempted theft and attempted robbery had received a nolle prosequi, but that other charges, theft, burglary, escape and handling stolen goods, would proceed.

Smith spent Christmas 1989 in A division at Pentridge. The same Sunday newspaper journalist reported the move: 'Smith was secretly transferred back to Melbourne on Monday to face charges still pending in Victoria.'

Smith eventually appeared to answer the Victorian charges. Effectively, only one month was added to his sentence. There were no more outstanding charges and he was in a stronger position to work towards his eventual release. That process began while he was still in Pentridge. But, before he could apply for a release date, his life sentence had to be re-determined under the Sentencing Act 1989 so that a set time could be applied to his 'life' conviction in the Godden matter. He returned to Sydney and Long Bay Jail.

ON 11 June, 1991, his sentence was re-determined from life to 15 years with an additional 10 years parole. Smith still wasn't

DOING TIME

happy. He complained that, at 15 years, the re-determined sentence was longer than most murderers got. The judgment had been influenced by a report from the Serious Offenders' Review Board which, in part, argued 'The Board submits that if an additional term is ordered it be lengthy. The Board and its predecessors have not been able to prepare Smith for rehabilitation and return to the community as a decent law-abiding citizen. This has been owing to his preoccupation with legal matters in New South Wales and Victoria. For the same reason the Board is not able to say whether he is rehabilitated'.

Under the 1989 Act, known as the 'Truth in Sentencing Act', the term 'life' would mean just that, for the term of natural life. The average term of a life sentence for murder before the new Act was 11.7 years.

Previously, some prisoners served no more than eight years. Smith felt cheated because, although he was serving a life term, many prisoners who had actually committed murder were being released having served less time than him.

Smith appealed the result and the minimum sentence was reduced to 14 years and three months, to expire on 13 December, 1991. However, in his finding, Justice Gleeson pointed out that the expiry date did not mean Smith would necessarily get out then. It was subject to his rehabilitation and good behaviour.

With his legal battles finished, Smith settled down to prison life. He'd kept away from trouble in the various prisons where he'd been a guest of Her Majesty and soon enough earned positions of trust including that of head sweeper.

There was little to complain about any more and it was important for him to be seen as rehabilitated. On 3 June, 1991, Brett Collins, by then managing director of Breakout Print in Sussex Street, Sydney, offered Jimmy Smith 'a job in our finishing section upon his release from prison'. It would attract 'award wages' and involve 'the completion and despatch of magazines and books'.

In October 1991, the Serious Offenders' Review Board recommended Smith's transfer to Silverwater Prison for work release consideration. It was coming together and Smith could smell the ocean air.

CHAPTER 12

Free as a jailbird can be

JIMMY Smith walked free from Silverwater Jail on 12 February, 1992. He was 49 and had been in custody 14 years and five months. His library of court transcripts, newspaper cuttings and correspondence were shipped to his brother Ron in Geelong. He headed straight for Valerie's flat in Bondi. But his long-awaited pleasure at being reunited with his true love didn't last long.

Less than 36 hours later, on 14 February – Valentine's Day – a masked gunman shot Smith several times at close range. The gunman lay in wait in the stairwell above Valerie's flat and started shooting when Smith and Valerie returned from a celebratory meal about 9pm.

Smith opened the security door and stepped back to allow Valerie to unlock the flat's front door. The gunman showed himself. There was no time for evasive action. Smith took five hits. Bleeding, Smith raced up the stairwell as the gunman raced down. Valerie found her husband collapsed on the top

CALL ME JIMMY

landing. She screamed as he lay prostrate, blood draining from his body. Three bullets had ripped apart his abdomen; two more had lodged in the chest and right thigh.

Valerie tore downstairs and across the road to a neighbour's house, screaming. The neighbour called the ambulance and the police. Smith was yelling, 'Where's Valerie? Is she all right? Is she all right?'

Smith was rushed to St Vincent's Hospital at Darlinghurst. The wounds were critical. He was placed on life-support while surgeons operated. Valerie didn't know whether he would live or die. She paced corridors and waiting rooms, asked for progress reports and waited. Staff made up a bed so she could be near her husband when he awoke from surgery.

The trauma to his body was such that Smith was in a coma when his mother Jean and brother Ron arrived from Geelong later that night. Jean stayed with him until midnight, talking to her son, and returned next morning to spend time with him. He told her later he knew they were there, but couldn't speak.

Meanwhile, police were combing the area for signs of the gunman. Tracker dogs picked up the scent at the scene, but lost it at the rear fence of the property.

Uniformed police patrolled the streets around Bondi. It was reported that a heavily-armed police guard maintained security around his hospital room and, in time, he regained consciousness. He was interviewed. Police asked who might have been responsible for the shooting. Smith said he had no idea, which proved that he was at least consistent – he had never been talkative in police interviews. No charges were ever laid over the shooting, which remains a mystery to this day, despite speculation.

Friends took up a collection and raised $30,000 to see him through. He gave this money to a mate to be passed on to brother, Ron, but the mate was arrested at Kings Cross and the money confiscated by police. It was eventually returned.

FREE AS A JAILBIRD CAN BE

A week or two after the shooting, Smith was well enough to revive his old gambling habits. He had friends go to the local tote to place bets of $1000 and up.

Apart from the faithful Val, hospital visitors included Tim Anderson, falsely convicted over the Sydney Hilton Bombing in 1978, who'd done hard prison time with Smith. There were people from the prison reform movements and there were crims. Not surprisingly, no one appeared to understand why anyone would want to gun down the likeable Jimmy Smith.

There were rumours about the shooting, none of them corroborated. One suggested the shooter had been Bertie Kidd, Val Smith's former husband. Another suggested the shooting had been planned by police close to Smith at the time of his arrest in Bomaderry and was a payback for the trouble he'd caused them in court.

One rumour combined both of these and had Bertie Kidd as the shooter under instructions from bent police. Still another related to something that had happened in prison. The details are hazy, but involved a dispute Smith had with another inmate where threats were made and, supposedly, the other inmate got in first when Smith was released.

Three and a half weeks after the shooting, Smith discharged himself. He wasn't fully recovered, but well enough to walk. He was worried the hospital offered little protection against a repeat attack. As Valerie Smith was to say: 'He didn't come here – naturally'.

Smith 'tooled up' with weapons and headed for the central coast, the Gosford area, a maze of thick bushland and inland waterways, somewhere to recuperate out of the limelight. Initially, he stayed with friends, possibly Julie Cashman and Garrick Joseph, but within two weeks flew to Queensland to meet his nephew, Barry Jones. He needed protection and the pair set up a rented house at Davistown, back in the Gosford area, a place almost surrounded by water and with only one way in. According to Jones, there were 'guns at every window'.

Smith and Jones spent their days training horses. Their stables were 300 metres from the house. Every morning they drove the horses to the Gosford track to work them and returned to muck out the stables. Smith loved betting and race meetings. They frequented the Erina Fair shopping complex and, Jones says, the security staff there knew them well enough.

The connection between Smith, Cashman and Garrick involved, according to Jones, selling some marijuana and speed for 'a bit of extra money'.

It is likely that Smith's association with the growing drug trade deepened over time. He was ageing, no longer a bank robber in his prime, but a man increasingly crippled by arthritis. There would come a time when he needed to make his money more easily.

But there was at least one more bank job in Smith. As Subzero stormed home in the 1992 Melbourne Cup, Smith was already planning an armed robbery in Melbourne with a tearaway crim, Christopher Dean Binse, who'd arrived at Davistown for a few weeks. The pair would meet up later at the farmhouse at Glenlyon in Victoria.

Valerie visited her man at Davistown on weekends and they weighed up the options, whether to move back to Victoria or live permanently on the central coast of New South Wales.

She had been against moving to the central coast, saying there was 'no future there.' She was at the Davistown house the weekend Garrick Joseph found the police bugging device. Smith had bolted a few hours earlier. The police moved in soon after and arrested Cashman and Joseph. They let Valerie go. 'They knew I'd arrived on the weekend and wasn't involved.'

Nine months after his release from Silverwater Jail, Jimmy

FREE AS A JAILBIRD CAN BE

Smith was once again a wanted man. He'd left the Davistown house, which was still under surveillance, gone to Erina Fair about six kilometres away and was caught shoplifting. Whether he had money in his pocket or not, Smith was a compulsive thief; what his brother Ron called a 'tea leaf'. It was the character flaw that had started him on crime's slippery slope 30 years earlier, and it would destroy him.

Security guards had followed him outside the shops, detained him and brought him back to the Grace Brothers store. If shoplifting was foolish, then Smith's next move was crazy ... he pulled a gun. And in that split second he went from being a middle-aged citizen with a colourful past to being a fugitive outlaw with not long to live.

As the security staff backed off, Smith bolted for the carpark. He bailed up an elderly couple still in their car and demanded they drive him out of the carpark. Abduction was added to the list of charges he would face if caught.

At the first intersection, the elderly couple fled from the car, telling Smith he could take it. The move must have disoriented Smith; he panicked, left the car as well, flagged down another, ousted the driver and escaped. The stolen car was found in the Kincumber area, across Brisbane Waters from Davistown. But Smith had vanished.

The Erina Fair debacle showed how desperate Smith was to avoid more time in prison. If he'd stopped to think rationally he would have realised that shoplifting was comparatively minor. But once he produced a gun, took hostages (however momentarily) and stole a car, the die was cast against him. He was on the run again.

Friends say Smith was paranoid after the shooting at Bondi and the years in prison, many of them in maximum security hell-holes. He feared corrupt police who, he believed, had set up the attempt on his life at Bondi. But to shoplift when he had money in his pockets was irrational and, ultimately, self-destructive.

More than likely Smith had a car waiting at Kincumber, a car left there some time earlier as part of the escape plan if he had to cross the Brisbane Waters. Assuming he did have a car at Kincumber, he would have driven to Gosford railway station and caught the train to Sydney, the safest way to travel given roadblocks and the potential for anonymity amongst fellow travellers.

In Sydney he was met by friends in a panel van. He took a mobile phone with him and maintained contact with more friends in Victoria while the van travelled down the Hume Highway, all the while watching for vehicles tailing it or stopped on the roadside. Every blind corner, every build-up in traffic, every small town was a potential trap.

He went to Glenlyon, in the central highlands, via Melbourne and Werribee, on the Geelong side of the city. It meant he'd been taken more than 100 kilometres extra. To get to Glenlyon from the Hume Highway there was no need to go through Melbourne. It would have been quicker to leave the Hume Highway at Broadford, about 60 kilometres on the Sydney side of Melbourne, cut through Kilmore and into the hills to Kyneton, where he could pick up the Daylesford Road.

The roundabout route might have been a smoke-screen for the last leg of the journey in case he was being followed. He changed vehicles at Werribee. It's possible he had to collect something there, perhaps even equipment for the planned bank robbery in Melbourne. That he went straight to Glenlyon is doubtful, because Christopher Binse apparently collected him in Ballarat and drove him along the 60 kilometres of winding country roads to the farmhouse.

FREE AS A JAILBIRD CAN BE

What the pair didn't know was that the supposed safe house was under surveillance by police. They were walking into a trap – although, oddly enough, that wasn't what sealed Smith's doom. His card was already marked.

At the farmhouse, Smith was introduced to Lorna 'Candy' Skellington and Binse showed him some guns and briefly outlined the plan for the robbery.

The farm yard was sheltered by trees, but the surveillance team was able to monitor some of the movements outside. A telephone bug was in place and, when somebody in the house called 'Tony' made arrangements to drive into Creswick, police at the operational headquarters in nearby Daylesford alerted the surveillance team to expect some movement soon.

'Tony' turned out to be Smith, but police didn't know who he was as he left the farm at 8.20pm on 5 December, 1992, in the white panel van Binse had arranged for him.

He drove cautiously on the narrow and unfamiliar roads. He turned left at the Midland Highway and entered the outskirts of Daylesford knowing a police car was following him. What he didn't know was that the van he was driving was stolen, but he must have wondered. He was driving well under the speed limit. He probably feared he'd been detected and any moment police cars would converge on him from everywhere.

There was nothing he could do but continue to drive sedately; any other action, especially speeding to get away, would certainly draw attention.

He must have considered the slim possibility that the patrol car was simply checking his speed and would move on when the officer realised no laws were being broken or, even more remote a possibility, the patrol car was simply heading in the same direction and in no hurry.

But the patrol car kept pace with Smith and followed him the

CALL ME JIMMY

28 kilometres to Creswick. It was enough to strain the nerves of any driver, let alone a wanted man who had spent a fair chunk of his adult life in prison. Smith kept one eye glued to the rear view mirror, the other on the road ahead and the speedometer. At Creswick, he would make his stand. He parked outside the Farmers Arms Hotel.

The patrol car pulled into the parking area, between the main street and the Farmers Arms Hotel, not far from Smith's van. Before he could move away from the panel van and into the hotel, the policeman was moving towards him.

There were two options – either pull the gun immediately or try to bluff his way out of it. Smith chose the latter but, when the officer asked to see some identification, Smith almost certainly presumed that his description had probably been broadcast to police in Victoria. From where he sat, the choice dwindled to one. Under the pretence of fetching his licence from the glove box, he produced a loaded gun covered by a folder.

In fact, Senior Constable Ian Harris thought it was a routine intercept of a suspected stolen car. He was taken by surprise and immediately raised his hands above his head. Smith moved towards the young officer and tried to take his gun, but Harris turned side-on, making it difficult for Smith to reach the holster. 'Don't touch the gun,' Smith warned repeatedly.

'No, no, I'm not ... someone help me,' pleaded Harris.

'I'm going to kill you,' screamed Smith.

As Smith pushed the policeman across the patrol car bonnet, Darren Neil drove his station wagon directly at Smith. Smith turned and aimed at Neil, but held his fire.

Neil stopped his car a metre short of Smith, who turned back to Harris in time to see the officer had his gun raised and was firing. Two bullets hit Smith almost at point blank range. He was probably dead before he hit the ground but hotel patrons,

FREE AS A JAILBIRD CAN BE

who rushed to the body, attempted resuscitation anyway. Moments later, support vehicles called in by D24 screamed into the carpark. It was all over.

THE death of 'Jockey' Smith was front page news across Australia. Photographs showing his dead body lying on bloodstained ground appeared in newspapers and a million television screens across the country.

There were other images as well, reminders of how he'd looked at varying stages of life, of him being bustled in and out of court flanked by police officers, and images of those who attended his funeral in Geelong.

Death notices appeared in Geelong, Melbourne and Sydney newspapers and 80 well-wishers sent cards to his mother Jean. Wreaths arrived from as far away as Long Bay. About 100 people, including police officers, attended the funeral at Geelong's Eastern Cemetery on Friday, 11 December, 1992. One officer described the funeral as 'fit for the Mayor of Geelong'.

Jean Smith believed her son had finally found 'peace' but, in the tradition of the Australian bushranger, the folklore lives on. So much so that, in March, 1996, even the folksy commercial television program *Burke's Backyard* saw fit to mention 'Jockey Smith' in two successive programs.

Jean Smith wrote to the host, Don Burke, wanting to know why he had mentioned 'Katingal and Jockey Smith' and asking 'what that has to do with gardening?'

Burke replied a couple of weeks later: 'We must say we had no intention of being hurtful to the family of your son and we do apologise if this was the result of our comments. However, much as you may dislike the situation, I suppose your son is now a part of Australia's history …'

CALL ME JIMMY

And that he is. Like Ned Kelly, 'Jockey' took on the coppers and was pipped at the post. He found his Glenrowan in a phone booth at Bomaderry.

But, even in defeat, there was something of the larrikin philosopher about him. As he once said to his mother: 'It's my burden to carry, mum. Don't you worry about it.' But, like any mother, she did and still does.